I0813806

THE TRUE EUROPE

BENEDICT XVI
JOSEPH RATZINGER

The True Europe

Its Identity and Mission

Selected Writings

Edited by Pierluca Azzaro and Carlos Granados
Translated by Michael J. Miller and Brian McNeil

IGNATIUS PRESS SAN FRANCISCO

Original Italian edition:
La vera Europa. Identità e missione
Published in 2021 by Edizioni Cantagalli, Siena, Italy

Cover design by Roxanne Mei Lum

ISBN 978-1-62164-595-5 (PB)
ISBN 978-1-64229-257-2 (eBook)
Library of Congress Control Number 2023949586
Printed in the United States of America ♾

CONTENTS

PART THREE
The Church and the Rebirth of Europe: Educational Challenge and New Evangelization

PART FOUR
The True Europe and Its Mission

INTRODUCTION

by His Holiness Pope Francis

I am happy to introduce the present volume, an anthology of selected texts by Joseph Ratzinger/Benedict XVI on Europe, published opportunely for the fiftieth anniversary of diplomatic relations between the Holy See and the European Union.

With his characteristic clarity, immediate accessibility, and at the same time depth, the Pope Emeritus magnificently outlines here the "idea of Europe" that undoubtedly inspired its Founding Fathers and is the basis for its greatness; the definitive dimming of this ideal would ratify its complete and irreversible decline.

He who decided to take the name Benedict, to call Europe back to its roots also, is perhaps precisely the one to teach us better than others the reason why: at the foundation of Europe, its creativity, its sound prosperity, and, above all, its humanity is the humanism of the Incarnation; Joseph Ratzinger writes that "the figure of Jesus Christ stands in the center of European history, and it is the foundation of true humanism, of a new humanity. For if God became man, then man receives an entirely new dignity. If man is merely the product of random evolution, then his humanity itself is an accident, and then he can also be sacrificed some day to seemingly higher purposes. But if God created and willed every individual human being, it is an altogether different matter. And if God himself became a man, if he even suffered for mankind, then man shares in God's own dignity. Someone who violates a human being then violates God himself." Despite the many words and high-sounding proclamations, today in Europe the very idea of respect for every human life is increasingly becoming lost, starting with the loss of the awareness of its sacredness, that is, starting precisely from the dimming of the awareness that we are creatures of God. Over the years Benedict XVI has not been afraid to denounce very courageously and farsightedly the many manifestations of this tragic rejection of the idea of creation, down to the current, final consequences, which are described in absolutely clear and convincing terms in the introductory text.

This volume, although imbued with great realism, does not conclude with pessimism and sadness; on the contrary: "The first reason for my hope", the author says, "consists in the fact that the desire for God, the search for God, is profoundly inscribed into each human soul and cannot disappear. Certainly we can forget God for a time, lay him aside, and concern ourselves with other things, but God never disappears. Saint Augustine's words are true: we men are restless until we have found God. This restlessness also exists today and is an expression of the hope that man may, ever and anew, even today, start to journey toward this God."[1] Thus, revealing to us the secret of his cheerfulness in these difficult times, Benedict XVI shows us also the road to travel for the rebirth of Europe.

Francesco

Vatican City, July 28, 2021

[1] Interview with Pope Benedict XVI for the film *Campane d'Europa* (October 15, 2012).

PREFACE

by His Holiness Benedict XVI

Doing Justice in God's Sight to Our Mission for Humanity

With the legalization of "homosexual marriage" in sixteen countries of Europe, the topic of marriage and family has acquired a new dimension that cannot be passed over in silence. It manifests a malformation of conscience, which plainly extends deep into Catholic circles of the population. It cannot be answered with a few little moralizations or with a few exegetical references. The problem runs deep and therefore must be considered fundamentally.

First, it seems to me important to state that the concept of a "homosexual marriage" contradicts all human cultures until now and therefore signifies a cultural revolution that opposes the entire tradition of mankind until now. No doubt there is extraordinary variety in the legal and moral conception of marriage and family in different cultures of the world. Not only the difference between monogamy and polygamy, but also other far-reaching differences can be observed. Nevertheless, one basic common element is never called into question: the fact that the existence of human beings in the form of man and woman is ordered to propagation and that the communion of man and woman and their openness to the transmission of life constitutes the essence of what we call marriage. The fundamental certainty that human beings exist as man and woman, that the task of transmitting life is assigned to human beings, and that precisely the communion of man and woman serves this purpose and that marriage consists essentially of this, above and beyond all differences, is a primordial certainty that exists to this day in mankind as a self-evident truth.

This primordial human certainty was shaken to its foundations when the Pill was introduced, making it fundamentally possible to separate fertility and sexuality. Here the crucial thing is not casuistry about whether and when the use of the Pill can be justified morally, but rather the fundamental novelty that it signifies as such—precisely the fundamental separation of sexuality and fertility. Indeed, this separation means that all forms of sexuality are thus equally legitimate. There is no fundamental standard now. If sexuality and fertility do not belong together on principle, then in fact all forms of sexuality are equally legitimate. This new message, which was contained in the invention of the Pill, transformed people's consciousness, only slowly at first, but then more and more evidently.

A second step then follows: If at first sexuality is separated from fertility, then conversely, fertility, too, can of course be thought of without sexuality. Then it seems right to stop leaving the propagation of mankind to accidental bodily passion and, instead, to plan and to produce human beings rationally. Thus human beings no longer are begotten and conceived but, rather, are made, and by now this process is in full swing. But then this means that a human being is no longer a gift that is given but, rather, is a planned product of our making. What can be made, however, can also be destroyed. In this respect the growing trend toward suicide as a planned end of one's own life is a component of the trend being depicted.

Thus, however, it becomes evident that the question about "homosexual marriage" is not just about more broad-mindedness and openness, but, rather, is about the fundamental question: What is a human being? Consequently, it also has to do with the question: Is there a Creator, or are we all just manufactured products? We are faced with the alternative: the human being as a creature of God, as an image of God, as a gift of God, or the human being as a product that he himself can manufacture and use as he pleases. When the idea of creation is abandoned, the greatness of the human being is abandoned, along with his un-availability [*Unverfügbarkeit*] and his dignity, which surpasses all plans to exploit it.

The whole thing can be expressed from another aspect, too. The ecological movement discovered the limit of feasibility [*Machbarkeit*] and recognized that "nature" prescribes for us a moderation that we cannot ignore with impunity. Unfortunately "human ecology" has still not been made concrete. A human being, too, has a "nature" that is prescribed for him, and violating or denying it leads to self-destruction. This is precisely what is at stake also in the case of the creation of human beings as man and woman, which is ignored in the hypothesis of "homosexual marriage".

It seems to me that it is important to reflect on the question in this dimension. Only in this way will we do justice in God's sight to our mission for mankind.

Benedict XVI

PART ONE

At the Sources of European Identity: Athens, Jerusalem, Rome

I

The "European Synthesis"

Homily at the Europe Day Celebration of the Pan-European Union of Bavaria, Munich, May 12, 1979

Reading: Philippians 4:6–9

The Acts of the Apostles (16:6–10) tell us a remarkable story which, like no other event, makes the foundations of Europe visible, its reason for being and its message for us. Paul is doing mission work in his native Asia Minor, and he clearly does not even think about crossing the channel that separates it from Europe. But then something remarkable happens. Wherever he tries to go, he feels that the Spirit of Jesus is preventing him, standing in his way everywhere like a wall. The new route opens up in a dream: Paul sees a Macedonian who calls to him and asks: Come over here and help us! The Macedonian stands for Greece, for Europe. His request is decisive for future history. In it, the mind of the Hellenic world calls for Jesus Christ. In its most highly purified form, the Greek mind had become yearning for him, yearning for the Gospel—an open vessel held out for it. And that is how Europe came to be, the Europe in which we live, the Europe that calls to us today. It is based on the union of Greek mind and Christian faith, on reason that has become yearning and in its privation senses what it lacks. And it is based on the answer of the Spirit of Jesus Christ, who grasps the open hand and becomes its guide.

We can learn in somewhat more detail what this vision signifies in practice from the reading that we have just heard (Phil 4:6–9). In it, Paul exhorts the Philippians to do all that is true, noble, right, all that is virtuous. The words that he uses come without exception from Greek moral philosophy —the whole sentence could be taken from it. What is written here is a product of those interior refinements of reason and its wisdom thich had developed in a long stream of historical struggles starting from Egypt—including some exchange with the biblical world—and concluding in Greece. Here we encounter something remarkable: Paul invites the Greeks to follow the wisdom of Greece; he invites them to follow reason and to do what is reasonable. Does that mean, perhaps, that the Christian faith ultimately makes itself superfluous, that it is only a preliminary step, until the Enlightenment no longer needs it and reason is self-sufficient? By no means. Rather, we find here the accomplishment of what the vision of the Macedonian in the dream represents figuratively: The Gospel has taken up the Greek mind; it has incorporated into itself the reason of the Greek world. It does not destroy reason but, rather, brings it around [restores it to consciousness]. Faith enables man to be reasonable. And conversely, reason does not make faith superfluous, but rather through faith reason receives the stability that protects it from falling headlong and keeps it rational. If reason loses this stability and then sees only itself, then it is like an eye that now sees only itself—such an eye is blind. Another image comes to my mind: reason that now sees only itself and no longer receives help is like a star that is torn out of its course and has only itself to follow. Having no place, it tumbles into the vacuum and plunges into nothingness. Faith keeps reason in the great fundamental realizations that reason can no longer prove but only see, and this is precisely how it keeps reason rational. Faith does not absorb it but, rather, sets it free.

This correlation of faith and reason is reflected in Saint Paul's catalogue of virtues, and this shows the true foundations of Europe, which gave this part of the earth its special mission and its special rank in world history. For this means that a new path has opened up between the barbarity of excessive reason and the barbarity of blind irrationality and blind superstition. The barbarity of reason without moderation—we are experiencing that today, and Paul was able to experience it in the Greek world of that time. The Acts of the Apostles tell us about the strong emotion that seized him when he discovered in Athens, the capital of ancient culture, an altar with the inscription: "To an unknown god" (Acts 17:23ff.). Where God is the Unknown, then the decisive thing is still unknown, and help is urgently necessary there. Paul experienced this when he encountered the misery of the dock workers in Corinth, the market for vice in the major cities, and the desperate perversity in the palaces of the wealthy. In the first chapters of the Letter to the Romans he describes this experience with words that remind us of the world of Jean Genet[1] and Pier Paolo Pasolini,[2] the desperate inner strife of modern existence. I will never forget the 1976 Dialogue on Humanism in Salzburg, at which a Commu-

[1] Jean Genet, French novelist and dramatist, born December 19, 1910, in Paris.

[2] Pier Paolo Pasolini, Italian author and film director, born March 5, 1922, in Bologna. His poems, novels, and films deal with social criticism and sexuality. Pasolini composed, among other things, a polemical poem against Pope Pius XII. He dedicated his controversial film *The Gospel according to Matthew* to Pope John XXIII. Pasolini was killed on November 2, 1975, in Ostia by a seventeen-year-old homosexual.

nist screamed at us: "Corrupt men of all lands, unite!" He pointed to the drug scene, the psychologically ill, and the suicides in Western society. It would not have been difficult to offset this with a more than abundant record of interior strife in the East—both cases illustrate the bankruptcy that wishes to see only itself and therefore must be blind. We find the counterpart—reason disconnected—obviously in Iran,[3] and somewhat differently in the worlds of superstition that once again are cropping up right in the middle of the autonomous rule of reason. Reason, when left alone, is blind, and fear of reason blinds a person. Christian faith, however, means that reason finds what is its own because faith upholds it and precisely thereby sets it free.

Politically, this means that from the beginning, Christian faith set the State free to do its own work and preserved its own space for itself: just as reason and faith do not dissolve into each other, so too Church and State must remain in their respective orders. We Christians are not striving for a theocracy or a dominion of the Church over the State, and we know that Church and party must not be confused—there is no need for external reminders about that. But we also know that State and Church can remain free only if the State's reason remains rational, if it does not lose its standards, which, after all, it cannot provide by itself. We have responsibility for keeping the moral values that today's reading speaks about as the inviolable guiding stars of life. That, of course, is the form of partisanship that we let no one take away from us: because we want freedom of reason, we

[3] On February 12, 1979, Prime Minister Bakhtiar, who had been appointed also by Mohammed Reza Shah Pahlavi, resigned. With the death by firing squad of former Prime Minister Hoveyda, the wave of executions inspired by Ayatollah Khomeini reached its first peak as early as April 7, 1979.

therefore oppose the mental extravagance that plunges the mind into unreason. Therefore, we stand up for the validity of those moral values with which the Christian message keeps reason on the starry path of humaneness.

Europe has reached a crisis of its history and of its mind. The Church's task, I repeat, is not to play party politics. But it is our task to work with all urgency for that purification of spirit and of minds which makes reason capable of the self-transcendence of yearning in which it opens itself and calls: "Come over . . . and help us!" (Acts 16:9). This is the petition with which we fill this Eucharist today. We pray to the Spirit of Jesus to travel across the sea of our doubts and our pride that separates us from him and to enlighten and strengthen us from within. This is the petition of Thomas, who after all the journeys of discipleship says to Jesus, at the same time desperately and confidently: "Lord, we do not know where you are going" (Jn 14:5). And the answer is true for us, too: "I am the way" (Jn 14:6)—he himself, Jesus Christ, is the true Way. Let us try to become more and more deeply reacquainted with him. Then we, too, will be able to perform correctly our service to this world in this time of ours.

2

The Heart of Europe: The "Humanism of the Incarnation"

Homily on the Occasion of a Visit of a Delegation of the German Bishops' Conference to the Polish Episcopate, Kraków, September 13, 1980

Dear brothers and sisters,

First I would like to express my heartfelt joy and gratitude for the opportunity to preach here in the venerable cathedral city of Kraków, which has become even dearer to us all, and to all Christendom, since its bishop was elected the Successor of Peter and the Supreme Shepherd of the whole Church two years ago. After the sinister history of relations between Germans and Poles that we now have behind us, this invitation is for me a particularly valuable sign for the unifying and reconciling power of faith, which gives the strength to forgive and creates fraternity where the spirit of disbelief had sown hatred and enmity. I would like to thank you cordially first of all for this gift of forgiveness, peace and faith-based fraternity.

For centuries Kraków was one of the great European metropolises. In the second half of the fifteenth century, its university had approximately the same number of foreigners and natives among its students. Allow me to recall just two great names that are closely connected with this city: Nicolaus Copernicus and Veit Stoss [a German sculptor]. The European dimension of this city is evident in both men; they illustrate for us the breadth and openness of an era in which Europe was a concrete reality. Therefore, this city itself suggests the question: What does the Christian faith have to do with Europe? What does Europe mean for the faith of Christians?

When we speak as Christians about Europe, what always comes to mind first is a remarkable story that is handed down to us in chapter 16 of the Acts of the Apostles. Paul is doing missionary work in his native Asia Minor, and he plainly has no intention of crossing the strait that separates it from Europe. But then something remarkable happens: he feels that the Spirit of Jesus is preventing him, wherever he tries to go; the Lord stands in his way like a wall everywhere. The new direction opens up through a vision that is granted to him in a dream: Paul sees a Macedonian standing there, who calls to him and begs: "Come over . . . and help us!" (Acts 16:9).

The Macedonian stands for Greece, for Europe. His request is decisive for future history. In its supreme refinement, the Greek mind had become yearning for Christ, an open vessel held out toward the Gospel of Jesus Christ. Europe became Europe through the Christian faith, which bears within it the heritage of Israel, but also adopted what was best in the Greek and Roman mind.

Later the Germanic and Slavic peoples entered into the space of this faith; they gave it new shapes and forms, but at the same time they received from it in the first place their history and identity. Every European people can and must acknowledge this fact about itself: The faith created our homeland, and we would lose ourselves if we threw the faith away.

But now we must ask: What are actually the particular

features that make Europe Europe? I would like to mention three sorts.

1. What Paul brought to the Macedonians was initially simply the figure of Jesus Christ, the Son of God made man. It was the encounter with him, who is true God from true God and at the same time true man, who suffered for us, was crucified and buried; who rose again on the third day and took human nature with him into the glory of God, so as to "prepare a place" for us all (Jn 14:2).

The figure of Jesus Christ stands in the center of European history, and it is the foundation of true humanism, of a new humanity. For if God became man, then man receives an entirely new dignity. If man is merely the product of random evolution, then his humanity itself is an accident, and then he can also be sacrificed some day to seemingly higher purposes. But if God created and willed every individual human being, it is an altogether different matter. And if God himself became a man, if he even suffered for mankind, then man shares in God's own dignity.

Someone who violates a human being then violates God himself. Reverence for human dignity and respect for the human rights of every individual human being are the fruits of faith in the Incarnation of God. Therefore faith in Jesus Christ is the foundation of all real progress. Someone who abandons faith in Jesus Christ for the sake of a supposedly higher progress is abandoning the foundation of human dignity.

2. Out of this Christian humanism, the humanism of the Incarnation, developed the peculiarity of Christian culture. Deep down, all its specific characteristics can be traced back to faith in the Incarnation and dissolve if you take this faith away. I would like to mention just a few of these characteristics.

a. Christian culture can never be exclusively a culture of having. It can never see material ownership and enjoyment as the highest value of a human being. It does not despise material things. After all, God's Son became a man. He lived a bodily life; he rose again in the flesh and took his body with him into heavenly glory: this is the highest promise imaginable for matter. Therefore, Christian culture takes care that every human being can live in dignity and receive a just share of the material goods of this earth. But man's highest good is not material possessions. We are experiencing in the West how the worship of consumption makes man worthless. He succumbs to selfishness; but contempt for other human beings almost necessarily results in self-contempt. If man has nothing higher to expect than material things alone, then the whole world becomes repulsive and empty to him. Therefore, Christian culture acknowledges the priority of moral values over material values. This is why the glory of God is a public value for Christian culture. The great cathedrals and churches, for instance here in Kraków the cathedral and Saint Mary's Basilica and so many others, are an expression of this conviction that the glory of God is a public and common good of man.

And in fact, precisely by giving God glory, man honored himself. Even today the great cathedrals are oases of humanity, or human dignity, because they are spaces of the publicly acknowledged glory of God. It is fundamental for the continued existence of a culture that the values in it remain in their correct order. The priority of moral values over material ones, the acknowledgment of God's glory—this is a fundamental common heritage of European culture, and today we Christians must once again make an effort to preserve and deepen it.

b. Part of Christian culture is the dignity of conscience

and the recognition of its rights. Conscience is the expression of the fact that God addresses each one of us individually and that each individual stands in the sight and in the heart of God. Thus conscience signifies also our duty to listen to God's call. Indeed, it does not mean that everyone can do what he wants but, rather, that everyone can know God's will and must be open to it.

Respect for conscience means also believing in freedom: no one can be forced to believe, because God wants man's free Yes. But everyone must have the right to believe and to live according to his faith. Contained also in the idea of conscience is the idea of tolerance, of proper respect for each other, of proper generosity with one another.

c. Among the foundations of European culture is the dignity of marriage and family, in the way in which the Lord renewed them according to the Creator's will, as a lifelong union of one man with one woman (Mk 10:1–12). Without Christian marriage, there is no Christian culture. Only when polygamy was overcome and marital fidelity became definitive could the specific features of European culture arise. It collapses when this fundamental form of ordering human affairs according to the Creator's purpose comes to an end.

You know, dear brothers and sisters, that the Synod of Bishops that will begin in around two weeks deals with the foundational topic of the Christian family. It does so in view of a deep crisis of the Christian family, which can be observed in all parts of the world. Something altogether decisive is at stake here, and I would like to take the opportunity to ask you all very sincerely to remember in your prayers the bishops at the synod, and ask God to bless our labors and to make them fruitful.

d. Christian culture is a culture of love of neighbor, a

culture of mercy, and for this same reason a culture of social justice, too. From the beginning, an altogether special component of it has been love for the weak and for the sick, the poor, the elderly—those who from an earthly perspective are useless. One of the greater barbarities of National Socialism was the murder of the mentally handicapped; behind this was their practice of measuring a human being by his usefulness for society. Thereby this worldview branded itself profoundly as a deviation from the Christian culture of Europe.

Christian culture not only built cathedrals for the glory of God, but also founded hospitals for the sick and the elderly, this too for the glory of God, whom it honored in suffering human beings. It placed these hospitals under the special protection of the Holy Spirit, who is Divine Love, the love between Father and Son: he was honored by this practice of loving along with his love; Christians entrusted to his consolation those who needed consolation in a special way.

True European culture is not only a culture of the intellect, but also a culture of the heart—a culture that is warmed by the Holy Spirit—and, therefore, a culture of mercy. From Christ crucified, it discovered the nobility of suffering, and that ennobled the culture itself. From this culture of works of mercy sprang up many religious foundations, which left their mark not only on the Church but also on European culture. Therefore, preserving Europe and developing it further means in particular also continuing to live and to foster this culture of works of mercy by accepting and taking up God's mercy.

3. This brings me to one last peculiar feature of what is European, in the Christian sense. Europe has always been at the same time national and supranational. It has always found

its quite particular expressions in the individual nations. The variety of national cultures is part of the richness of the concept of Europe. But in Europe's best eras, the nations were not closed off from one another, but, rather, above and beyond the national boundaries there were foundational organizations of common interest in which Europe's unity was experienced. Thus diversity was not opposition but, rather, the fructification of all for each other's sake.

I have already spoken about the universities and the artists, for whom there were no boundaries. Just as Veit Stoss, who was from Nuremberg, created his greatest work in Kraków, so too Jan Polack from Kraków matured as an artist in Munich and created works of everlasting beauty there. The religious orders, the councils, and the fundamental elements of the European legal system transcended the nations. Beyond all the boundaries, above all, Rome was the connecting center.

After all the destruction that National Socialism wreaked in the first half of this [twentieth] century, we must again relearn this original European character: respect for the uniqueness of the other and commonality in diversity. This is why a common faith is so important, a faith that joins us in the unity of one single Church, above and beyond the boundaries. This is why unity with the Holy Father in Rome is so important, in which the supranational character of the faith is expressed.

But when faith in Christ is lived out correctly, then it will also automatically produce, as one of its fundamental virtues, fraternal unity with Christians of other denominations and with all people who are seeking God.

In the center of my cathedral city of Munich stands the Marian Column that the Bavarian Elector Maximilian set up in 1638 during the terrible tribulation of the Thirty Years'

War. It was meant to be not only the center of this city, but also the center of the whole land, and in fact all distances in our city are measured from this point; Mary has remained the silent hub of all our streets.

The image of the Mother of the Lord is part of the heart and soul of European culture. It is part of the heart and soul of our faith. In the Mother's presence, we all understand one another; in her presence, we all recognize ourselves as children. From her we learn trust; with her we learn to believe and to pray. Our common Mother gives us a common language, however different the hymns and the prayers may be in the individual countries—in the heart they all have the same sound: When we look up to our Mother, defiance ends and enmity is over. She gives us reconciliation; she leads us to her Son.

And so during these days, when for the first time after the calamitous Second World War a whole delegation from the German Bishops' Conference officially visits the Catholic Church in Poland and the Polish bishops, full of confidence in our common Mother, the Mother of the Lord, let us pray that she will bless the path of reconciliation on which we are walking toward each other.

Let us pray to her to protect our countries from war and from all evil, but especially from the temptation of disbelief and from its consequences. Let us ask her to lead us on the basis of faith to true peace, to true culture, and thus to obtain for Europe a new future based on faith.

3

Europe and Anti-Europe: True and False Democracy, True and False Modernity

In the vicissitudinous history of the concept and reality of "Europe", it is significant that the idea of Europe has made a conspicuous entrance whenever danger threatened "the peoples who were to be united under this collective concept".[1] This is true not only in our time, when, after two world wars, considering the destruction in the European world, the question about the West and about the restoration of a united Europe has become urgent. Heinz Gollwitzer pointed out that the passage of the term "Europe" from learned language into popular speech, which occurred as early as the beginning of the modern era, should probably be viewed not only as a result of the widespread influence of humanistic thought, which owed much to antiquity, but also as a reaction to the threat from the Turks.[2] Europe comes to know its identity most clearly when it is forcibly confronted with something that represents its very opposite. One can most readily approach the essence of a thing by determining first what it is not. The problem with the contemporary debate about Europe and also with the political struggle for Europe consists largely of the fact that

[1] H. Gollwitzer, "Europa, Abendland", in *Historisches Wörterbuch der Philosophie*, ed. J. Ritter (Basel and Stuttgart: Scheidegger und Spiess, 1972), 2:826.

[2] Ibid.

it remains unclear what people actually mean by "Europe" or intend it to be. Is it more than a somewhat nebulous romantic dream? Is it more than a community of political and economic interests for former world powers that have been pushed to the sidelines? What is actually meant by Europe must lie somewhere between nebulous idealism and a merely pragmatic community of interests. Only when it is more than both of these can it represent over the long term a real and, at the same time, an ideal goal for political action that is informed by morality. Mere *Realpolitik* without a formative, moral idea does not hold up; yet mere idealism that has no concrete political content remains ineffective and empty. Thus an initial thesis that can serve as a basis for this lecture might be formulated as follows: Only when the term "Europe" represents a synthesis of political reality and moral ideality can it become a dynamic force for the future.

Accordingly, we must look for a concept of Europe that fulfills these requirements. Methodologically, the history of European thought and of European reality itself has just offered us a way, namely, by finding out first from the counterimages what Europe is not. Then, in a second section, I will attempt to formulate the positive components of the concept "Europe". The third section will briefly define the tasks faced by someone who wants Europe.

I. Counterimages to Europe

When we begin to ascertain the counterimages to what, based on history and on the ethos preserved within it, must be called "Europe", I see three in particular, each of which represents a different historical departure from the historical dynamic of the European thing. First, today there is a strong, worldwide psychological and political trend that would like to go back in history to a time before the European element. It wants to cleanse history, so to speak, of the incursion of the European thing, which is regarded as an alienation from one's own thing or in general as the original sin of history, as the reason for the life-threatening crisis in which mankind finds itself today. Second, there is a forward-looking trend that outruns and escapes European history, as it were, continuing its trajectory in such a way as to loosen its intrinsic hold on traditional elements. Third, there is a trend that combines these two movements and thereby aims at a complete fusion of realism and ideal driving forces and thus also becomes the most drastic alternative blueprint to Europe.

In the following remarks, I will attempt to outline briefly these three trends, which, I believe, can mark off the boundaries of the concept "Europe".

1. Back before Europe

From the end of antiquity until well into the early modern era, Islam proved to be the real counterpart to Europe. The contrast between Europe and Asia, between *Erebos* (evening) and *Oriens* (sunrise),[3] which can be found as early as the sixth century before Christ in the writings of Hecataeus of Miletus and which was not meant as a merely geographic distinction, continues in modified form in this confrontation. From its very origins, Islam is in certain respects a return to a monotheism that does not accept the Christian turn to a God who has become man, and it likewise shuts itself off from Greek rationality and the resulting culture, which by way of the idea of God's Incarnation had become a compo-

[3] H. Treidler, "Europe", in *Der kleine Pauly, Lexikon der Antike* (Stuttgart: Druckenmüller, 1967), 2:448.

nent of Christian monotheism. Of course, one may object that again and again over the course of history there has been rapprochement between Islam and the intellectual world of Greece, but it has never lasted. Above all, this means that the separation of faith and law, of religion and tribal authority, was not completed in Islam and cannot be accomplished without disturbing Islam at the very core. Put differently: the faith is presented in the form of a more or less archaic system of civil and penal laws and corresponding practices in everyday life. Islam is defined, not in terms of nationality, but, rather, by a legal system that fixes its ethnic and cultural features and at the same time sets limits to rationality where the Christian synthesis sees that reason has its place.[4]

Since the eighteenth century, Islam obviously had lost much of its political and moral importance, and from the nineteenth century on it increasingly came under the rule of European legal systems that considered themselves universally applicable because, as enlightened law, they had detached themselves from their Christian foundations and now presented themselves as pure, rational law. But, for that very reason, these legal systems are necessarily perceived as godless and contrary to the faith wherever Islam is or becomes alive as a faith. Considering the unity of religion and of ethnicity, they appear to be an attack that is both ethnic and religious, to be an alienation not only from what is one's own but from what is real. The combination of these two affronts causes the vehemence of the reaction we can observe today.

There are certainly many reasons for the intensification of this trend, but they cannot be discussed here in detail.

[4] See, for example, the presentation by Ringgren and Ström, *Die Religionen der Völker* (Stuttgart: Alfred Kröner, 1959), 98–142.

Most importantly, on the one hand, the Arab world has grown stronger politically and economically, and, on the other hand, European rational law is in a crisis, now that it has completely relinquished its religious foundations and de facto runs the risk of turning into a rule of anarchy. The moment Europe calls its own spiritual foundations into question or abolishes them, separates itself from its history and declares it a cesspool, the response of a non-European culture can only be a radical reaction and a return to the time before the encounter with Christian values.

Furthermore, I consider this reaction of the Islamic world to be only the most visible and politically most effective segment of a movement that, in many varied forms, is powerfully at work within the European consciousness itself. The work of Lévi-Strauss—to mention only one example—expresses for its part the longing in the European mind to put its Christian domestication behind it, precisely as domestication—as slavery, in contrast with which the *monde sauvage* can be seen as the better world.[5]

On another level, granted, yet structurally related in many respects, is the cruelest and most terrifying form of a return to a pre-Christian world: what Germany experienced in the first half of the twentieth century and exhibited to the rest of mankind. For in keeping with its basic tendency, National Socialism was a renunciation of Christianity as alienation from the "beautiful" Germanic "savagery" and the desire to go back to a time before the Judeo-Christian "alienation", when such savagery was celebrated as the true culture.[6]

[5] This notion is critically examined in a book by my student B. Adoukonou, *Jalons pour une théologie Africaine* (Paris: Lethielleux, 1980).

[6] On this subject, see, for example, R. Baumgartner, *Weltanschauungskampf im Dritten Reich* (Mainz: Grünewald, 1977).

2. Escape into the future

A second antithesis to the historical and moral entity called Europe developed—quite unlike what has been described thus far—from the nature of the European mind itself and probably should be characterized today as the prevalent finding in the political thought of the so-called Western world in general. Typical for Europe is the separation of faith and law (a separation with a Christian basis) that includes the rationality of law and its relative autonomy with respect to the religious realm but also, generally speaking, the duality of Church and State. While the political realm is subject to religiously based ethical norms, it does not have a theocratic constitution.

This independence of reason has led in the modern era with increasing rapidity to its total emancipation and to an unlimited autonomy of reason. Reason thereby assumes the form of positive reason, as Auguste Comte understood it, which takes as its only standard what is experimentally verifiable. The radical consequence of this, however, is that the entire realm of values, the entire realm of what "is above us", drops out of the sphere of reason, that the sole binding standard for reason and thus for man, politically as well as individually, becomes what "is under him", namely, the mechanical forces of nature that can be manipulated experimentally. Granted, God is not rejected absolutely, but he belongs to the realm of what is purely private and subjective. In a highly problematic essay that nevertheless frames the issue suggestively, Friedrich Wilhelm Bracht tries to depict the real revolution of 1789 as the fact that God ceased to be the public *summum bonum* (highest good), that he was replaced first by the nation and then, from 1848 on, by the proletariat or else the world revolution. In his opinion, one would have to say about modern consumer society that its God is its belly.[7] In a society, however, in which God can no longer be the common, public *summum bonum* but is relegated to the private sphere, God's status is changed for the individual as well. A society in which the movement we have just described has taken over completely I would call "post-European". In such a society, the things that constituted Europe as a spiritual reality have been abandoned. In this sense, today's Western societies appear to me to be largely post-European societies already, which of course live on the aftereffects of the European heritage and to that extent are still European. The plurality of values that is legitimate and European is noticeably exaggerated into a pluralism that increasingly excludes every moral mainstay of law and every public embodiment of the sacred, of reverence for God as a value that is communal, too. Even to question this is considered, in most circles, an offense against tolerance and against the society founded on reason alone. But a society in which this is radically the case cannot, I am convinced, remain a society of law for long. It will open the door to tyranny when it is sufficiently weary of anarchy. Rudolf Bultmann, in a very astute analysis of the problem of law, which he undertakes within the context of his commentary on the trial of Jesus, formulates the extremely thought-provoking statement: "An unchristian State is possible in principle, but not an atheistic State."[8] Western societies are going through

[7] F. W. Bracht, "Die Abkehr von Gott in der Politik", *Zeitbühne* 8 (1979): 4–14, 41–48. I consider neither the political nor the ecclesial notions of Bracht acceptable, but the question about God's position in public consciousness deserves attention, even if one cannot agree with the author on anything else.

[8] R. Bultmann, *The Gospel of John: A Commentary* (Philadelphia: Westminster Press, 1971), 660–61.

this learning experience today. The Islamic reaction against Europe is very closely connected with it, as we have already indicated.

3. Marxism

The two trends described above are combined in a remarkable manner in Marxism, the third and most impressive form of turning away from the historical scheme of Europe. Marxism, on the one hand, harks back to a situation prior to Christian faith; it is a return to the salvation that was begun in Christ, an entrance into the still open-ended structure of Israel's hope. But it does so, not by anchoring itself in Israel's great religious heritage, but merely by drawing upon its religious dynamic and the full force of a hope that transcends rationality; then, however, it applies as its instrument the totally emancipated reason of the modern era, which has been freed from metaphysical connections of any sort. It sees its *summum bonum* in the world revolution, that is, in the total renunciation of the world as it has been until now, whereby the world that is to be newly created, as the negation of a negation, must be totally positive. Inasmuch as it combines the two countermovements to what is European, Marxism qualifies as the most radical antithesis not only to what is Christian as such, but also to the historical scheme that has been shaped by Christianity. What has been until now is viewed simply as an anti-value, and for that very reason the revolution is considered the absolute value. What has been until now takes its place in the historical process, once it has been understood, but that in no way alters the fact that overcoming it is the only progressive action possible that will lead history onward to its goal. Accordingly, Marxism is the product of Europe but at the same time the most decisive rejection of Europe, in the sense of that inner identity which it has developed over the course of its history.

II. Positive Components of the Concept of Europe

In the second section, I will attempt to outline positively what Europe is. I intend to do so by examining the history of the meaning of the word "Europe", in which the inner stratification of the complex structure of Europe becomes visible. It seems to me that we can discern four such strata.

1. The Greek heritage

Europe, as a word and as a geographical and intellectual-spiritual concept, is a construct of the Greeks. The term in itself is indicative. It probably goes back to a name for evening (*ereb*) that was common to several Semitic languages and thus refers to the fateful dialogue of the Semitic mind and the Western mind, which belongs to the essence of what is European.[9] Geographically, the space described as Europe gradually widened. At first it included only the region of Thessaly, Macedonia, and Attica. As early as Herodotus, however, it was part of the threefold division of the earth into Europe, Asia, and Libya, one of the three great geographical and cultural zones that are contiguous in the region of the Mediterranean Sea.[10]

Europe, accordingly, appears to be constituted at first by the spirit of Greece. If it were to forget its Greek heritage, it could no longer be Europe. While the myth of Europa points to the area of the chthonic [underworld] religions

[9] Treidler, "Europe", 2:448.

[10] Ibid.

and of Minoan religious circles, the formation of Europe was based on overcoming the chthonic religion through the Apollonian form. Greece is a heritage with obligations, although they are difficult to describe in detail. I would regard as the central feature what Helmut Kuhn has called the Socratic difference: the difference between the good and goods and, thus, the difference in which both the right of conscience and also the reciprocal relation of *ratio* and *religio* are present.[11]

The heritage of Greece can also be formulated from another perspective that is somewhat more comprehensible to us. One of its discoveries, which is valid for all ages (despite the many different connotations of the term today), is democracy, which of course, as Plato explained, is essentially connected with *eunomia*, with the validity of good law, and which can remain democracy only in that connection.[12] Thus democracy is never merely majority rule, and the mechanism by which majorities are established must be subject to the common rule of the *nomos*, of what is intrinsically right, that is, to the recognition of values that are an obligatory prerequisite for the majority also.

2. *The Christian heritage*

The second stratum of the concept "Europe" becomes evident in the well-known episode in Acts 16:12. After this extremely odd and dramatic account, the Spirit of Jesus forbids Saint Paul to continue his missionary journey within the confines of Asia. Instead, a Macedonian appears to him in a

[11] H. Kuhn, *Der Staat* (Munich: Kösel Verlag, 1967), 25–26.

[12] Cf. C. Meier, "Demokratie", in *Geschichtliche Grundbegriffe: Historisches Lexikon zur politisch-sozialen Sprache in Deutschland* (Stuttgart: Klett-Cotta Verlag, 1973), 829ff.

vision one night and calls to him: "Come over to Macedonia and help us." The passage then continues: "And when he had seen the vision, immediately we sought to go on into Macedonia, concluding that God had called us to preach the gospel to them." Although it is depicted in this way only in the Acts of the Apostles, I still think that this has a broader basis in the New Testament. In my opinion, what is being said here intrinsically touches upon a saying from the Gospel of John that occupies a significant place there. Before the Passion, after Jesus' entrance into Jerusalem, at the very moment when there is talk about the fulfillment of Jesus' glory, the request of the Greeks arrives: "Sir, we wish to see Jesus" (Jn 12:21). Bishop Graber has pointed out that in Saint Luke's account of Pentecost, in the list of peoples who represent the whole world (Acts 2:9ff.), only Asian peoples are named at first. Not until the very last place is there any mention of the Romans who are present.[13] The point of departure for the Gospel, therefore, is in the Orient. Like John and the whole New Testament, Luke emphasizes the root, which is Israel: salvation comes from the Jews (Jn 4:22). But Luke adds a path that opens up a new door. The path traced out in the Acts of the Apostles, all told, is a path from Jerusalem to Rome, a pathway to the pagans by whom Jerusalem is destroyed and who nevertheless adopt it in a new way.

Christianity, accordingly, is the synthesis brought about in Jesus Christ between Israel's faith and the Greek mind. Wilhelm Kamlah has portrayed this very impressively.[14] Europe is based on this synthesis. The Renaissance attempt to

[13] R. Graber, *Ein Bischof spricht über Europa* (Regensburg: Josef Kral, 1978), 10–11, 22–23, along with the reference to the relation to John 12:21.

[14] W. Kamlah, *Christentum und Geschichtlichkeit* (Stuttgart: Kohlhammer, 1951).

distill and restore the Greek element in a pure form by removing the Christian element is just as hopeless and absurd as the more recent attempt to manufacture a de-Hellenized Christianity. In my opinion, Europe in the narrower sense originates from this synthesis and is founded upon it.

3. The Latin heritage

A third stratum of the concept is evident in the fact that during the sixth century "Europe" was understood as a term for Gaul and that the Carolingian Empire then claimed to be Europe and to exhaust the meaning of this word.[15] In the further course of the development, this identification, which was never universally accepted, loosened up again to a great extent. An equation of the medieval *Imperium sacrum* with Europe did not result. The concept "Europe" was more capacious than that of the Holy Roman Empire, which considered itself to be the Christian transformation of the *Imperium Romanum*. On the contrary, Europe now coincided with the Occident, that is, with the sphere of the Latin culture and Church, whereby this Latin territory included not only the Romance peoples but also the Germanic, Anglo-Saxon, and some of the Slavic peoples, especially the Poles. The *res publica christiana*, which the Christian West considered itself to be, was not a politically constituted structure but, rather, a real and living whole in its cultural unity, in its "legal systems, which transcended tribes and nations, in its councils, in the institution of its universities, in the founding and spread of its religious orders, and in the circulation of its intellectual and ecclesial life through Rome as the ventricle of its heart".[16]

[15] Gollwitzer, "Europa, Abendland", 826.

[16] Ibid., 825.

The medieval *res publica christiana* cannot be restored, and to restore it as such is not a reasonable goal, either. History cannot be turned back. A future Europe must carry within itself the fourth dimension also, that of the modern era, and above all must surpass the all-too-narrow framework of the West, of the Latin world, so as to include the Greek world and the Eastern Christian world, or at least it will have to be open to them. But conversely, there can be no future Europe that would jettison the Latin heritage, the heritage of the Christian West in the sense that we have just described. If that were to happen, we would no longer be talking about Europe but would already have bid farewell to it.

4. The heritage of the modern era

As the fourth stratum of what constitutes Europe we should mention the indispensable contribution made by the spirit of the modern era. Granted, the ambivalence inherent in each of the individual strata is perhaps most plainly in evidence here. But by no means should this lead to a rejection of the modern era, a temptation that one could encounter both in nineteenth-century Romanticism with its nostalgia for the Middle Ages and also in Catholic circles between the two world wars.

I consider it to be the characteristic feature of the modern era, in the positive sense, that the separation of faith and law, which in the medieval *res publica christiana* was rather hidden, is now carried out consistently; as a consequence, freedom of religion gradually and clearly takes shape in a variety of bourgeois legal systems, and, thus, the interior claims of the faith are distinguished from the fundamental claims of the ethos upon which the law is based. The human values that are fundamental for the Christian world view make it possible, in a productive dualism of Church and State, to have a free, humane society in which freedom of conscience and, with it, fundamental human rights are secured. In this society, different expressions of the Christian faith can coexist and make room for different political positions, which nevertheless have in common a central set of standard values, the binding force of which simultaneously safeguards a maximum of freedom.

As we know from our own experience, this is a rather idealized picture of the modern era, as it wanted to see itself but never quite was concretely. The ambivalence of the modern era is based on the fact that it obviously failed to appreciate the roots and the real-life basis of the idea of freedom and urged an emancipation of reason that intrinsically contradicts the nature of human reason (which is not divine) and therefore necessarily became unreasonable itself. The epitome of the modern era appears—wrongly, in the final analysis—to be that completely autonomous reason which no longer recognizes anything but itself and has thereby gone blind and, through the destruction of its own foundations, becomes inhumane and hostile to creation. This sort of autonomous reason is, granted, the product of the European mind, but at the same time it should be regarded as essentially post-European, indeed anti-European, as the inner destruction of what is not only constitutive for Europe but is the prerequisite for humane society in general. Thus, we must adopt from the modern era, as an essential and indispensable dimension of what is European, the relative separation of Church and State, freedom of conscience, human rights, and reason's responsibility for itself, while resisting its radicalization by holding fast to the foundations of reason in reverence for God and for the fundamental moral values that come from the Christian faith.

III. Theses for a Future Europe

From the discussion thus far it is probably clear that not every political or economic union that takes place in Europe constitutes per se Europe's future. A mere centralization of business or legislative jurisdictions can also lead to an accelerated deconstruction of Europe, if it leads, for instance, to a technocracy that takes increased consumption as its sole standard. Conversely, such institutions have their value in a larger context as a way of overcoming nation-worship and as part of a peaceful order in which all have a share in this world's goods. Of course, then, their fundamental rule cannot be an extended group-egotism of the rich nations as they defend their advantages. Their shared wealth must be understood as a shared responsibility for the world as a whole, and in this sense Europe has to be an open-ended system in its economic mechanisms as well. The idea of ruling the world and of dividing up the other parts of the world into colonies must be replaced by the idea of an open society and of reciprocal responsibility. This fundamental orientation, which results from the concept of Europe that has been elaborated thus far, can be developed in four theses from the four dimensions of Europe I have tried to outline.

First thesis: One constitutive element of Europe from its beginnings in Hellas is the intrinsic correlation of democracy and *eunomia*, that is, laws that cannot be manipulated.

As opposed to party rule and dictatorship (arbitrary rule), Europe has had a high regard for the rule of reason and of freedom, which can last only as the rule of law. The limitation of power, checks on power, and transparency in wielding power are constitutive elements of the European community. As a prerequisite for these, the law must be immune to manipulation and must have its own inviolable sphere of action. The prerequisite for this, in turn, is what the Greeks called *eunomia*, which means that the law is based on moral standards. Therefore, I consider it undemocratic to turn the expression "law and order" into abusive language. Every dictatorship begins with disparagement of the law. We should agree with Plato also when he says that it is less important to have a particular type of mechanism for forming the majority than it is to actualize as securely as possible under the given circumstances the *content* of democratic mechanisms, that is, the control of power by law, the inviolability of law by those in power, and the normalization of law in accordance with ethics. Accordingly, anyone who fights for Europe is fighting for democracy, but for democracy in its indissoluble connection with *eunomia*, as the concept has just been described.

Second thesis: If *eunomia* is the prerequisite for the viability of democracy, as opposed to tyranny and mob rule, then the fundamental prerequisite for *eunomia* in turn is a common—and, for public law, obligatory—reverence for moral values and for God.

Once more I recall Bultmann's important statement: "An unchristian State is possible in principle, but not an atheistic State"—at least, not as a State that simultaneously continues to be ruled by law. This implies that God is *by no means* relegated to the private sphere but is recognized publicly also as the supreme value. This certainly includes—and I would like to emphasize this very strongly—tolerance and a place for the atheist, and it must have nothing to do with coercion in matters of faith. It is just that, the way things are beginning to develop now, in many respects they should be the other way around: atheism is starting to be the fundamental public dogma, and faith is tolerated as a private opinion, yet this arrangement ultimately does *not* tolerate faith in its essence. Ancient Rome, too, granted such private tolerance to faith; sacrificing to Caesar was supposed to be only an admission that faith had no public rights and, in any case, made no fundamental claim.

I am convinced that in the long term the rule of law has no chance of survival in a State that is radically and dogmatically atheistic and that it is necessary to reconsider this question fundamentally—as a matter of survival. I likewise venture to declare that democracy is capable of functioning only when conscience is functioning and that the latter has nothing to say if it is not oriented to the validity of the fundamental moral values of Christianity, which can be put into action even without a Christian profession of faith, indeed, even in the context of a non-Christian religion.

Third thesis: The rejection of the dogma of atheism as a prerequisite for public law and the formation of a State, along with a publicly recognized reverence for God as the basis for ethics and law, means rejecting both the nation and also the world revolution as the *summum bonum*.

Nationalism not only brought Europe to the brink of destruction de facto and historically; it also contradicts what Europe essentially is, spiritually and politically—even though it has dominated recent decades of European history. Hence, international political, economic, and legal institutions are necessary; these naturally cannot be intended as building blocks for a super-nation but, instead, should restore and strengthen the proper identity and importance of the individual regions of Europe. Regional, national, and supranational institutions should mesh in such a way that both centralism and particularism are excluded in like manner. Above all, open exchange and unity in variety should be revitalized to a great extent through nongovernmental cultural and religious institutions and forces.

In the universities, religious orders, and Church councils, the Middle Ages were acquainted with European institutions as a concrete, nongovernmental reality that was effective precisely as such. Recall that Anselm of Canterbury, for instance, came from Aosta in Italy and served as abbot in Brittany and as archbishop in England; that Albert the Great came from Germany and was able to teach just as well in Paris as in Cologne and then became the bishop of Regensburg; that Thomas Aquinas taught in Naples, Paris, and Cologne and that Duns Scotus was an instructor in England as well as in Paris and Cologne, to mention only a few examples. There should be a revival of this; if these cultural entities are not decisively strengthened as vital, nongovernmental institutions, then in my opinion the merely governmental and economic mechanisms can ultimately have no positive effect. From this perspective, Christian ecumenism has a specifically European significance, too. Just as nationalism is opposed to the future of Europe, so too does Marxism, at least in its pure form, contradict what is essential to Europe. Its rejection of history, which in its entirety is demoted to the status of a mere prehistory of the world that is yet to be created, its methods, and its goals lead to a tyrannical society in which law and ethics can be manipulated and, therefore, freedom is turned into its opposite.

Fourth thesis: For Europe, the recognition and the preservation of freedom of conscience, human rights, academic freedom, and hence of a free human society must be constitutive.

These achievements of the modern era should be safeguarded and developed, without falling into the bottomless pit of a rationalism devoid of transcendence, which abolishes its own freedom from within. By these standards, the Christian will evaluate European policy, and based on them he will fulfill his political task.

4

"Might Makes Right" and the Right to Life: Toward a European Idea of Law

Address at the Convention
on the Right to Life and Europe,
Held in Rome, December 18–19, 1987

Why continue to advocate publicly in this tragedy?

To a wide spectrum of self-proclaimed moderates in public opinion today it may seem excessive and inopportune, indeed downright tiresome, that anyone should continue to reiterate as a decisive question the problem of respect for recently conceived preborn life. After the harrowing debates associated with the legalization of abortion that have occurred within the last fifteen years in almost all Western countries, should we not consider the issue resolved now and therefore avoid reopening ideological conflicts from the past? Why not resign ourselves to the fact that we have lost this battle and devote our energies instead to initiatives that might win the favor of a larger social consensus? Viewing things superficially, we could be convinced that, basically, the legal approval of abortion has changed little in our private life and in the life of our societies. Basically everything seems to continue exactly as before. Everyone can follow his conscience: someone who does not want to abort is not forced to do so. Someone who does so with the approval of a law—so they say—might have done so anyway. It is all done in the silence of an operating room, which at least guarantees a certain degree of safety for the procedure. The fetus that will never see the light is as though it had never existed. Who notices it? Why continue to advocate publicly in this tragedy? Would it not be better to leave it buried in the silence of the conscience of the individual actors in the drama?

In the Book of Genesis, there is a passage that speaks to this problem with impressive eloquence. It concerns the blessing that the Lord God gives to Noah and to his sons after the flood, which reestablishes forever those laws which alone can guarantee the continuation of life for the human race after original sin. The creation that had come from God's hands absolutely perfect became involved in disorder and degeneration after the fall of our first parents. Violence and unlimited killing and revenge spread throughout the world, henceforth making a well-ordered, just social life impossible. Now, after the great cleansing of the Flood, God puts down the bow of his anger and once again embraces the world in his mercy, showing it the essential norms for survival, with a view to its future redemption: "For your lifeblood I will surely require a reckoning; of every beast I will require it and of man; of every man's brother I will require the life of man. Whoever sheds the blood of man, by man shall his blood be shed; for God made man in his own image" (Gen 9:5–6). With these words, God claims the life of a human being as his peculiar possession: it remains under his direct and immediate protection. Human blood is something "sacred"; when it is shed, it cries out to God (cf. Gen 4:10), because man is made in his image and likeness. The authority of society and in society was instituted by him precisely for the purpose of guaranteeing respect for this fundamental right, which is endangered by the wicked human heart.

Acknowledging the sacredness of human life and its inviolability, with no exceptions, is therefore not a little problem or an issue that we can consider relative, given the pluralism of the opinions present in modern society. The passage from Genesis orients our reflection in two senses, which neatly corresponds to the dual dimension of the demands that had been made on us in the beginning: (1) there are no "little murders": respect for every human life is an essential condition for making possible a society worthy of this name; (2) when in his conscience man loses respect for life as something sacred, inevitably he ends up losing his own identity, too.

Might makes right or the might of what is right?

In today's pluralistic societies, in which various religious, cultural, and ideological orientations coexist, it is becoming increasingly difficult to guarantee a common basis of ethical values shared by all and capable of serving as an adequate foundation for democracy itself. On the other hand, there is a rather widespread conviction that we cannot do without a minimum of moral values that are acknowledged and sanctioned in social life; yet when it comes down to determining them through the play of the consensus that they must obtain at the social level, they become less and less stable. One single value seems undisputed and indisputable, to the point where it becomes the filter for selecting the others: the right of individual freedom to express oneself without impositions, at least as long as one does not injure the rights of others.

And thus even the right to an abortion is invoked as an essential part of the right to freedom for women, for men, and for society. A woman has the right to continue practicing her profession, to safeguard her reputation, to maintain a certain life-style. Man has the right to decide on the purpose of his life, to have a career, to enjoy his work. Society has the right to control the numerical level of the population so as to guarantee widespread well-being for its citizens, through the balanced management of its resources, jobs, etc.

All these rights are real and well founded. No one denies that sometimes the concrete situation in life in which the choice of an abortion is made can be tragic. Nevertheless, the fact remains that individuals claim to exercise these real rights to the detriment of the life of an innocent human being, whose rights are not even taken into consideration. In this way, people become blind to the right to life of another smaller, weaker person who has no voice. The rights of some are affirmed at the expense of the fundamental right to life of another. All legalization of abortion, therefore, implies the idea that might makes right.

In this way, inadvertently for the most part, but really, the very foundations of an authentic democracy based on the order of justice are undermined. The constitutional charters of the Western countries, the product of a complex process of cultural maturation and secular struggles, are based on the idea of an order of justice, on the awareness of a fundamental equality of all people in our common humanity. At the same time, they express an awareness of the profound injustice entailed in making the real but secondary interests of some prevail over the fundamental rights of others. The Universal Declaration of Human Rights, signed by almost all the countries in the world in 1948, after the terrible trial of the Second World War, fully expresses, even in its title, the awareness that human rights (of which the fundamental one is precisely the right to life) belong to a human being by nature, that the State recognizes them but does not confer them, that they belong to all human beings as human beings and not because of their other secondary characteristics that others would have the right to determine arbitrarily. We can understand, then, how a State that arrogates to itself the prerogative to define who is a subject of rights and who is not, and which consequently identifies some as having the power to violate the fundamental right to life of others contradicts the democratic ideal—which it continues to cite, however, while undermining the very foundations on which it stands. In fact, by accepting the violation of the rights of the weakest, it also accepts the fact that might prevails over right.

"Ecce Homo"

But besides the legal problem, at a more fundamental level, there is the moral problem that runs through the heart of each one of us, in that hidden interiority where free will makes a decision for good or for evil. I said a moment ago that the decision in favor of abortion necessarily involves a moment in which one agrees to become blind to the right to life of the little one who was recently conceived. The moral tragedy, the decision for good or for evil, begins with one's outlook, with the choice of whether or not to look at the other's face. Why is infanticide rejected almost unanimously today, while people have become almost unfeeling about abortion? Maybe just because in abortion we do not see the face of the one who will be condemned to never seeing the light of day. Many psychologists have pointed out that in those women who want to abort, the spontaneous fantasies of an expectant mother (naming the child, imagining its face and future) are repressed. And these very same fantasies that are dismissed or repressed often return later as feelings of unresolved guilt to torment their conscience.

The face of another is fraught with an appeal to my freedom to welcome him and to take care of him, because it affirms his value in himself and not insofar as he happens to coincide with some interest of mine. Moral truth, as a truth about the unique and unrepeatable value of the human person who is made in God's image, is a truth fraught with demands on my freedom. To decide to look this truth in the face is to decide to convert, to allow myself to be challenged, to go out of myself, and to make space for another person. Therefore, even the evident character of the moral value depends in large part on a secret decision of free will, which agrees to see and therefore to be provoked and to change.

In his preface to the well-known book by the French biologist Jacques Testart, *L'oeuf transparent* [The transparent egg], the philosopher Michel Serres (apparently a nonbeliever), in confronting the question about the respect owed to the human embryo, asks himself the question: "Who is man?"

He points out that there are no unambiguous and truly satisfactory answers in philosophy and in today's culture. However, he notes that, although we have no precise theoretical definition of a human being, we nevertheless know very well in our concrete experience of life who a human being is. We know it above all when we are confronted by someone who is suffering, who is a victim of the abuse of power, who is defenseless and condemned to death: "*Ecce homo!*" Yes, this nonbeliever quotes, of all things, the statement of Pilate, who had all the power, in the presence of Jesus, who had been stripped, scourged, crowned with thorns, and was now condemned to the Cross. Who is man? He is precisely the weakest and most defenseless, the one who has neither the power nor the voice with which to defend himself, the one whom we can pass by in life while pretending not to see him. The one to whom we can close our hearts and say that he never existed. And thus, spontaneously another passage from the Gospel comes to mind that was meant to respond to a similar request for a definition: "Who is my neighbor?" We know that in order to recognize who our neighbor is, it is necessary to agree to become a neighbor, that is, to stop, to get off the horse, to come over to the one who is in need, and to take care of him. "As you did it to one of the least of these my brethren, you did it to me" (Mt 25:40).

A look at the other person safeguards the truth and the dignity of the human being

I would like to read to you an excerpt by a great Italian-German thinker, Romano Guardini:

> Man is not inviolable merely in virtue of the fact that he exists. An animal, too, could lay claim to such a right, since it, too, exists. . . . Man's life remains inviolable because *he is a person*. . . . To be a person is not a psychological but an existential fact: it does not depend fundamentally on one's age or psychological condition or on the gifts of nature with which the subject is provided. . . . The personality may remain below the threshold of consciousness—for example, when we are sleeping—but it remains, nevertheless, and must be taken into account. The personality may as yet be undeveloped—for example, when we are children—but it has a claim to moral respect from the very beginning. It is even possible that the personality in general may not emerge in one's acts, since the psycho-physical presuppositions are lacking—as in those who are mentally ill. . . . Finally, the personality can also remain hidden—as in the embryo—but it exists in the embryo from the outset

> and has its own rights. It is this personality that gives men their dignity. It distinguishes them from material objects and makes them *subjects*. . . . We treat a thing like a thing when we possess it, use it, and finally destroy it—or, if we are speaking of human beings, kill it. *The prohibition against taking human life expresses in the most acute form the prohibition of treating man as if he were a thing.*[1]

Thus it is also clear that the look that I freely agree to direct toward the other has a decisive effect on my own dignity. Just as I can agree to reduce the other to an object, to be used and destroyed, so, too, I must accept the consequences of my way of looking—consequences that have repercussions on me. "The measure you give will be the measure you get" (Mt 7:2). The look that I direct toward another has a decisive effect on my humanity. I can treat him as a thing only by forgetting his dignity and mine, the fact that both he and I are the image and likeness of God. The other is the custodian of my dignity. This is why morality, which begins with this look at the other, safeguards the truth and the dignity of the human being: man needs morality in order to be himself and not to lose his identity in the world of things.

There is a final, decisive passage to consider in our reflection, a passage that takes us back to the excerpt from Genesis from which we set out. How is it possible for man to look in this way that is capable of welcoming and respecting the dignity of the other person and at the same time of guaranteeing his own? The tragedy of our time lies precisely in our inability to look at one another in this way, and as a result the look of the other becomes a threat from which we

[1] Romano Guardini, "I diritti del nascituro," *Studi cattolici*, nos. 159–60 (May/June 1974), cited in Joseph Ratzinger, *Christianity and the Crisis of Cultures*, trans. Brian McNeil (San Francisco: Ignatius Press, 2006), 68–69.

must defend ourselves. In reality, morality is always part of a broader religious horizon, which constitutes its life breath and sphere of activity. Outside of this sphere it becomes asphyxiated and formal, it weakens and then dies. The ethical recognition of the sacredness of human life and the commitment to respect life both need faith in creation as their perspective. Thus, just as a child can confidently be open to love, if he knows that he is loved, and can develop and grow, if he knows that his parents look at him lovingly, so too we succeed in looking at others with respect for their dignity as persons if we experience God's loving look at us, which reveals to us how valuable our person is. "Then God said: 'Let us make man in our image, after our likeness. . . . And God saw everything that he had made, and behold, it was very good" (Gen 1:26, 31).

Christianity is the memory of the Lord's look of love at mankind, which safeguards the full truth about us and the ultimate guarantee of human dignity. The mystery of the Nativity reminds us that in Christ who is born, every human life, from its first beginnings, is definitively blessed and welcomed by God's merciful look. Christians know this and in their own lives stand beneath this look of love; with that look itself, they receive a message that is essential for the life and the future of mankind. So then they can take up today, with humility and pride, the good news of the faith, without which human life cannot exist for long. In this task of proclaiming human dignity and the duties to respect life that result from it, they will probably be ridiculed and hated, but the world could not live without them.

I would like to conclude with the astonishing words of the ancient letter to Diognetus, which describes the irreplaceable mission of Christians in the world:

Christians are indistinguishable from other men either by nationality, language or customs. . . . With regard to dress, food and manner of life in general, they follow the customs of whatever city they happen to be living in, whether it is Greek or foreign. And yet there is something extraordinary about their lives. They live in their own countries as though they were only passing through. They play their full role as citizens, but labor under all the disabilities of aliens. Any country can be their homeland, but for them their homeland, wherever it may be, is a foreign country. Like others, they marry and have children, but they do not expose them. They share their meals, but not their wives. They live in the flesh, but they are not governed by the desires of the flesh. They pass their days upon earth but they are citizens of heaven. Obedient to the laws, they yet live on a level that transcends the law. Christians love all men, but all men persecute them. . . . To speak in general terms, we may say that the Christian is to the world what the soul is to the body. . . . Christians love those who hate them just as the soul loves the body and all its members despite the body's hatred. It is by the soul, enclosed within the body, that the body is held together, and similarly, it is by the Christians, detained in the world as in a prison, that the world is held together. . . . Such is the Christian's lofty and divinely appointed function, from which he is not permitted to excuse himself.

5

Beyond Liberalism and Communism: Toward a European Idea of the Economy

Introduction to the Symposium "Church and Economics in Our Responsibility for the Future of the Global Economy"

In the name of the two other sponsors also, Cardinal Höffner and Cardinal Etchegaray, I cordially welcome all who have gathered here for the Symposium on Church and Economics. I am glad that the collaboration of the Pontifical Council for the Laity, the International Association of Catholic Universities, the Institute for German Economics, and the Konrad Adenauer Foundation has made possible a discussion on a global scale about a question that concerns us all. For the economic inequality between the Northern and the Southern Hemispheres is increasingly becoming an internal threat to the cohesiveness of the human family; in the long term it could endanger the course of our history no less than the arsenals of weapons with which East and West confront each other. Therefore, new efforts must be undertaken to overcome this tension, because all methods so far have proved inadequate for the purpose; on the contrary, poverty in the world has continued to grow in the last thirty years to a truly disturbing extent. In order to find truly forward-looking solutions, new economic ideas will be necessary, that, however, for their part seem to be inconceivable and most importantly incapable of realization in the absence of new moral impulses. At this juncture arises the possibility and the necessity of a dialogue between Church and economics.

Allow me to try to make clear in somewhat greater detail the point at issue that will be discussed in the next few days. For at first glance—just in terms of a classic economic theory—it is not evident what Church and economics are actually supposed to have to do with one another, apart from the fact that the Church, too, is responsible for business enterprises and to this extent is a market factor. But it is not in this capacity, as an element in the economy, that she is not supposed to enter into the dialogue here, but, rather, in her capacity as Church. Yet here we face the objection that according to the Second Vatican Council, too, the autonomy of secular departments is to be respected first and foremost, and therefore economics has to proceed according to its own rules and not according to moral deliberations applied to it from outside. But according to the tradition inaugurated by Adam Smith, the market is considered incompatible with ethics, because voluntary "moral" actions would contradict the rules of the market and would simply drive the moralizing entrepreneur out of the marketplace.[1] So for a long time, economic ethics was considered wooden iron [i.e., a contradiction in terms], because, after all, economics is about efficiency and not about morality.[2] The inner logic of the market supposedly frees us from the necessity of having to build on the greater or lesser morality of the individual

[1] See P. Koslowski, "Über Notwendigkeit und Möglichkeit einer Wirtschaftsethik", in *Scheidewege, Jahresschrift für skeptisches Denken* 15 (1985–1986): 301. To this fundamental essay I owe ideas that are essential for my presentation.

[2] Ibid., 294.

economic agents: The correct play of the market rules best guarantees progress and also distributive justice.

For a long time, the great results of economic theory caused people to overlook its limitations. In an altered situation, *its unspoken philosophical presuppositions and, thus, its problems* become clearer. Although this understanding is oriented toward the freedom of the individual economic agents and in this respect can be called liberalist, the core concept is actually deterministic. It presupposes that, given the characteristics of human beings and of the world, the free play of market forces can work only in one direction, namely, that supply and demand will tend to regulate themselves along the lines of economic efficiency and economic progress.

However, this determinism—in which man, although apparently free, in reality acts entirely under the necessary laws of the market—includes another and perhaps even more astonishing presupposition, namely, that the natural laws of the market (if I may put it that way) are essentially good and necessarily work for the good, regardless of the moral state of the individual human beings. These two presuppositions are not entirely wrong, as the results of the market economy show, but neither do they have unlimited applicability or unlimited accuracy, as the problems of today's global economy demonstrate.

Without elaborating the problem in detail here—which is not my task—I would merely like to underscore a statement by Peter Koslowski that makes the point on which the whole thing depends: "The economy is not only ruled by economic laws but is determined by human beings. . . ."[3] Even though the market economy is based on the placement

[3] Ibid., 304; cf. ibid., 301.

of the individual into a certain force field of interconnected rules, it cannot make the human being superfluous or eliminate his moral freedom from the economic event. Today it is becoming increasingly clear that the development of the global economy has to do also with the development of the global community, of the worldwide family of humanity, and that the development of mankind's spiritual faculties is of essential importance for the development of this global community. The rules of the market function only when a fundamental moral consensus exists and supports them.

Although so far I have tried to point out the tension between a purely liberal economic model and an ethical inquiry and, thus, to sketch a preliminary range of problems that will probably play a role in this symposium, I must now allude also to the opposite tension. Today the question about markets and morals has long since ceased to be a merely theoretical problem.

Since the intrinsic inequality of the individual major economic regions endangers the play of the market, there have been attempts since the 1950s to produce an economic equilibrium through development projects. Today, we can no longer overlook the fact that this attempt, in the form that it has taken until now, has failed and that the inequality has even been aggravated. The consequence is that broad sectors of the Third World, that at first looked with great hope to developmental aid now see the market economy as the reason for their poverty and regard it as a system of exploitation that has become a structural sin and injustice.

From this perspective, then, *a centrally managed economy* appears to be *the moral alternative to which the Third World turns with an almost religious fervor*; indeed, it literally becomes the content of a religion. For whereas the market economy bets on the beneficial operation of selfishness and its automatic limitation by other selfish competitors, here the predominant idea seems to be a just guidance in which the goal is the same privilege for all and the equitable division of goods among all. Certainly the examples thus far are not encouraging, but this cannot refute the hope that this moral concept can nevertheless be successfully implemented: If the whole thing were to be attempted on a stronger moral foundation, so the reasoning goes, it would necessarily succeed in reconciling morality and efficiency in a society that is geared, not to maximizing profits, but rather to self-restraint and service of the common good. Thus, the dispute between economics and ethics in this sphere is increasingly becoming a dispute *against* the market economy and its intellectual foundations *in favor of* a centrally managed economy, which some think can now finally be set on its correct moral foundation.

The whole scope of the question under discussion here, however, becomes visible only when we include now also the third sphere of economic and theoretical considerations that characterize the panorama of the situation today: *the Marxist world.* In terms of its economic-theoretical and practical structure, the Marxist system as a centrally managed economy is the radical antithesis to the market economy.[4] The social benefit expected from it is that there is no private power to dispose of the means of production, supply and demand are not harmonized by competition in the marketplace, and consequently there is no room for the private profit motive, but instead all regulations are issued by a central economic management. But despite this radical contrast in the concrete economic mechanisms, there are *also common elements in their deeper philosophical presuppositions.*

[4] See Cardinal J. Höffner, *Wirtschaftsordnung und Wirtschaftsethik: Richtlinien der katholischen Soziallehre* (Bonn: Sekretariat der Deutschen Bischofskonferenz, 1985), 34–44.

The first element is that Marxism, too, is a form of determinism and that, conversely, it too promises complete liberation as the product of determinism. For this reason, it is fundamentally an error to assume that the system of central management is a moral system as compared to the mechanistic system of the market economy. This becomes quite clearly evident, for example, in the fact that Lenin agreed with Sombart's thesis that in Marxism there was not one grain of ethics but only economic legalities.[5] Indeed, the determinism here is far more radical and more principled than in liberalism: the latter at least acknowledges the realm of the subjective and sees it as the space of ethics; in Marxism, in contrast, becoming and history are totally reduced to the economy, and the attempt to cordon off a special subjective realm appears to be resistance to the solely valid laws of history and, thus, a reaction hostile to progress, which cannot be tolerated. *Ethics is reduced to the philosophy of history, and the philosophy of history deteriorates into Party strategy.*

But let us return once again to the common elements in the philosophical foundations of Marxism and capitalism (understood in the strict sense).

The second common element—as the preceding discussion has already suggested—is that determinism includes the renunciation of ethics as an independent factor relevant to the economy. In Marxism, this is evident in a particularly dramatic way in the fact that religion is traced back to economy: it is said to be the reflection of a particular economic system and, thus, also an obstacle to correct knowledge and correct action, an obstacle to the progress at which the natural laws of history aim. Here, too, it is assumed that history,

[5] Koslowski, "Über Notwendigkeit", 296, citing Lenin, *Werke* (Berlin, 1971), 1:436.

which proceeds in the dialectic of negative and positive, by its intrinsic nature (which cannot be further substantiated) must finally have a totally positive outcome. From this perspective the Church can contribute nothing positive to the global economy—that is clear; she plays a role for the economic issue only as something that must be overcome. Consequently, however, she can be *used temporarily as a means of her own self-destruction and, thus, as an instrument of the "positive forces of history"*; this is an insight that has cropped up only in recent times; obviously, it in no way changes the basic thesis.

Moreover, the whole system lives, in practice, on the apotheosis of the central management, in which the world spirit itself would have to be at work if the thesis were to be correct. It is simply an empirical observation to say that this is *a myth in the worst sense of the word*, and the statement is continually borne out by further evidence. Thus, the radical rejection of any concrete dialogue between Church and economics, which underlies this kind of thinking, is itself a confirmation of the need for it.

In attempting to map the constellation of factors impinging on a dialogue between Church and economics, I stumbled on another, fourth aspect. It is illustrated in the famous remark made by Theodore Roosevelt in 1912: "I think that the assimilation of the Latin American countries into the United States will be long and difficult as long as these countries are Catholic." Along the same lines, Rockefeller, during a lecture in Rome in 1969, recommended replacing the Catholics there with other Christians[6]—an undertaking that is notoriously under way. Plainly in both statements,

[6] I owe the reference to these two remarks to the essay by A. Metalli, "La grande epopea degli evangelici", *30Giorni* 3, no. 8 (1984): 9.

religion, or in this case a Christian denomination, is presupposed as a socio-political and thus also an economic-political factor, which is foundational for the way in which political structures and economic possibilities develop. This recalls Max Weber's thesis about the intrinsic connection between capitalism and Calvinism, between the shaping of the economic order and the religious idea that determines it. Here Marx's notion seems almost to be stood on its head: economics does not produce religious ideas, but, rather, the fundamental religious orientation decides which economic system can develop.

The idea that only Protestantism can bring forth a free economy, while Catholicism includes no suitable education in freedom and in the self-discipline necessary for it, but rather favors authoritarian systems, is no doubt still very widespread even today, and much in recent history appears to support this view. On the other hand, today we can no longer so unabashedly regard the liberal-capitalistic system, even with all the corrections that it has adopted meanwhile, as the salvation of the world as was still the case in the Kennedy era with its Peace Corps optimism: the questions that the Third World has about this system may be one-sided, but they are not unfounded.

Therefore, a self-critique by the Christian denominations with regard to their political and economic ethics would probably be required first, but this cannot proceed as a purely intra-ecclesial discussion but can be fruitful only if it is conducted as a dialogue with those who are Christians and are responsible for the economy. Due to a long tradition, in many cases, they view the fact that they are Christian as their subjective sphere, while as economists they follow the laws of the economy; these two spheres appear to have no point of tangency in the modern separation of the subjective and the objective world. But it would depend on the point of contact between them, where the two would have to come together without mixture or separation.

It is becoming an ever clearer economic-historical fact that the development of economic systems and their correlation with the common good depends on a particular ethical discipline, which for its part can be produced and sustained only by religious forces.[7] Conversely, it is meanwhile becoming evident that the decline of such discipline can also bring about the collapse of the market laws. An economic policy that is ordered not only to the welfare of the group, indeed, not only to the common good of a particular State, but rather to the *common good of the human family demands a maximum of ethical discipline and thus a maximum of religious strength*. Political consensus-building that applies the intrinsic laws of the economy to this end seems today almost impossible, despite all the great humanitarian declarations; it can be feasible only if altogether new ethical forces are released for this purpose.

A kind of morality that thinks that it can skip over competency in the laws of economics is not morality, but moralism and, therefore, the opposite of morality.

Practicality that thinks it can do without ethics is a misunderstanding of human reality and, thus, impracticality. Today we need a maximum of economic competency, but also a maximum of ethics, so that the economic competency is put at the service of the correct goals and its knowledge becomes politically feasible and socially tolerable.

[7] For a lengthy discussion of this subject, see P. Koslowski, "Religion, Ökonomie, Ethik: Eine sozialtheoretische und ontologische Analyse ihres Zusammenhangs," in P. Koslowski, ed., *Die religiöse Dimension der Gesellschaft, Religion und ihre Theorien* (Tübingen: J. C. B. Mohr, 1985), 76–96.

With all these observations, I did not intend to give any answers to the questions that prompt us, nor could I: for that I lack the economic competency. But I tried to point out the question that has brought us together here. It is of the utmost urgency. The very fact that we are talking together is a great result. Let us hope that we succeed in taking a step forward in the necessary correlation of ethics and economics and that this leads to more knowledge and better action and, so, ultimately to more peace, more freedom, and more unity of the human family.

PART TWO

Europe: Downfalls and Rebirths

6

War, Reconstruction, and the Heritage of the Postwar Period

Four Talks on the Occasion of the Sixtieth Anniversary of the Landing of the Allied Forces in France

(a) In Search of Peace

Europe at war and after the war

On June 6, 1944, when the Allied troops began to land in France, which was occupied by the German Wehrmacht, it was for the whole world—but also for many, many Germans—a sign of hope that soon there would be peace and freedom in Europe. What had happened? A criminal and his fellow Party members had managed to seize power in Germany. And once the Party was in power, law and injustice became intertwined, one often being inextricably confused with the other, because the government headed by a criminal had also assumed the jurisdictional prerogatives of the State and of its ordinances. Thus it could, in a certain sense, demand from its citizens obedience to the law and respect for the authority of the State (cf. Rom 13:1ff.) while at the same time using the law as a means to criminal ends. The same legal order that continued to some extent to function as usual in everyday life had become simultaneously a force that was destroying the law. The perversion of the ordinances that ought to have served the cause of justice but instead were consolidating the rule of injustice and making it inscrutable was in actual fact a dominion of lies that darkened consciences. Facilitating this dominion of lies was a system of intimidation, in which no one could confide in anyone else, because everyone, in a way, had to protect himself under a mask of lies that, on the one hand, served the purpose of self-defense but tended, on the other hand, to strengthen the power of evil. Thus it was necessary for the whole world to intervene in order to break the cycle of criminality and to reestablish liberty and law. We give thanks at this hour that that indeed happened, and it is not only the countries that were occupied by the German troops and delivered from Nazi terror that give thanks. We Germans, too, give thanks that liberty and law were restored to us through that military operation. If ever in history there was a just war, this was it: the Allied intervention ultimately benefited also those against whose country the war was waged. Such an observation, it seems to me, is important, because it demonstrates on the basis of a historical event that absolute pacifism is unsustainable. This, of course, in no way diminishes the duty to ask very carefully whether and under what conditions something like a "just war" is still possible today: that is to say, a military intervention conducted in the interests of peace and according to moral criteria against unjust regimes. Above all, though, what we have said should make it quite clear, we hope, that peace and law, peace and justice are inseparably connected with each other. When law is trampled on and injustice comes to power, peace is always threatened and is already to some extent broken. In this sense, a commitment to peace is above all a commitment to a form of law that guarantees justice for the individual and for the entire community.

In Europe, after the end of the hostilities, in March of 1945, a long period of peace was granted to our continent, such as it has rarely experienced in all of its history. This is due in large measure to the first generation of politicians after the war—Churchill, Adenauer, Schuman, De Gasperi, whom we must thank in this hour. We must be grateful that the decisive factor in rebuilding the Western world after the war was ultimately, not the thought of revenge or of humiliating the conquered, but rather the duty of guaranteeing the rights of all, so that instead of competition there would be collaboration, a reciprocal exchange, mutual acquaintance, and friendship within a diversity in which each nation preserves its identity while sharing the responsibility to respect the law, after the previous perversion of it. The driving force behind this politics of peace was the connection between political action and morality. The inner criterion of all politics is found in those moral values which we do not invent but only recognize and which are the same for all men. Let us say it plainly: these politicians drew their moral concept of the State, of peace and responsibility, from their Christian faith, a faith that had overcome the challenges of the Enlightenment and to a great extent had been purified in its confrontation with the distortion of the law and of morality caused by the Party. They wanted to set up, not a denominational State, but, rather, a State informed by ethical reasoning; still, their faith had helped them to revive and reestablish the rule of reason that had been subjected and perverted by an ideological tyranny. They developed a politics of reason—of moral reasoning; their Christianity had not distanced them from reason but, rather, had illuminated their reason.

Of course we should add the fact that Europe was divided by a border that cut not only our continent but also the entire world in two. A large part of Central and Eastern Europe found itself under the rule of an ideology that exploited the Party and subjected the State to the Party, thus transforming it into a party. Here, too, the result was a rule of lies and the destruction of mutual trust. Since the collapse of those dictatorships, we have seen what enormous economic, ideological, and spiritual disasters these regimes caused. In the Balkans, armed conflicts broke out in which the whole historical weight of the past provoked new explosions of violence. Although we emphasize the criminal character of these regimes and are glad that they have been overthrown, we must nevertheless ask ourselves why the majority of the African and Asian peoples, the so-called non-aligned [neutral] states, considered the system in the East more moral and more realistic for their own political development than the political and legal order in the West. This no doubt indicates shortcomings in our political structures on which we should reflect.

The development of the world situation after the war

Although Europe since 1945, with the exception of the conflicts in the Balkans, has experienced a period of peace, the world situation overall has been anything but peaceful. From Korea to Vietnam, from India to Pakistan, in Bangladesh, Algeria, and the Congo, from Nigeria (Biafra) to the hostilities in the Sudan, Rwanda and Burundi, Ethiopia, Somalia, Mozambique, Angola, Liberia, and in Afghanistan and Chechnya, a blood-stained arc of armed conflicts has developed, to which must be added the battles in and for the Holy Land and in Iraq. This is not the place to analyze and classify these conflicts, the wounds from which are still bleeding. I would like to examine in more detail, however, two phenomena that are in a certain sense new, because in them a specific threat comes to light and, along with it, the particular task of our times in the search for peace.

One of these phenomena is the sudden apparent decline in the cohesive force of the law and in the ability of different communities to coexist. A typical example, it seems to me, of the breakdown of the force of the law that plunges society into chaos and anarchy is Somalia. But Liberia, too, presents an example of the way in which a society disintegrates from within because the national government is incapable of establishing its credibility as a force for peace and freedom, and therefore everyone tries to take justice into his own hands. We witnessed something similar in Europe after the collapse of the united Yugoslav government. Ethnic populations that for generations, despite many tensions, had lived together peaceably suddenly rose up against each other with an unimaginable cruelty. It was like a breach in a spiritual dam: the protective barrier no longer withstood the pressures of a new situation, and the arsenal of hostility and violence that lurked in the depths of men's souls, held back until then by the forces of law and of a common history, exploded without restraints. Of course, in that region different historical traditions, among which there had always been latent tensions, lived side by side: there both Latin and Greek forms of Christianity could be found in addition to the active presence of Islam, thanks to centuries of Turkish rule. But all these tensions had not prevented a peaceful coexistence that now was disintegrating and headed for anarchy. How could it happen? How was it possible that suddenly, in

Rwanda, the coexistence between the Hutu and Tutsi tribes turned into bloody hostilities everywhere? There were certainly many causes for that collapse of law and of the capacity for reconciliation. We can mention several. Cynicism and ideology had darkened consciences in all these regions: the promises of ideology justified any and all means that might seem suited to its purposes, thus abolishing, so to speak, the very idea of law or even the distinction between good and evil. Besides the cynicism of the ideologies (and often closely connected with it) there is the cynicism of business interests and of the major markets, the shameless exploitation of the earth's natural resources. Here, too, the common good is set aside by the profit motive, and power takes the place of law. In this way, the positive influence of ethics dissolves from within, and finally the material advantage that was being pursued is itself destroyed. At this level we are confronted with a major task for Christians today: we must begin by learning from each other to want to be reconciled and to do everything possible to ensure that conscience has an authoritative voice, instead of being crushed by ideology and financial interests. Especially in the Balkans (although the same thing is true for Ireland), the task of genuine ecumenism should be to seek together the peace of Christ, to offer it to one another, and thus to consider the very ability to make peace as a genuine criterion for truth.

The other phenomenon that weighs heavily on us especially today is terrorism, which meanwhile has become a sort of new world war—a war with no definite front, which can strike everywhere and no longer recognizes the distinction between combatants and the civilian population, between the guilty and the innocent. Given the fact that terrorist agents, or even conventional organized crime (which is constantly strengthening and extending its network), could gain access to nuclear arms and biological weapons, the peril that threatens us has reached frightening dimensions. As long as this potential for destruction remained exclusively in the hands of the major powers, one could always hope that reason and the awareness of the dangers weighing upon the people and the State would rule out the use of this type of weaponry. Indeed, despite all the tensions between East and West, we were spared a full-scale war, thanks be to God. But in dealing with the terrorist forces and organized crime we can no longer count on such reasoning, because the readiness to engage in self-destruction is one of the basic components of terrorism—a kind of self-destruction that is exalted as martyrdom and transformed into a promise.

In search of peace: The question of the right relation between reason and religion

What can we do, what must we do in this situation? First of all, we need to consider several fundamental truths. One cannot put an end to terrorism—a force that is opposed to the law and cut off from morality—solely by means of force. It is certain that, in defending the law against a force that aims to destroy law, one can and in certain circumstances must make use of proportionate force in order to protect it. An absolute pacifism that denies the law any and all coercive measures would be capitulation to injustice, would sanction its seizure of power, and would abandon the world to the dictates of violence, as we have already explained briefly at the beginning. But in order to prevent the force of the law itself from becoming injustice, it must be subjected to strict criteria that should be acknowledged as such by all. It must inquire into the causes of terrorism, which very often is rooted in injustices that are not countered by effective measures. Therefore it must strive by all means to remove the preexisting injustices. Above all, it is important to offer forgiveness again and again in order to break the vicious circle of violence. Where the principle of "an eye for an eye" is ruthlessly put into practice, there is no way out of the violence. Humanitarian gestures, which break with violence and see a fellow man in the opponent and appeal to his own humanity, are necessary, even when they seem at first to be a waste of time. In all these cases, it is important that there not be just one political power that maintains law and order. Particular interests then become too easily mixed up in the intervention and obscure the clear vision of justice. A genuine *ius gentium* [international law] is urgently necessary, without hegemonic dominion and its accompanying interventions: only in this way can it be evident that it is a matter of protecting the rights common to all, even those who find themselves, so to speak, on the opposite side. This is precisely what succeeded in convincing those who had fought against each other in World War II and brought about a true peace. It was a question by no means of reinforcing one particular law, but rather of establishing freedom for all and the rule of genuine law, even though, of course, this was not able to prevent the development of new hegemonic structures.

But in the present clash between the major democracies and Islamist terrorism, even more profound questions come into play. There seems to be a collision of two major cultural systems, which manifest, nevertheless, quite different forms of power and of moral perspective: the "West" and Islam. What is the West, however? And what is Islam? Each one is a complex world including great differences within it, and these two worlds are also, in many respects, mutually interactive. To that extent it is wrong to generalize in opposing the West and Islam. Yet some commentators tend to describe the contrast in even starker terms: Enlightened reason, they say, is confronting here a fanatical, fundamentalist form of religion. Therefore, in their view, we must defeat fundamentalism in all its forms and promote the victory of reason so as to leave the coast clear for enlightened forms of religion (which are considered enlightened provided they are subject in everything to the standards of that reason).

It is true that in this situation the relationship between reason and religion is of decisive importance and that the search for the right balance between them is at the heart of our efforts on behalf of peace. Modifying a famous remark by Hans Küng ("Keine Weltfriede ohne Religionsfriede!" [There will be no peace in the world without peace among religions]), I would say that there can be no peace in the world without genuine peace between reason and faith, because without peace between reason and religion, the sources of morality and law dry up. To explain what I mean to say by this, I will formulate the same idea in negative terms. There are pathologies of religion, as we can see, and there are pathologies of reason, as we can also see. Both sorts of pathologies pose a fatal threat to peace, and even to mankind as a whole, in our age of global power structures. Let us look at this more closely. God or the Divinity can become a way of making absolute claims for one's own authority and interests. Such a partisan image of God, which identifies God's absolute character with a particular community or its areas of interest and thereby raises things that are empirical and relative to the status of absolutes, dissolves law and morality. Good is then whatever serves my own power, and the difference between good and evil collapses in practice. Morality and law become partisan. This is further aggravated when the will to fight for one's own causes acquires all the weight of absolutist fanaticism, of religious fanaticism, and thereby becomes brutal and blind. God is transformed into an idol in which man adores his own will. We can see something of this sort in the terrorists and their ideology of martyrdom, an ideology that, to tell the truth, in certain cases can also be quite simply an expression of despair in dealing with the injustice in the world. Furthermore, closer to home, in the sects of the Western world, we find examples of irrationalism and a distortion of the religious dimension that show how dangerous a religion that loses its bearings can be.

But there is also a pathology of reason that is entirely cut off from God. We have seen it in the totalitarian ideologies that cut themselves off from God and wanted henceforth to construct a new man, a new world. Hitler, certainly, must be described as an irrationalist. The major prophets and practitioners of Marxism, however, likewise considered themselves to be rebuilding the world based on reason alone. Perhaps the most dramatic example of this pathology of reason was Pol Pot, in whom the cruelty inherent in such a reconstruction of the world is quite evident. Spiritual developments in the West, too, are tending more and more toward devastating pathologies of reason. Did not the atomic bomb, with which reason sought power in the ability to destroy instead of being a constructive force, already overstep the boundaries? Furthermore, when reason gets its hands on the origins of life through research into the genetic code, it increasingly tends to see man no longer as a gift of the Creator (or of "Nature") but as a product. Man is "produced", and what we "produce" we can also destroy. Human dignity vanishes. In what, then, are human rights supposed to be anchored? How can we maintain respect for human life, for the disadvantaged, the weak, the suffering, and the disabled? At the same time the notion of reason is becoming more and more attenuated. For example, ancient philosophers distinguished between *ratio* and *intellectus*, between reason in relation to empirical reality and man-made things and that reason which penetrates the deepest levels of being. Now, only reason in the more restricted sense remains. Only what is verifiable, or, more precisely, what can be proved, is said to be reasonable; reason is reduced to what can be confirmed by means of experimentation. The entire field of morality and religion is thus relegated to the domain of the "subjective" —it falls outside the scope of commonsense reason. Religion and morality no longer pertain to reason; there are no more common, "objective" criteria for morality. This is not viewed as being particularly tragic, in the case of religion: everyone has to choose his own. But this means that it is regarded, in any case, as a sort of subjective ornament that may have useful motives. In the study of morality, general rules are sought. Of course, if reality is nothing but the result of mechanical processes, then it contains no moral criteria. The "good in itself", which Kant was still so concerned about, no longer exists. "Good" simply means "better than", as it was once remarked by a moral theologian who is now deceased. But if that is so, then there is no longer anything that is always and in itself evil. Good and evil depend, then, on a calculus of consequences. And this is precisely how the ideological dictatorships have acted: in certain cases, if it is in the interest of building the future world of reason, it can be a good thing to kill innocent people. In any case, their absolute dignity no longer exists. Sick reason and manipulated religion eventually lead to the same result. To sick reason any statement about permanent values, every defense of reason's capacity to know truth, seems to be fundamentalism. Nothing remains but dissolution or "deconstruction", the key concept in the writings of Jacques Derrida. He "deconstructed" hospitality, democracy, the State, and finally even the idea of terrorism, only to find himself terror-stricken by the events of September 11. Reason that can no longer recognize anything but itself and what is empirically certain is paralyzed and self-destructive.

Faith in God, the idea of God can be manipulated, and then it becomes destructive: this is the risk that religion runs. But reason that cuts itself off from God completely and tries to confine him to the purely subjective realm loses its bearings and thus opens the door to the forces of destruction. Whereas the Enlightenment was searching for moral foundations that would be valid "*etsi Deus non daretur*" [even if God did not exist], we must invite our agnostic friends today to be open to a morality "*si Deus daretur*" [as if God did exist]. Kolakowski, drawing on his experiences in an atheistic, agnostic society, has demonstrated masterfully that without this absolute point of reference, man's action becomes lost in uncertainty and is inevitably at the mercy of the forces of evil.[1] As Christians, we are called today, certainly not to set limits to reason and to oppose it, but rather to refuse to reduce it to the level of practical reason and to defend instead its ability to perceive good and the One who is Good, what is holy and the One who is Holy. Only in this way can we fight a real battle on behalf of man and against inhumanity. Only reason that is still open to God, only reason that does not banish morality to the subjective sphere and does not reduce it to a calculus, can counter the manipulation of the idea of God and the pathologies of religion and offer remedies.

[1] Leszek Kolakowski, *Religion: If There Is No God—On God, the Devil, Sin, and other Worries of the So-Called Philosophy of Religion* (South Bend, Ind.: St. Augustine Press, 2001).

The task of Christians

And so it is plain that Christians today face a great challenge. Their task and ours is to see to it that reason is fully functional, not just in the realm of technology and material progress in the world, but also and especially as a faculty of truth, promoting its capacity to recognize what is good, which is a necessary condition for law and therefore also a prerequisite for peace in the world. Our task as contemporary Christians is to make sure that our idea of God is not excluded from the debate about man. This idea of God has two essential characteristics: God himself is the Logos—the rational origin of all reality, the creative reason from which the world came forth and which is reflected in the world. God is Logos—meaning, reason, the Word—and therefore man complies with this Logos by keeping an open mind and defending a type of reason that is not blind to the moral dimensions of being. For *logos* means a reason that is not simply mathematical but is at the same time the foundation and guarantee of the good. Faith in God as Logos is also faith in the creative power of reason; it is faith in God the Creator, which means believing that man is created in the image of God and that he therefore shares in the inviolable dignity of God himself. Here the idea of human rights has its ultimate foundation, even though it has developed in various ways and has not always been well received over the course of history.

God is Logos. But there is a second characteristic. The Christian faith in God tells us also that God—eternal Reason—is Love. It tells us that he is not a being turned in on himself, without relations to others. Precisely because he is sovereign, because he is the Creator, because he embraces everything, he is Relation and he is Love. Faith in the

Incarnation of God in Jesus Christ, and in his suffering and death for mankind, is the supreme expression of a conviction that the heart of all morality, the heart of being itself and its deepest principle, is love. This affirmation is the most resolute refusal of every ideology of violence; it is the true *apologia* for man and for God. Let us not forget, however, that the God of reason and of love is also the Judge of the world and of mankind—the guarantor of justice, to whom men must render an accounting. Given the temptations to power, it is a fundamental obligation to keep in mind the truth about the Judgment: every one of us must someday give an account. There is a justice that is not abolished by love. In the *Gorgias* of Plato we find a striking parable for it that is not nullified but rather fully validated by the Christian faith. Plato explains how the soul, after death, at last finds itself naked before the Judge. Now it no longer matters what rank it held in the world. Whether it is the soul of the king of Persia or of any other ruler: the Judge sees the scars of his perjuries and crimes:

> with which each action has stained him, and he is all crooked with falsehood and imposture, and has no straightness, because he has lived without truth. [The Judge sees that he is] full of all deformity and disproportion, which is caused by license and luxury and insolence and incontinence . . . Or, again, he looks with admiration on the soul of some just one who has lived in holiness and truth; he may have been a [free] man or not, . . . and sends it to the Isles of the Blessed."[2]

Wherever such convictions are strong, law and justice are also in force.

[2] Plato, *Gorgias* 525a–526c; cf. Christoph Schönborn, *God Sent His Son: A Contemporary Christology*, trans. Henry Taylor (San Francisco: Ignatius Press, 2010), 365.

I would like to mention yet a third element of the Christian tradition that is of fundamental importance in the difficult circumstances of our time. The Christian faith—following the way shown to us by Jesus—banished the ideal of political theocracy. To put it in modern language, it promoted the secular character of the State, in which Christians live together in freedom with those who hold other beliefs, united by the common moral responsibility founded on human nature, on the nature of justice. The Christian faith distinguishes this from the Kingdom of God, which does not and cannot exist in this world as a political reality, but rather comes into being through faith, hope, and charity and must transform the world from within. In the conditions of this world, the Kingdom of God is not a worldly kingdom but, rather, an appeal to man's freedom and a support for reason so that it can accomplish its task. This distinction is what is ultimately at stake in the temptations of Jesus: the rejection of political theocracy, the relative importance of the State, the law that is proper to reason and at the same time freedom of choice, with which every human being is endowed. In this sense, the secular State is a result of the fundamental Christian decision, even though it took a long struggle to understand all of its consequences. This secular, "lay" character of the State includes by its very nature this balance between reason and religion that I tried to demonstrate earlier. Therefore it is also opposed to ideological secularism, which tries to establish a State run by reason alone, a State that is cut off from all historical roots and hence no longer recognizes any moral foundations other than those that are evident to that reason. Eventually it has nothing left but the positivistic criterion of the majority principle, leading to the decadence of a law governed by statistics. If the nations of the Western world were to commit themselves entirely to this path, they would be unable in the long run to resist the pressure of ideologies and political theocracies. A State, even a secular State, has the right and even the obligation to rely on the moral traditions in which it is rooted and that shaped it; it can and must acknowledge the fundamental values which made it what it is and without which it cannot survive. There is no such thing as an ahistorical State based on abstract reason.

In practice this means that we Christians must strive, together with all of our fellow citizens, to give law and justice a moral foundation inspired by fundamental Christian ideas, however the individual may interpret their origins and harmonize them with his entire life. But in order to make such common rational convictions possible, in order to prevent "right reason" from losing its sight, it is important for us to live out our own heritage with vigor and purity, so that it might be made visible and effective, with all its intrinsic power of persuasion, in society as a whole. I would like to conclude with the words of Kurt Hübner, a German philosopher from Kiel, which clearly express this concern:

> We will be able to avoid conflict with the cultures that are hostile to us today only on the condition that, by becoming once again fully conscious of how deeply rooted our culture is in Christianity, we disprove their vehement reproach that we have forgotten God. Of course that will not be enough to dispel the resentment caused by the superiority of the West in many fields that shape broad sectors of life today, but it can play an important role in extinguishing the flames of the religious conflagration that feeds on it.[3]

[3] K. Hübner, *Das Christentum im Wettstreit der Weltreligionen* (Tübingen: Mohr Siebeck, 2003), 148.

Indeed, if we do not recall the God of the Bible, the God who has come close to us in Jesus Christ, we will not find the path of peace.

(b)

Faith in the Triune God and Peace in the World

The feast of the Holy Trinity is different from all the other feasts of the liturgical year, such as Christmas, Epiphany, Easter, and Pentecost, when we celebrate the wondrous works of God in history: the Incarnation, the Resurrection, the Descent of the Holy Spirit, and consequently the birth of the Church. Today we are not celebrating an event in which "something" of God is made visible; rather, we are celebrating the very mystery of God. We rejoice in God, in the fact that he is the way he is; we thank him for existing; we are grateful that he is what he is and that we can know him and love him and that he knows and loves us and reveals himself to us. But the existence of God, his being, the fact that he knows us—is that really a cause for joy? Certainly it is not something easy to understand or experience. Many gods in the different religions of peoples throughout the world are terrible, cruel, selfish, an inscrutable mixture of good and evil. The ancient world was characterized by a fear of the gods and a dread of their mysterious power: it was necessary to win the favor of the gods, to act in such a way as to avoid their whims or their bad humor. Part of the Christian mission was a liberating force that was able to drive out a whole world of idols and gods that are now considered empty, illusory appearances. At the same time it proclaimed the God who, in Jesus, became man, the God who is Love and Reason. This God is mightier than all the dark powers that the world can contain: "We know that 'an idol has no real existence', and that 'there is no God but one'. For although there may be so-called gods in heaven or on earth—as indeed there are many 'gods' and many 'lords' —yet for us there is one God, the Father, from whom are all things and for whom we exist" (1 Cor 8:4–6). Even today this is a revolutionary, liberating message with respect to all the ancient traditional religions: No longer is there reason to fear the spirits that surround us on all sides, coming and going ceaselessly, eluding our vain efforts at exorcism. Anyone who "dwells in the shelter of the Most High, who abides in the shadow of the Almighty" (Ps 91:1), knows that he is safe, guarded tenderly by the One who welcomes him and offers him refuge. Someone who knows the God of Jesus Christ knows that the other forms of fear in the presence of God have disappeared also, that he has overcome all the forms of harrowing existential anguish that spread through the world in ever new ways. In view of all the horrors of the world, the same question unceasingly arises: Does God exist? And if he exists, is he truly good? Might he not be instead a mysterious and dangerous reality? In modern times this question is posed differently: the existence of God seems to be a limit to our freedom. He is perceived as a sort of supervisor who pursues us with his glance. In the modern era, the rebellion against God assumes the form of a fear of an omnipresent, all-seeing God. His glance appears as a threat to us; indeed, we prefer not to be seen, we just want to be ourselves and nothing more. Man does not feel free, he does not feel that he is truly himself, until God is set aside. The story of Adam already notes this: he sees God as a competitor. Adam wants to lead his own life, all alone, and tries to hide from God "among the trees of the garden" (Gen 3:8). Sartre, too, declared that we must deny God, even if he must exist philosophically, because the concept of God is opposed to man's freedom and greatness.

But has the world really become more brighter, freer, happier after setting God aside? Or has man not been stripped of his own dignity and condemned to an empty freedom that makes cruel and ruthless choices of all sorts? God's glance only frightens us if we think of him as reducing us to some kind of servitude or slavery; but if we read in it the expression of his love, we discover that he is the fundamental requirement for our very being, that it is he who makes us live. "He who has seen me has seen the Father", Jesus said to Philip and to us all (Jn 14:9). Jesus' face is the face of God himself: this is what God is like. Jesus suffered for us, and by his death he has given us peace; he reveals to us who God is. His glance, far from being a threat, is a glance that saves us.

Yes, we can rejoice that God exists, that he has revealed himself to mankind, and that he does not leave us alone. How consoling it is to know the telephone number of a friend, to know good people who love us, who are always available and never aloof: at any time we can call them and they can call us. This is precisely what the Incarnation of God in Christ says to us: God has written our names and phone numbers in his address book! He is always listening; we do not need money or technology to call him. Thanks to baptism and confirmation, we are privileged to belong to his family. He is always ready to welcome us: "Behold, I am with you always, to the close of the age" (Mt 28:20).

But the Gospel reading for today adds a particularly important statement: Jesus promises the Holy Spirit (Jn 16:13), whom he calls, several times, the "Paraclete". What does that mean? In Latin, the word is translated as *Consolator*, the Comforter. Etymologically, the Latin word means: the one who stays by us when we feel lonely. Thus our solitude ceases to be loneliness. For a human being, solitude is often a place of unhappiness; he needs love, and solitude makes the absence of it conspicuous. Loneliness indicates a lack of love; it is something that threatens our quality of life at the deepest level. Not being loved is at the core of human suffering and personal sadness. The word *Consoler* tells us precisely that we are not alone, that we can never feel abandoned by Love. By the gift of the Holy Spirit, God has entered into our loneliness and has shattered it. Indeed, this is genuine consolation; it does not consist merely of words but has the force of an active and effective reality. During the Middle Ages this definition of the Spirit as Consoler led to the Christian duty of entering into the solitude of those who suffer. The first hospices and hospitals were dedicated to the Holy Spirit: thus men undertook the mission of continuing the Spirit's work; they dedicated themselves to being "consolers", to entering into the solitude of the sick, the suffering, and the elderly, so as to bring them light.

This is still a serious duty for us today, in our time.

Moreover, the Greek work *parakletos* can be translated in yet another way: it also means "advocate". A verse from the Book of Revelation might help us to understand it better: "And I heard a loud voice in heaven, saying, 'Now the salvation and the power and the kingdom of our God and the authority of his Christ have come, for the accuser of our brethren has been thrown down, who accuses them day and night before our God" (Rev 12:10). Someone who does not love God with all his heart does not love man, either. Those who deny God quickly become persons who destroy nature and accuse men, because accusing other men and nature enables them to justify their opposition to God: a God who has made this cannot be good! That is their logic. The Holy Spirit, the Spirit of God, is not an accuser; he is an advocate and defender of mankind and creation. God himself takes the side of men and creatures. Within creation, God affirms and defends himself by coming to our defense. God is for us; we see that clearly throughout the earthly life of Jesus: he is the only one who takes our side, becomes one with us even unto death. Saint Paul's awareness of this prompted an outburst of joy:

> If God is for us, who is against us? [. . .] Who shall bring any charge against God's elect? It is God who justifies; who is to condemn? Is it Christ Jesus, who died, yes, who was raised from the dead, who is at the right hand of God, who indeed intercedes for us? [. . .] For I am sure that neither death, nor life, nor angels, nor principalities, nor things present, nor things to come, nor powers, nor height, nor depth, nor anything else in all creation, will be able to separate us from the love of God in Christ Jesus our Lord (Rom 8:31–39).

This God is for us a cause of joy, and we want to celebrate him. To know him and to acknowledge him is of great importance in our time. We are remembering the terrible days of the Second World War, happy that the dictator Hitler has disappeared along with all his atrocities and that Europe has been able to regain its freedom. But we cannot forget the fact that, even today, the world suffers from atrocious threats and cruelties. To corrupt and exploit the image of God is as dangerous as the denial of God that was part and parcel of the twentieth-century ideologies and of the totalitarian regimes that sprang from them, turning the world into an arid desert, outside and inside, to the very depths of the soul. Precisely at this historical moment, Europe and the world need the presence of God that was revealed in Jesus; they need God to stay close to mankind through the Holy Spirit. It is part of our responsibility as Christians to see to it that God remains in our world, that he is present to it as the one and only force capable of preserving mankind from self-destruction.

God is One and Three: he is not an eternal solitude; rather, he is an eternal love that is based on the reciprocity of the Persons, a love that is the first cause, the origin, and the foundation of all being and of every form of life. Unity engendered by love, trinitarian unity, is a unity infinitely more profound than the unity of a building stone, indivisible as that may be from a material perspective.

This supreme unity is not rigidly static; it is love. The most beautiful artistic depiction of this mystery was left to us by Andrei Rublev in the fifteenth century: the world-renowned icon of the Trinity. Of course, it does not portray the eternal mystery of God in himself; who would dare to do that? It attempts, rather, to represent this mystery as it is reflected in the gift of itself in history, as in the visit of the three men to Abraham by the oaks of Mamre (Gen 18:1–33). Abraham immediately recognized that they were not just like any other men, but that God himself was coming to him through them. In Rublev's icon, the mystery of this event is made visible, presented as an event that can be contemplated in its many dimensions: thus the mystery as such is respected. The artistic richness of this icon allows me to underscore another characteristic: the natural surroundings of this event, which express the mystery of the Persons. We are near the oaks of Mamre, which Rublev depicts in stylized form as a single tree representing the tree of life; and this tree of life is none other than the trinitarian love that created the world, sustains it, saves it, and is the source of all life. We see also the tent, the dwelling of Abraham, which recalls the Prologue of John's Gospel: "And the Word became flesh and dwelt among us" (Jn 1:14). The body of the incarnate Word of God became itself the tent, the place where God dwells: God becomes our refuge and our dwelling place. Finally, the gift that Abraham offers, "a calf, tender and good", is replaced, in the icon, with a cup, a symbol of the Eucharist, a sign of the gift in which God gives himself: "Love, sacrifice and self-immolation preceded the act by which the world was created and are the source of that creation."[4] The tree, the tent, and the cup: these elements show us the mystery of God, allow us to immerse ourselves in the contemplation of its intimate depths, in his trinitarian love. This is the God that we celebrate. This is the God who gives us joy. He is the true hope of our world. Amen.

(c)
The Responsibility of Christians for Peace

On this day, June 6, we remember the battle for Europe and for its freedom that entered into its crucial phase sixty years ago. But our commemoration does not just look only to the past; it should also be an orientation toward the future.

But first let us pause for a moment and look back. Sixty years ago armies fought to liberate Europe and the world from a brutal dictatorship that despised human beings. The human person was trampled on, exploited, treated as an object by the madness of a regime that wanted to create a new

[4] P. Evdokimov, *The Art of the Icon: A Theology of Beauty*, trans. Steven Bigham (Redondo Beach, Calif.: Oakwood Publications, 1990), 247.

world. People spoke about God, but his name was used as a slogan that served the will of an absolute power. God's will did not count; what mattered instead was one's personal will to power, which no longer recognized in man the image of God that deserved respect, but simply considered him as "human material" to be exploited; in fact, man was disdained and disfigured in exactly the same way as God himself was being disdained and disfigured. Countless persons were used as raw material in the concentration camps. A vast array of young men fell on the battlefields; today we are here to honor their graves. We know that all those who fell on both sides are now in the merciful goodness of God. They are all children of God; each one is personally known by God, is loved and willed by him, is called by name. Every single person left an empty space behind; for each of them there were so many tears and so much sorrow. But we know that now they are in good hands; they are in God's hands, in his goodness, which is mercy and reconciliation. Today this should be for us a heritage that helps us to consider anew the dignity of man, of every human person; it helps us to reflect in a new way on death and on eternal life. We must learn to recognize the image of God in the face of every man, however disagreeable or strange he may seem to us. In every human being we should see a companion in the life hereafter, a fellow traveler whom we will meet again in the next world. And we should foster a new awareness of our vocation to eternal life, living in such a way that we will be able to meet God face to face and present to him our earthly life. For the generation to which I belong, the idea of the hereafter and of eternal life was increasingly set aside and considered marginal, even in the preaching of the Church. Perhaps both the faithful and those who proclaimed the Word were afraid that thinking too much about the hereafter would cause Christians to neglect this world and its concrete, historic realities. It seemed that Christians were only half-heartedly concerned with building up this world. For centuries it had been said that life would be better and more humane if Christians did not live as though they had to flee the world. And then people imagined that there would be plenty of time, in any case, to think about the hereafter, whereas the present moment was worth the trouble of striving to make the world more livable at last. But surely the world has not become more livable or more humane as a result of this ideology; on the contrary, the person who lives the present moment in light of his responsibility with regard to eternal life is the one who gives full meaning to these present days. The parable of the talents shows us that the Lord has not called us to a life of comfortable tranquility; rather, he has called us to trade with the talents that have been given to us and to increase them (see Mt 25:14–30). Furthermore, to live with the thought of eternal life is to be free of the desire to enjoy everything right away, to use up everything right away; for then one knows that now is the time to work and afterward comes the great feast. These cemeteries before which we stand today exhort us to remember death and thus invite us to live the present moment well with a view to eternity.

There are three key words that could very well sum up our reflection: reconciliation, peace, and responsibility. After the bloody confrontations of the Second World War, a process of reconciliation began, for which we are deeply grateful, with heartfelt appreciation. The United States undertook a vast and compelling program of foreign aid to help their former adversaries get back on their feet and to promote reconstruction. Great Britain and France shook hands as a sign of reconciliation with those who had been their enemies during World War II. Charles de Gaulle once explained the meaning of this: Although there was a time when it was our duty to be enemies, now it is our joy that we can be friends. The process of reconciliation that has taken place in Europe, thanks in particular to the North Atlantic Treaty Organization [NATO], has changed the course of world history; this process has its origins in the Christian spirit.

Only reconciliation can create peace; it is not violence that can resolve situations but, rather, justice. This must be the normative criterion for all political action in the conflicts of the present time. The Letter to the Hebrews speaks about Christ's blood, which utters a cry different from the one that came from the blood of Abel (12:24). This cry calls, not for retaliation and revenge, but for reconciliation. The Letter to the Ephesians speaks to us about this same reality: Christ is our peace. By his death, he has broken down the wall of separation and enmity. By his blood, which is to say, by his love, which extends unto death and endures even in the experience of death, he unites those who were far off and those who were near (cf. Eph 2:14–22). This is the God whom we proclaim, and this is the image of man that should guide us. The peace of Christ surpasses the boundaries of Christianity and is valid for all, both near and far. Our ways of acting, both in little things and in great matters, should proceed from him as their source and bear his imprint.

And with that, we come to the final key word of our reflection: the word "responsibility". Already with the conclusion of World War I and even more forcefully after the experience of World War II, the cry arose: "War never again!" Unfortunately, the reality has proved to be quite different: the decades following 1945 were afflicted with bloody wars in various parts of the world. And unfortunately we must fear that evil injustice will rear its head once more and that it might again be necessary to defend law and justice against evil and injustice, even by resorting to military measures. What, then, can we hope for? What should we do? The totalitarian ideologies of the twentieth century promised us that they would build a free and just world, and in order to reach that objective they demanded the slaughter of countless victims. But the utopian dream has exerted a powerful attraction on the Christian consciousness and left a deep impression on it. The expectation of Christ's return refers to a salvation that takes place beyond history, whereas people want a hope within history and for the sake of history. They prefer to remove the word "God" from the New Testament expression, "the Kingdom of God", and to speak only about the "kingdom" to describe a new utopia that embraces both Christians and non-Christians: the "kingdom", that is, a better world has to come about within history. Nothing else about our faith is preached, then, and the prescriptions for building this "kingdom" are rather indefinite, so that they are open to any ideological misinterpretation. But utopias and ideologies are deceptive phantasms that lead men into error. And once again we ask ourselves: "What is being promised us?" "What should we do?"

The Christian answer involves three aspects. First, there is the promise of the heavenly Jerusalem that is not built by men but is given by God. Connected with it, in a manner that transcends history, is the ancient prophecy that human freedom would time and again be misused, and so evil would time and again gain power in the world. The Book of Revelation expresses this by means of terrifying images. Beyond the obscurity of these images we can catch a glimpse of the other side of the story, which is essential: even though God allows a lot of room to the freedom that chooses evil (there are all too many proofs of this, different ones in every age), he will never let the world fall completely out of his hands. Although the Book of Revelation speaks about destruction, it is for a limited time, and in a certain sense disaster strikes only a relatively small percentage, for instance one-third.

The world belongs to God and not to the Evil One, however much territory the latter may acquire. This certitude is fundamental, and it is a decisive point in the apocalyptic imagery. Indeed, it presupposes that the earth-shaking events narrated in the Book of Revelation are already well known; they will never manage to take complete possession of the world and will never succeed in destroying it: this is the real heart of the message.

Finally, the third aspect of the Christian response to the question regarding the future is called *ethics* or responsibility. This is not the magic charm of a progressive historical development that tends to build a world that is finally just, even though it may have to be without freedom. God sustains the world, but he does this essentially by means of our freedom; this should be freedom to do good, which is capable of opposing freedom to do evil. Faith does not create a better world, but it awakens and strengthens those ethical forces that construct embankments and bulwarks against the tide of evil. Faith awakens the freedom to do good and fortifies it against the temptation to use freedom in a distorted way to choose evil. The graves of the Second World War commend to us the task of strengthening the forces of good: it is an invitation to work, to live, and to suffer for the propagation and reinforcement of those values and truths that build a united world with God as its fulcrum. God promised Abraham that he would not destroy the city of Sodom if at least ten just men could be found there (Gen 18:32). We must make sure, then, that there will never be a day without those ten just men who can save an entire city.

(d)

The Grace of Reconciliation

This is the moment to get down on our knees with the utmost respect for those who died in World War II, remembering the countless young men from our country who, along with their future and their hopes, were destroyed in the bloody massacre of the war. And as Germans we are grieved by the fact that their idealism, their enthusiasm, and their loyalty to the State were exploited by an unjust regime.

But this does not stain the honor of those young men; only God was able to look into their conscience. Every one of them stands before God as an individual, with the course of his life and with his death; each one stands before the God whose merciful goodness, as we know, protects all our dead. They only sought to do their duty, and often this involved tremendous interior struggles, with many doubts and questions. But they look at us and question us: "And you? What will you do so that young men will no longer be forced to go to war? What will you do so that the world will not be devastated again by hatred, violence, and lies?"

But although this is an hour for sorrow and an examination of conscience, it is also a moment for profound gratitude, because over these graves reconciliation was born. Former enemies became friends, and now they walk hand in hand along their common path. The sacrifice of our dead was not in vain, even if we consider it solely from the perspective of history. After the First World War, rancor and hostility remained among the nations that had fought one another, especially between the French and the Germans. This hatred poisoned souls. The Treaty of Versailles had deliberately planned to humiliate Germany and impose enormous burdens on it, which reduced its people to dire straits, thus opening the door to extremist ideologies and dictatorship. Those lying promises to restore Germany to its freedom, dignity, honor, and greatness spread widely and gained a hearing. But, as we have seen, the principle of "an eye for an eye, a tooth for a tooth" cannot lead to peace. Thank God, nothing like that happened again after World War II. With the Marshall Plan, the Americans provided enormous amounts of foreign aid to us Germans, enabling us to rebuild our country and fostering its freedom and well-being. In the new world order that followed the collapse of colonialism, and during the extremely difficult period of the "Cold War" between East and West, people quickly realized that only a united Europe could have a say in history and in its own future. They understood that the various nationalist ideologies that had torn apart our continent had to vanish so as to make room for a new solidarity. And so it happened after the conflicts between France and Germany that for centuries had left their bloody mark. Thanks be to God, an increasingly close friendship has been established between the French and the Germans, and thus, since the late 1950s, Europe has developed, starting with that central unity and then expanding in ever larger circles. And today we stand before these graves that remind us of the fatal discord of the past, but now we are here as friends, as persons who have been reconciled with one another.

As we look back now on the process of mutual reconciliation and gradually developing solidarity, it appears to us as a logical development that was demanded and made structurally possible by the new world order. But we cannot overlook the fact that this logic per se was not understood in the same way by all and was not self-actualizing. History shows us that too often men act in ways contrary to all logic and reason. The fact that the politics of reconciliation triumphed is to the credit of a whole generation of politicians: let us recall the names of Adenauer, Schuman, De Gasperi, De Gaulle. These were objective, intelligent men who had a healthy political realism. But their realism was rooted in the firm ground of the Christian *ethos*, which they recognized as an *ethos* of reason, an *ethos* of enlightened, refined reason. They knew very well that politics cannot be mere pragmatism but must be a moral endeavor: the objective of politics is justice and, along with justice, peace. The political order and power itself must acknowledge their origins in the fundamental criteria of the law. But if the essence of politics is making power moral, along with the order that has the principles of law as its source, then in this twofold foundation we find a fundamental ethical category. But where do the fundamental criteria of justice come from? Where can we find them? For these men, it was quite clear that the Ten Commandments are the fundamental point of reference for justice, a reference that is valid for all times; and they had reread, elaborated, and reinterpreted this reference in the light of the Christian message. There is no disputing the historical role of the Christian faith in giving life to Europe. It is to the great credit of Christianity that it gave birth to Europe after the decline of the Greco-Roman Empire and after the period of the barbarian invasions. Not only that, but the rebirth of Europe after World War II was likewise rooted in Christianity and, therefore, in man's responsibility before God: we are very much aware that this is the deepest foundation of a government of laws, as it is clearly stipulated in the German Constitution that was framed after the collapse of Nazism. Anyone who wants to build Europe today as a bastion of law and justice that is valid for all men of all cultures cannot rely on an abstract reason that knows nothing about God and belongs to no particular culture, an abstract reason that pretends to measure all cultures according to the yardstick of its own judgment. But what yardstick are they talking about? What sort of freedom can reason of this sort safeguard? What can it reject? Even today, responsibility before God and being rooted in the great values and truths of the Christian faith—values that transcend the individual Christian denominations because they are common to all—are indispensable forces in the construction of a unified Europe that is much more than a single economic bloc: a community of law, a bastion of law, not only for itself but also for all of mankind.

The dead of La Cambe call to us: they rest in the peace of God, but they continue to ask us: "What are you doing for peace?" They warn us that the State is capable of losing its foundations in law and of cutting itself off from its roots. The memory of the sorrow and of the evils of the Second World War, together with the memory of the great work of reconciliation that, thank God, has been accomplished in Europe, show us where to find those forces that can heal Europe and the world. The earth can be a brighter place and the world can be humane only if we let God into the world.

7

1968 and Years of Violence and Disillusionment: Diagnosis and Rudiments of a Response

The image of man that dominates in modern literature, in visual arts, cinema, and theater is primarily a gloomy image. The great and the noble are suspect from the outset; they must be torn from their pedestal so that one can see through them. Morality counts as hypocrisy, joy as self-deception. Anyone who simply puts trust in the beautiful and the good is either inexcusably ingenuous or acting with evil intent. The truly moral attitude is suspicion, and its greatest success is in exposing. Criticism of society is obligatory; it is impossible to find words lurid and brutal enough to describe the dangers that threaten us. This delight in the negative is not, however, unlimited. There exists at the same time an obligation to be optimistic, and the failure to observe this obligation does not go unpunished. For example, anyone who expresses the view that not everything in the intellectual development of the modern period has been correct, that it is necessary in some essential areas to reflect on the shared wisdom of the great cultures, has chosen to make the wrong kind of criticism. He finds himself suddenly confronted with a resolute *apologia* for the fundamental decisions of the modern age; no matter how much delight one may take in negation, he is not permitted to call into question the view that the fundamental trajectory of historical development is progress and that the good lies in the future—and nowhere else.

The strange schizophrenia of today's criticism of society becomes palpably clear in the radically contradictory ways in which dominant opinion has reacted to the two events that were perceived recently to be the strongest moral challenges to our society. The first of these was the disaster at Chernobyl. If one wished to appear enlightened, one could not find words drastic enough to portray the danger of what had happened. One had to see a monstrous threat hanging over every living creature, and the only sufficient response could be the total abandonment of atomic energy. The second event was the rapid advance of the new viral illness AIDS. There can be no doubt that many more people will become sick and die (or have already died) of AIDS than of the consequences of Chernobyl and that the risk caused by this new scourge of mankind stands much nearer to the door of each individual than the risk caused by nuclear power plants. But anyone who dares to say that mankind should set itself free from the chaotic sexual libertinism that gives AIDS its offensive potential is dismissed by public opinion as a hopeless obscurantist: such an idea can only be deplored by one's enlightened contemporaries, who pass over it in silence. All this shows us that there exists today a permissible criticism of society and a forbidden criticism of society; but the permissible criticism goes only as far as the threshold of fundamental decisions, which may not be called into question.

1. The Moral Problems of Our Age— An Attempt at a Diagnosis

The theme proposed here naturally demands a reflection that does not allow itself to be intimidated by such prohibitions. Nevertheless, it would be wrong, conversely, to see our society and its moral situation as a whole only in tones of unrelieved gray. We must not let ourselves be affected by the superficial obligatory optimism of certain trends, but, equally, we must not yield to the temptation to overlook the positive elements in the total complex of our age. It is, of course, not possible here to give an exhaustive description of the moral physiognomy of our age. The aim of our reflections is to find support and healing, that fundamental orientation with which to survive the present and thus open the path into the future. We are inquiring about the characteristic elements of *our* age, in order to recognize what hinders and what serves access to the correct path. Thus, in this first part of our analysis, we are not discussing defects or virtues that have always existed and no doubt always will exist but rather characteristic signs of our own times. In a negative perspective, there are two striking elements here that do not belong in the same way to other periods: terrorism and drugs. On the positive side, a strong moral consciousness is being asserted, concentrating essentially on values of the social sphere: freedom for the oppressed, solidarity with the poor and disadvantaged, peace and reconciliation.

a. The problem of drugs

Let us attempt to look somewhat more closely at these phenomena. I recall a debate I had with some friends in Ernst Bloch's house. Our conversation chanced to hit on the problem of drugs, which at that time—in the late 1960s—was just beginning to arise. We wondered how this temptation could spread so suddenly now, and why, for example, it had apparently not existed at all in the Middle Ages. All were agreed in rejecting as insufficient the answer that at that period the areas where drugs were cultivated were too far away. Phenomena like the appearance of drugs are not to be explained by means of such external conditions; they come from deeper needs or lacks, while dealing with the concrete problems of procurement follows later. I ventured the hypothesis that obviously in the Middle Ages the emptiness of the soul, which drugs are an attempt to fill, did not exist: the thirst of the soul, of the inner man, found an answer that made drugs unnecessary. I can still recall the speechless indignation with which Mrs. Bloch reacted to this proposed solution. On the basis of dialectical materialism's image of history, she found the idea almost criminal that past ages could have been superior to our own in not wholly inessential matters; it was impossible that the masses could have lived with greater happiness and inner harmony in the Middle Ages—a period of oppression and religious prejudices—than in our age, which has already made some degree of progress along the path of liberation: this would entail the collapse of the entire logic of "liberation". But how, then, is one to explain what has happened? The question remained unanswered that evening.

Since I do not share the materialistic image of the world, I continue to believe that my thesis was correct. Naturally, however, it must be made more concrete, and it is precisely the thinking of Ernst Bloch that can offer a helpful starting point here. For Bloch, the world of facts is a bad world. The principle of hope means that man energetically contradicts the facts; he knows he is obliged to overcome the bad world of facts in order to create a better world. I would put it in this way: drugs are a form of protest against facts. The one who takes them refuses to resign himself to the world of facts. He seeks a better world. Drugs are the result of despair in a world experienced as a dungeon of facts, in which man cannot hold out for long. Naturally, many other things are involved, too: the search for adventure; the conformity of joining in what others are doing; the cleverness of the dealers, and so on. But the core is a protest against a reality perceived as a prison. The "great journey" that men attempt in drugs is the perversion of mysticism, the perversion of the human need for infinity, the rejection of the impossibility of transcending immanence, and the attempt to extend the limits of one's own existence into the infinite. The patient and humble adventure of asceticism, which, in small steps of ascent, comes closer to the descending God, is replaced by magical power, the magical key of drugs—the ethical and religious path is replaced by technology. Drugs are the pseudo-mysticism of a world that does not believe yet cannot get rid of the soul's yearning for paradise. Thus, drugs are a warning sign that points to [something] very profound: not only do they disclose a vacuum in our society, which that society's own instruments cannot fill, but they also point to an inner claim of man's nature, a claim that asserts itself in a perverted form if it does not find the correct answer.

b. Terrorism as a moral problem

Terrorism's point of departure is closely related to that of drugs: here, too, we find at the outset a protest against the world as it is and the desire for a better world. On the basis of its roots, terrorism is a moralism, albeit a misdirected one that becomes the brutal parody of the true aims and paths of morality. It is not by chance that terrorism had its beginning in the universities, and here once again in the milieu of modern theology, in young people who at the outset were strongly influenced by religion. Terrorism was at first a religious enthusiasm that had been redirected into the earthly realm, a messianic expectation transposed into political fanaticism. Faith in life after death had broken down, or at least had become irrelevant, but the criterion of heavenly expectation was not abandoned: rather, it was now applied to the present world. God was no longer seen as one who genuinely acts, but the fulfillment of his promises was demanded just as it had always been, and, indeed, with a new vigor. "God has no other arms but ours"—this now meant that the fulfillment of these promises can and must be carried out by ourselves. Disgust at the intellectual and spiritual emptiness of our society, yearning for what is completely different, the claim to unconditional salvation without restrictions and without limits—this is, so to speak, the religious component in the phenomenon of terrorism, which gives it the impetus of a passion focused on a totality, its uncompromising character, and the claim to be idealistic. All this becomes so dangerous because of the decisively earthly character of the messianic hope: something unconditional is demanded of what is conditional, something infinite is demanded of what is finite. This inherent contradiction indicates the real tragedy of this phenomenon in which man's great vocation becomes the instrument of the great lie.

The false dimension in terrorism's promise was, however, concealed, as far as the average participant was concerned, by connecting the religious expectation to modern intellectuality. This means, first, that all traditional moral criteria are dragged before the tribunal of positivistic reason, "called into question", and "seen through" as unproven. Morality does not lie in Being but in the future. Man must devise it himself. The sole moral value that exists is the future society in which everything that does not exist now will be fulfilled. Thus morality in the present consists in working for this future society. Accordingly, the new moral criterion states: "Moral" is what serves to bring about the new society. What serves to do this, however, can be ascertained with the scientific methods of political strategy, with psychology, and with sociology. Morality becomes "scientific": its goal is no longer a "phantom"—heaven—but a phenomenon that can be constructed, the new age. Thus the moral and the religious have become realistic and "scientific". What more could one want? Is it any wonder that it was precisely idealistic young people who felt challenged by these promises?

It is only on closer inspection that one sees the cloven hoof in its entirety and hears Mephistopheles sneering. "'Moral' is whatever creates the future": on this criterion, even murder can be "moral"; even the inhuman must serve on the path to humanity. Fundamentally, this is the same logic as that which says that even embryos may be sacrificed for "genuinely high-quality scientific results". And the concept of freedom here is the same as that which teaches us that it must be a part of a woman's freedom to get rid of a child that stands in the way of her self-realization. Thus terrorism moves on today, without any restriction, to somewhat more elevated battlefields, with the full blessing of science and of the enlightened human intellect. Certainly the coarse terrorism of those who would change society has been brought under control in Western societies: it has been too great a threat to the accustomed life of these societies, and the immorality of its morality has become too obvious. But a genuine dissociation from its foundations has still not taken place; one sign of this is the fact that terrorism is still recommended without any embarrassment to Third World countries that lie sufficiently far removed from us. Today, just as earlier on, one is regarded as virtually immoral if one fails to praise slogans for the Third World that one would not like to see applied in one's own surroundings. Taking the side of militant ideologies of liberation seems a kind of moral compensation for accepting a comfortable life in which one wants to see nothing essential changed. We can thank God that the praxis of terrorism has been reduced in Europe, but its intellectual foundations have not been overcome, and, until this happens, its flames can be kindled anew at any time.

c. The new turning to morality and religion

We are now confronted very emphatically with the question: What is it that is really false in these intellectual foundations that we have only sketched briefly here? Exactly where does the error lie? Before we examine this question in depth, we must complete our inventory of today's society. We have said that the outstanding negative phenomena are the advances made by drugs and the threat posed by terrorism; but there also exists, as a positive phenomenon, a strong new will to work for great moral values like freedom, justice, and peace. Can this perhaps supply the answer to the threats that hang over our age? We must begin by noting that the values that have the greatest prominence here are largely identical with those that have been and are proclaimed as well by the supporters of violent movements as the values at which they aim. But this misuse does not discredit the values as such. What is new in many of the young generation of today is the fact that these goals are now projected onto the level of concrete political and social action and thereby stripped of their irrational and violent character. The ideologies are cut away, so that it becomes possible to see the good in its purity once again. One may in truth call this an element of hope: the deep divine message in man can be buried and disfigured, but it breaks out again and again and creates a path for itself. In this context, we must also note that a new desire for recollection, for contemplation, for true sacrality, indeed, for contact with God is perceptible.

Thus forces are emerging that permit us to hope. But just as the spring of water must be contained to prevent it from drying up, so these impulses, too, need to be purified and given structure, so that they can have their true effect. The new religious interest can very easily be diverted into the esoteric; it can evaporate into mere romanticism. It is extremely difficult for this religious interest to leap over two hurdles: it seems to be difficult to accept the continuity of a steady discipline, of a straight path that does not allow itself to be diverted from the ordering of the will and of the reason into quick satisfactions through techniques based on feelings. But it seems to be even more difficult to lead such a religious interest into the context of the common life of an "institution" of faith in which religion, as faith, has become the form and path of a community. But where this double hurdle is not surmounted, religion degenerates into a luxury; it does not develop any binding moral force for the community or for the individual. Understanding and the will disappear from religion; all that remains is feeling alone, and that is too little.

The new moral impulses, too, are at risk in similar ways. Their exposed flank is the general lack of individual-ethical values. The gaze is directed to the great totality, to what concerns the community. Certainly, one must acknowledge that the attention paid to marginalized groups often finds expression, too, in a personal readiness to help, which gives rise to the motivation to serve and to give assistance in admirable ways. But on the whole, one observes, rather, a weakness in personal motivating force. It is easier to demonstrate for the rights and freedoms of one's own group than to practice in daily living the discipline of freedom and the patience of love for those who suffer or, indeed, to bind oneself to such service for the whole of one's life, with the concomitant renunciation of a great part of one's own individual freedoms. It is noticeable that the motivating force to serve in the Church, too, has clearly become decisively weaker: there are scarcely any vocations now for Orders that dedicate themselves to caring for the sick and the elderly. One prefers to work in more "pastorally" ambitious services. But what is in fact more truly "pastoral" than the unpretentious existence at the service of those who suffer? No matter how important the professional qualification for these services is, without a deep moral and religious foundation, they congeal into mere technology and no longer perform what is critical in human terms.

Thus, the weak side of today's moral awakening lies first of all in the weakness of the individual-ethical motivating force. But something deeper lies behind this: moral values have lost their evidential character, and thus also their compelling claim, in a society conditioned by technology. They indicate goals for the totality, goals that awaken enthusiasm and zeal; but it is not clear to me why they should continue to be obligatory when this has negative consequences for me, threatening my own freedom and my personal peace. But this means that these goals remain largely ineffective, and the public vigor with which they are proclaimed in demonstrations and continually defended in speeches is surely itself a compensation for this lack of concrete effectiveness. So this brings us once again to the question that we left unanswered above: Where precisely is the beginning of the error in that kind of moralism which ends in terrorism? For this error is the real root of almost all the other problems of our epoch; its practical consequences extend far beyond the areas affected by terrorism.

2. Elements of an Answer

a. The essence of what is moral

Let us try to feel our way slowly toward the facts of the case. I said that that which is moral has lost its evidential character. Only a small number of people in modern society still believe in the existence of divine commandments, and still fewer are convinced that these commandments—if they exist—are communicated to us without error through the Church, through the religious community. The idea that another will, the will of the Creator, calls us and that our being is right when our will is in harmony with his will is an idea that is foreign to most people. The only function remaining for God at best is that of having set the primal Big Bang in motion; the notion that he is actively present in our midst and that man is subject to his will seems to most people a naïvely anthropomorphic concept of God in which man overestimates himself. The idea of a personal relationship between the Creator God and each individual person is certainly not wholly absent in the religious and ethical history of man, but in its pure form it is limited to the sphere of biblical religion. But there is an objective connection between this and the conviction that was common to almost the whole of mankind before the modern period, the conviction that man's Being contains an imperative; the conviction that he does not himself *invent* morality on the basis of calculations of expediency but, rather, *finds* it already present in the essence of things. Long before the outbreak of terrorism and the invasion by drugs, the English author and philosopher C. S. Lewis pointed to the fatal danger of the abolition of man that lies in the collapse of the foundations of our morality, emphasizing the evidential character of mankind as a whole on which the existence of man *qua* man rests. He reviews all the great cultures to show the existence of this evidential character. Not only does he refer to the moral inheritance of the Greeks, as this was articulated especially by Plato, Aristotle, and the Stoics, who wish to lead man to perceive the rationality of Being and, therefore, demand an education in "connaturality with reason"; he recalls also the idea of *Rta* in early Hinduism, which speaks of the harmony of the cosmic order, the moral virtues, and the ceremonial of the temple. He emphasizes especially the Chinese teaching of the Tao: "It is Nature, it is the Way, the Road. It is the Way in which the universe goes on. . . . It is also the Way which every man should tread in imitation of that cosmic and supercosmic progression, conforming all activities to that great exemplar."[1] But Lewis also refers to the law of Israel, which links cosmos and history and intends to be an expression of the truth of man as well as of the truth of the world as a whole. There are differences in detail within this knowledge shared by the great cultures, but stronger than the differences is the great

[1] C. S. Lewis, *The Abolition of Man* (New York: Macmillan, 1947), 28.

common area that presents itself as the primal evidential character of human life: the doctrine of objective values expressed in the Being of the world; the belief that attitudes exist that correspond to the message of the universe and are true and therefore good and that other attitudes likewise exist that are genuinely and always false because they contradict Being.

Men in the modern period have been persuaded that the moralities of mankind contradict each other radically, just as the religions do. In both cases, the simple conclusion has been drawn that all of this is a human construction, whose inconsistencies we now at last see through and can replace with rational knowledge. But this diagnosis is extremely superficial. It clings to a series of details that are lined up alongside each other in no particular order and thus arrives at its banal know-it-all attitude. In reality, the fundamental intuition about the moral character of Being itself and about the necessary harmony between the human being and the message of nature is common to all the great cultures, and therefore the great moral imperatives are likewise held in common. C. S. Lewis has stated this emphatically:

> This thing which I have called for convenience the *Tao*, and which others may call Natural Law or Traditional Morality or the First Principles of Practical Reason or the First Platitudes, is not one among a series of possible systems of value. It is the sole source of all value judgements. If it is rejected, all value is rejected. If any value is retained, it is retained. The effort to refute it and raise a new system of value in its place is self-contradictory.[2]

[2] Ibid., 56.

b. The falsification of scientism: The abolition of man

The problem of the modern period, that is, the moral problem of our age, consists in the fact that it has separated itself from this primal evidential character. In order genuinely to understand this process, we must describe it still more precisely. It is characteristic of thought marked by the natural sciences to posit a gulf between the world of feelings and the world of facts. Feelings are subjective, facts are objective. "Facts", that is, that which can be established as existing outside ourselves, are as yet only "facts", naked facticity. It belongs to the world of pure fable to attribute any qualities of a moral or aesthetic nature to the atom beyond its mathematical determinations. But the consequence of this reduction of nature to facts that can be completely grasped and therefore controlled is that no moral message outside ourselves can now come to us. Morality, just like religion, now belongs to the realm of the subjective; it has no place in the objective. If it is subjective, then it is something posited by man. It does not precede vis-à-vis us: we precede it and fashion it. This movement of "objectification", which permits us to "see through" things and to control them, essentially knows no limits. Auguste Comte called for a physics of man: gradually, even the most difficult object of nature—man—must become scientifically comprehensible, that is, subordinate to the knowledge of the natural sciences. Thus one would see through man in precisely the same way as one has already seen through matter.[3] Psychoanalysis and sociology are the fundamental ways to fulfill this demand. One can now (so it seems) explain the mecha-

[3] Cf. Henri de Lubac, *The Drama of Atheist Humanism* (San Francisco: Ignatius Press, 1995), 131–267; Hans Urs von Balthasar, *The God Question and Modern Man* (New York: Seabury Press, 1967).

nisms whereby man came to believe that nature expresses a moral law. Naturally, the man who has been "seen through" is no longer a man at all—it belongs to the essence of such knowledge that he, too, can be only pure facticity now: "If you see through everything, then everything is transparent. But a wholly transparent world is an invisible world", writes Lewis.[4] The theories of evolution, developed into a universal view of the world, confirm this optic and attempt at the same time to compensate for it.[5] Naturally (so they say), everything has become what it is without any logic or, more correctly, through the sheer logic of facts. But it is now possible to reconstruct this purely mechanical origin of the world's coming into being in theories about chance and necessity, in the perfect doctrine of evolution. The consequences drawn from "evolution", imitations of its successes, would then be the new morality: the goal of evolution is the survival and the optimization of the species. The optimal survival of the genus "man" would now be the fundamental moral value; the rules for accomplishing this would be the only moral regulations. It is only in appearance that this is a return to listening to the moral instruction that nature gives: in reality, it is now the god Meaningless who rules, for evolution on its own terms is meaningless. Calculation rules, and power rules. Morality has surrendered, and man *qua* man has surrendered. It no longer makes sense to cling to the survival of this particular species. Let us listen to C. S. Lewis once again. Already in 1943, he described this process with razor-sharp acuteness:

[4] Lewis, *Abolition of Man*, 91.

[5] Cf. on this, R. Spaemann, R. Löw, and P. Koslowski, *Evolutionismus und Christentum* (Weinheim: VCH, 1986); W. Bröker, "Schöpfung als Auftrag", in *Weisheit Gottes—Weisheit der Welt*, ed. W. Baier et al. (St. Ottilien: EOS Verlag, 1987), 115–26.

> It is the magician's bargain: give up our soul, get power in return. But once our souls, that is, our selves, have been given up, the power thus conferred will not belong to us. . . . It is in Man's power to treat himself as a mere "natural object". . . . The real objection is that if man chooses to treat himself as raw material, raw material he will be.[6]

Lewis formulated these warnings during the Second World War, because he saw the destruction of morality as something that threatened the ability to defend one's native land against the oncoming storm of barbarity. But he was objective enough to add: "I am not here thinking solely, perhaps not even chiefly, of those who are our public enemies at the moment. The process which, if not checked, will abolish Man, goes on apace among Communists and Democrats no less than among Fascists. . . ."[7] This remark seems to me to be very important: the most opposite modern views of the world share the same starting point: the denial of the natural ethical law and the reduction of the world to "mere" facts. The measure of what they illogically retain of the old values is variable, but they are threatened by the same danger in their central point.

The real untruth of the world view of which drugs and terrorism are symptoms consists in the reduction of the world to facts and in the narrowing-down of reason to the perception of what is quantitative. That which is most specific to man is shoved aside into the subjective realm and thus lacks reality. The "abolition of man", which results from the attribution of absoluteness to one single mode of knowledge, at the same time clearly falsifies this world view. Man exists, and anyone who, on the strength of his own

[6] Lewis, *Abolition of Man*, 83–84. (The first British edition of *The Abolition of Man* was published by Oxford University Press in 1943.)

[7] Ibid., 85.

theory, has to pull man down into the sphere of a machine that is "seen through" and can be assembled lives in a constriction of perception that misses precisely what is essential. If the aim of science is the most universal knowledge possible, the knowledge most in accordance with reality, then such an absolutized form of method is the opposite of science. This means, in other words, that practical reason, too, on which genuinely ethical knowledge is based, is truly reason and not merely the expression of subjective feelings without any value as evidence. We must again learn to understand that the great ethical insights of mankind are just as rational and just as true as—indeed, more true than—the experimental knowledge of the realm of the natural sciences and technology. They are more true, because they touch more deeply the essential character of Being and have a more decisive significance for the humanity of man.

c. Reason of morality and reason of faith

Two consequences derive from this. The first is that moral obligation is not man's prison, from which he must liberate himself in order finally to be able to do what he wants. It is moral obligation that constitutes his dignity, and he does not become more free if he discards it: on the contrary, he takes a step backward, to the level of a machine, of a mere thing. If there is no longer any obligation to which he can and must respond in freedom, then there is no longer any realm of freedom at all. The recognition of morality is the real substance of human dignity; but one cannot recognize this without simultaneously experiencing it as an obligation of freedom. Morality is not man's prison but, rather, the divine element in him.

In order to present the second consequence, we must

again reflect on the fundamental insight we reached earlier: practical (or moral) reason is reason in the highest sense, because it penetrates the real mystery of reality more deeply than does experimental reason. But this means that the Christian faith is not a limitation or paralysis of reason: on the contrary, it is only this faith that sets reason free to perform its own proper work. For practical reason, too, needs the confirmation of an experiment, but of one too large to be carried out in laboratories: it needs the experiment of a human existence that has stood the test, and this can come only from history that itself has stood the test. This is why practical reason was always given its place in the great context of experience and testing of holistic ethical-religious visions. And just as the natural sciences live from brilliant breakthroughs made by great individuals, so, too, these systematizations of the ethical view depend both on the experience of community and on the exceptional vision of individuals who succeeded in gaining a glimpse of the whole. The great ethical constructs of Greece, of the Near and the Far East, of which we have spoken briefly above, have lost none of their validity in the core of what they say, but today we can see them as tributaries that ultimately flow into the great river of the Christian interpretation of reality.

The ethical vision of the Christian faith is not in fact something specific to Christianity but is the synthesis of the great ethical intuitions of mankind from a new center that holds them all together. This agreement in ethical wisdom is often put forward today as an argument against the obligatory character of the commandments of God that are proclaimed in the Bible. It is argued that this agreement shows that the Bible does not possess any ethical instruction at all of its own but simply adopts the moral insights of its milieu at the time. Accordingly, only what is recognized at a specific time as reasonable has validity in morality—and thus one has already arrived at the reduction of morality to a mere calculation, that is, at the abolition of the "moral" in the proper sense of the word. It is the opposite that is true: the inner harmony of the fundamental moral instruction, which was of course developed and purified step by step, is the best proof of its validity—the best proof that it was not invented but found already in existence. Found—how? It is here that the realms of revelation and reason penetrate one another very closely. This knowledge was found, on the one side, as we have said, by those who were able to see more deeply. We call such sight, which goes beyond one's own capacity of knowledge, revelation. But that which is seen here is, in the ethical realm, essentially the moral message that lies in creation itself. For nature is not—as is asserted by a totalitarian scientism—some assemblage built up by chance and its rules of play but is rather a creation. A creation in which the *Creator Spiritus* expresses himself. This is why there are not only natural laws in the sense of physical functions: the specific natural law itself is a moral law. Creation itself teaches us how we can be human in the right way. The Christian faith, which helps us to recognize creation as creation, does not paralyze reason; it gives practical reason the life-sphere in which it can unfold. The morality that the Church teaches is not some special burden for Christians: it is the defense of man against the attempt to abolish him. If morality—as we have seen—is not the enslavement of man but his liberation, then the Christian faith is the advance post of human freedom.

I should like to add one more reflection. The Roman poet Juvenal has formulated in an unsurpassable way my concern here:

Summum crede nefas animam praeferre pudori
et propter vitam vivendi perdere causas—

"Believe that it is the worst crime to prefer your physical life to reverence and to destroy, for the sake of living, the reasons for living." This means that there are values worth dying for, because a life purchased at the cost of betraying these values is based on the betrayal of the reasons for living and is therefore a life destroyed from within. We could express what is meant here as follows: where there is no longer anything worth dying for, life is no longer worthwhile; it has lost its point. And this is not only true for the individual; a land, too, a common culture, has values that justify the commitment of one's life; if such values no longer exist, we also lose the reasons and the forces that maintain social cohesion and preserve a country as a community of life.

This brings us once more to the reflections on which we first touched in our remarks about drugs. Man needs transcendence. Immanence alone is too narrow for him. He is created for more. The denial of an afterlife led initially to a passionate glorification of life, the assertion of life at any price. For everything must be attained in this life—there is nothing else. The lust for life, the lust for all kinds of fulfillment, was intensified to the utmost. But at once, an enormous devaluation of life came from this: life is no longer surrounded by the seal of the holy; one throws it away when it no longer pleases. The misshapen triplets—abortion, euthanasia, suicide—are the natural progeny of this fundamental decision, which is the denial of eternal responsibility and of eternal hope. Lust for life changes into disgust with life and into the emptiness of its fulfillments. Here, too, the abolition of man is the consequence.

Man needs morality in order to be himself. But morality requires faith in creation and immortality, that is, it needs the objectivity of obligation and the definitiveness of responsibility and fulfillment. The impossibility of a human existence cut off from these is the indirect proof of the truth of the Christian faith and of its hope. It is this hope that saves man, today as ever—indeed, precisely today. The Christian is entitled to be glad in his faith. Without the good news of faith, human existence does not survive in the long run. The joy of faith is its responsibility: we should seize it with new courage in this hour of our history.

8

The Lesson of 1989: The Political Force of Metapolitical Realities

The year 1989 led to dramatic changes in the political and spiritual panorama of Europe that no one could have predicted even a short time ago. This revolution—and this is the true novelty of it—took place, not by military force or political violence, but rather by virtue of new beginnings and spiritual upheavals that simply swept the ground out from underneath the traditional power structures and caused them to collapse as though overnight.

This process not only concerns the states that until now were dominated by the Marxist ideology, but it has a global significance. It extends far beyond the confines of politics, all the more so because the process itself was set in motion in the metapolitical sphere and then brought to light the political force of factors that originally were not of a political nature.

The first version of this essay, in Italian, was presented on December 16, 1989, in Rieti, Italy—while still under the vivid impression of the events that had just occurred in Eastern Europe—as an attempt at an initial reflection on the causes and consequences of what had happened. The version reprinted here is the one used for a conference at Sapienza University in Rome on February 15, 1990. As part of the celebrations of the 1,400th anniversary of the Third Council of Toledo, the author presented in Madrid on February 24, 1990, a subsequent version that was modified to suit the specific occasion. [Translated from Italian.]

It would be out of place, however, to harbor cheap feelings of satisfaction because of the downfall of others. We are all called to reflect: On what spiritual foundations can we build roads capable of going forward to meet the future, and on what foundations is that not possible?

Consequently, the reflections on the following pages will certainly refer to the political events of 1989, but they will be directed above all toward the metapolitical dimension, which on this occasion was manifested in all its pressing current relevance.

I. The Crisis of Marxism as Calling the West into Question

1. The metapolitical presuppositions of the political and economic crisis

We wish, therefore, to begin our investigation with the facts that occurred so as to identify the forces that propelled them internally and, thus, to seek valid benchmarks for the further journey.

The first question that we must ask is: What actually went wrong over the course of the years 1989 and 1990?

First of all, we can and must simply say that Marxism, as an all-encompassing interpretation of reality and as a guide to historical action, was completely repudiated. Its promises of liberty, equality, and well-being for everyone were not proved true by the facts; instead, their falsity was unmasked precisely by the factual data of politics and economics.

However accurate these initial observations may be, though, they would stop at the surface if we were to be content with them. We must, instead, take another step and ask ourselves:

What, then, is false in this interpretation of the world and in the praxis that is deduced from it?

A precise observation of the phenomenon leads immediately to the heart of the matter: the force of the spirit, the energy of personal convictions, sufferings, and hopes caused the existing structures to collapse. This means: the brand of materialism that tried to conceive the spirit in a reductive way as a mere consequence of material structures, as a mere superstructure of the economic system, was definitively repudiated. At this point, though, we are speaking no longer only about the problem of Marxism and its political-institutional ramifications, but also about ourselves in the first person. Materialism, indeed, is a problem that concerns all of us; this shipwreck compels us without exception to reflect conscientiously. It is necessary, then, to dwell again for a moment on this question and to ask ourselves: What is, strictly speaking, the nucleus of a materialist ideology?

It does not consist in the absolute negation of the reality of the spirit. Materialism too admits that at a certain point in history spirit appeared and that, from then on, it must be distinguished from what is simply matter. The essence of modern materialism is subtler: it consists in the way in which the relation between matter and spirit is conceived. Matter is the first and original thing; in the beginning was matter, and not the *Logos*. From it everything develops in a causal process, which is then raised to a necessary process. Spirit has never been anything other than a product of matter. When its laws are known and one is able to manipulate them, then one can direct the course of the spirit, too. The spirit is changed by transforming the material conditions for its existence. In this way, mechanically, that is, by composing and transforming the structural framework of material conditions, history itself can be changed and transformed.[1]

[1] Obviously it would be necessary to elaborate in greater detail and to explain further this general diagnosis about the essence of modern materialism by referring in particular to dialectical and historical materialism—something that is not possible within the limits of this talk. The peculiar characteristic of this type of materialism results above all from the introduction of the "labor" factor into the materialist consideration of reality. The fundamental premise, however, still remains the thesis of the primacy of matter over consciousness—a thesis that, thanks to the dialectical view of the relation between nature and consciousness, is broadened, without being resolved, though. By means of labor—this is the thesis—man acts upon nature, transforming it and being transformed by it, and in this dialectic antithesis he is said to have in turn the development of his consciousness. Dialectical materialism tries in this way to overcome a purely mechanistic materialism; it claims to "replace a mechanistic (or even pantheistic) consideration of nature and of man with a fundamentally materialistic theory of man's development, which embraces all spheres of reality and at the same time respects their specific peculiarities." The philosophical dictionary edited by G. Klaus and M. Buhr at the Bibliographic Institute in Leipzig (1965) describes in these terms the claim to novelty and definitive validity of the kind of materialism founded by Marx and Engels (cf. 329a). In this way, their followers try to manage to classify history and society completely under a set of norms that can be investigated scientifically and manipulated, which remained beyond the scope of the preceding, more "contemplative" or "metaphysical" forms of materialism. In this sense, the above-cited dictionary continues: "For the first time in human intellectual history, the possibility thus presented itself of applying materialism to the explanation of social life and discovering its material motive forces and laws. In this way for the first time a scientific theory of society was founded" (ibid., 329a–b). This very claim to being "scientific" was refuted by the most recent events, which pitted against the alleged "laws of social life" a freedom that in itself annulled those "laws". Both articles, "Materialism" (325–30), and "Historical and Dialectical Materialism" (330–40), as well as the further article on "Matter" (341–44) from the dictionary just cited rate as a quasi-official presentation of Marxist philosophy. Informative articles with extensive bibliographies are: W. Nieke, "Materialismus", in J. Ritter and K. Grunder, eds., *Historisches Wörterbuch der Philosophie*, vol. 5 (Basel and Stuttgart: Scheidegger und Spiess, 1980), 843–50; W. Knispel, W. Goerdt, and H. Dahm, "Materialismus, dialektischer", in Ritter and Grunder, *Historisches Wörterbuch*, 5:851–59.

This materialist arrogance has proved that it is false. Of course, spirit depends to a great extent on its material conditions; nevertheless, it is also superior to them. It is not possible to liberate man from his personal freedom by covering with cement the paths along which it must move. The pretense of building the perfect man and the perfect society by prescriptions of a structural sort is the specific nucleus of contemporary materialism, and this nucleus has proved its own falsehood. Anyone who trusts the mechanical factor, rather than the spiritual, eternal one, in the long run keeps his own accounts wrong.

If this is true, at the same time it calls into question as well a certain type of faith in science that, on the other hand, makes its own effects felt far beyond the sphere of Marxist influence.

Science, in the more restricted sense of the term, refers to the sphere of what is necessary; in other words, what can be reduced to ironclad rules of causal explanation. By means of this procedure, it attains objectively verifiable certainties. This means, however, that science, understood in this way, cannot deal adequately with the dimension of freedom or, therefore, with what is specifically human in man and in his social formations.

Yet the fascination with an all-encompassing concept of science that would allow scientists to study man, too, no less exactly than physical realities drove them to dispute this limitation of science. Already in the writings of Auguste Comte, every effort was made to conceive of man, too, as a being determined by necessary laws, so as to leave no more unexplored territories on the map of the scientific world. This was the origin of that common fundamental concept—despite the differences in the details—of "social science", which appears in the East as Marxist socialism and in the West as positivist sociology. In both cases, it represents—as Jürgen Habermas puts it—the "project of modernity".[2]

It would go beyond the scope of our considerations to try to elucidate here in more detail the fundamental methodological arrangement that is at work behind all the differences between Marxism and positivism and is common to both. We are talking about a model of "human science" in which this discipline is understood as a modern metaphysics, as an interpretation of the fundamentals of the human condition. A citation from Habermas may suffice once again; he says that being a person must be considered, not an "independent variable", but rather "a generic essence that (first of all) is realized in a historic process and within an epoch and a society that are absolutely determined". The notion of individual person is then "an individual who has become such through and by virtue of a process of socialization and who therefore cannot quite be conceived of apart from society. He is, so to speak, produced or generated by means of the mechanisms of socialization."[3]

The attempt to manipulate man "scientifically"—in the stricter sense of the term—implies determinism, which results from the presupposition of materialism. A notion of science that had been elaborated in relation to something in which there is no freedom is transposed here to the level of what is free, of what is properly human, so as to make

[2] I draw the references to Habermas from the important essay by R. Hofmann, "Soziologie als theologische Grunddisziplin? Zur vergessenen Metaphysik der Sozialwissenschaften", in *Communio*, German edition, 19 (1990): 453–66 at 456.

[3] Thus B. Hamann defines Habermas' position. *Sozialisationstheorie auf dem Prüfstand* (Bad Hellbrunn: Klinkhardt, 1981), 46; see also R. Hofmann, "Soziologie als theologische Grunddisziplin?", 461.

possible a "human physics" made up exclusively of necessary laws and exact forecasts.[4]

At this point, the theory—if accepted consistently—essentially requires the exclusion of the freedom factor. The Marxist system was nothing but an absolutely rigorous application of these fundamental presuppositions to political action: the repression of freedom wrought by the system therefore must not be deemed an abuse but, rather, the logical consequence of this principle.

The concrete rebirth of freedom in the struggle against the system, which played out in the streets of the capitals of Eastern Europe, acquires for this reason a decisive theoretical significance. It not only calls Marxist thought into question but also challenges our way of basing the human sciences on methodical presuppositions that exclude the *humanum*. What happened here in the arena of politics is thus an invaluable and effective contribution to the fundamental question: What is freedom and what is man?

There is also a third aspect of the phenomenon that we are examining that seems to me quite obvious. What happened has called into question also a certain connotation of the idea of progress.

The term "progress" has become a necessary corollary of post-Hegelian philosophies of history. It presupposes the mechanistic interpretation of history that we just subjected to a critique. "Progress" is therefore a slogan that can easily be utilized as a label for facile partisan classifications. In the past, the socialist camp simply believed that progress was whatever served to build up socialism. Yet there is also

[4] Other clarifications of this problematic area can be found in M. Kriele, *Befreiung und politische Aufklärung* (Freiburg, 1980), 78–82.

a superficial, no less sectarian and unilateral liberalism in which freedom is identified with the absence of restraints, and "progress" appears to be that which cuts all sorts of ties. And finally there is also the technological variant of faith in progress: it views the increase of technology's power per se as a form of human progress. In this connection, Romano Guardini spoke about the "folly of faith in progress".[5]

Whenever progress is considered a necessary process of the orderly development of history, it remains beneath what is properly human and, in the final analysis, is an anti-human concept. Individual freedom and personal ethical responsibility cannot then be considered factors disturbing such deterministic processes. The fact that in 1989–1990, this "disturbing factor" pounced so widely and overwhelmingly onto the historical scene is a process that gives hope and is, at the same time, a factual datum that ought to compel us to reflect and to modify our convictions.

It is inevitable at this point to ask ourselves whether we are ready for and capable of such a change. To what point are we truly in a position to develop new, fruitful holistic visions and to repudiate the implicit or manifest materialism that led to the painful flirtation of Western intellectuals with Marxism, which they no longer want to hear anything about today?

[5] Romano Guardini, *Die Lebensalter*, 10th ed. (Mainz: Grünewald, 1986), 97. The critical discussion of faith in progress runs through all the works of Guardini. Particularly urgent are several considerations in this connection that he expressed in a speech to university students in 1956, after the Hungarian Uprising was repressed. Just one citation: "It is false and dangerous to define man as the being who makes progress. No, he is the being that no form of progress ever makes safe against dangers, but rather must again and again . . . decide between good and evil." R. Guardini, *Wahrheit und Ordnung: Universitätspredigten*, vol. 11 (Würzburg: Werkbund, 1956), 262.

2. *The forces that promoted the changes*

We must turn now to an investigation of the effective forces that promoted the changes in the states of Eastern Europe.

Here, too, we are not talking about a political analysis in the strict sense of the word. After asking ourselves a little earlier what truly ran aground and proved to have no future, let us inquire now about the positive side: What are the energies capable of bringing about the change? Here, of course, our analysis cannot be in any way exhaustive but can be only an initial attempt to survey the field.

What caused the change? Let us dwell in the first place on the concrete political processes, so as then to be able to set them into a broader context of meaning.

We need to mention first, as an obvious factual datum and as a factor that became the most powerful driver of the recent transformations, the material failure of the Marxist system precisely in the economic and social sphere. Marxism, indeed, failed on its own turf—as an economic theory—and today it is no longer possible to take it seriously in that scientific field. The theorists of the system and its functionaries had already known this for some time; faith in it had decreased little by little in those who represented it when faced with the evidence of the facts. For some time now, the system has managed to stand, no longer on an actual conviction, but solely due to the self-assertion of the authorities.

The duration of naked power, which is founded on itself alone without leaning on spiritual values, is necessarily limited. At the moment when the "loss of faith" of those in authority converged with their citizens' loss of confidence and the pure and simple lack of wealth, the fragile construct necessarily started to collapse onto itself.

The second factor that must be mentioned, then, in this connection is the force of religion. It had been predicted that religion would vanish by itself, when progress had changed the social relations that gave rise to the alienating projection of the religious element. The ideologues had long since ended up admitting that the rapidity of this process had been overestimated; then little by little the hypothesis that religion would never definitively disappear became acceptable. Finally, something surprising happened: the question about God emerged again precisely among the intellectuals dedicated to the natural sciences. This science, having become conscious of its own limits, acknowledged that the real answers were found beyond what it was capable of affirming by itself.

The problem of God flashed like lightning in the midst of the investigations of the strictest scientific rationality, and at the same time from the depths of human existence sprang once again the longing for eternity that is profoundly imprinted on our soul. We know from many testimonies that even in our day God has become a provocative topic of discussion among the young people at the universities, who were educated in the totalitarian regimes to State-sanctioned atheism.[6] This has not always led to conversion, to the full Christian faith. But this questioning has spontaneously given

[6] A particularly impressive testimony is found in the writings of T. Goritschewa, for example, *Von Gott zu reden ist gefährlich* [Talking about God is dangerous], 3rd ed. (Freiburg: Herder, 1984), and *Die Kraft der Ohnmächtigen. Weisheit aus dem Leiden* [The power of the helpless: wisdom from suffering] (Wuppertal: Brockhaus Verlag, 1987). Still important for the journey of gradual conversion to God are the works of Aleksandr Solzhenitsyn, particularly *The First Circle*.

rise to a new ability to accept the mystery through the message of icons and to experience the closeness of the divine in the Orthodox liturgy, which is entirely dedicated to the mystery itself.

The splendor of religion's promises, at first obscured by the enchantment of the ideological utopias, then made itself noticeable and proved capable of orienting people toward other higher practical forms of human life than a desacralized world could offer, perhaps by making use of various surrogates typical of moral libertinism. Religion, which until a short time ago was considered the quintessence of superstition and oppression, reemerged as a genuine authority on freedom; and once again it burst onto the scene as a social force that relativized the dominant power. It infused its spiritual energies, which ultimately were stronger than physical violence.

There is another, third factor that we cannot overlook, and its nature is much different from the preceding ones: the influence of the communications media. Here we encounter a remarkably ambiguous reality, which we must not minimize in diagnosing the current historical moment, unless we want to be guilty of oversimplifying the phenomenon.

No doubt, the communications media proved to be factors in destabilizing dictatorships. With their minute analyses and their structural tendency to demystify events, they relativize everything; they present contrasting images of every fact and in this way make everything debatable. They set before our eyes ideals in life, and thus they affirm a unit of measurement that prompts us to challenge the status quo. They form consciousness as well as the unconscious and drive viewers toward the realization of what they have seen and heard. In this way, they certainly contributed to forming a mentality that is less and less willing to resign itself to an unchangeable status quo. Probably they are also partly to thank, then, for the most positive and most surprising aspect of the changes: namely, that they almost always took place without violence.

Of course we cannot conceal the fact that the communications media, with their trivialization of violence—which they present as altogether normal and habitual human behavior—have a serious responsibility for the levity with which the threshold of violence between individuals and groups is crossed nowadays. However, there is also the reverse side of the coin of their power to influence: what happens in any part of the world becomes visible everywhere. Military violence against people who are protesting peacefully, which we saw in China and which was documented for us on our television screens in Romania, was shown throughout the world in its horror and brutality. This cannot hide behind the mask of a commitment to making society better; instead, it has clearly revealed the brutal face of a bloody dictatorship, which is repugnant to the civil conscience of the whole world.

When these images are broadcast worldwide, it lends powerful support to the local events and becomes timely protection for the unarmed protesters. These are positive effects of mass society, to which we had given no thought at all until now. But no doubt there is also another aspect of the same phenomenon.

The power of images, their ability to relativize events is exerted far beyond the sphere of dictatorships and tends toward indiscriminate skepticism. We get the impression that we know it all and can judge everything; but this can lead to the loss of the ability to perceive the deeper dimensions of life. We run the risk of flattening our sensibility, of closing ourselves off from outside things, of making demands with regard to life that not only cause dictatorships to totter, but also destabilize the very depths of the human soul itself. There is a looming danger that the soul might become incapable of the patience that leans on the truth and incapable also of that connection without which truth is not revealed and the response of love cannot blossom.

The phenomenon of the communications media, ultimately, cannot be judged as either exclusively positive or as simply negative. Precisely in their ambiguity, they are a sign of the historic destiny assigned to our era, the power of which can extend in an ever-increasing way in the most varied directions.

II. Analogies and Differences in the Western World

Our preceding reflections started from the events in Eastern Europe but were also an attempt to reflect on our problems: the problems of the Western world and of its ideologies.

This aspect of our study should be explored now in greater depth, before we can draw conclusions from it for the paths of faith today. Therefore, I would like to address three questions: the crisis of faith in science, the new demand for spirituality and ethics, and the new thirst for religion.

1. The crisis of faith in science

In the last decade, creation's resistance to letting itself be manipulated by mankind has been manifested as a novel element in our overall cultural situation. The question about the limits of science and the criteria that it should hold has become unavoidable. It seems to me that particularly telling signs of this change in the intellectual climate are the different ways in which the Galileo case is judged.

This fact, although relatively unremarkable in the seventeenth century, was raised already in the next century to the status of an Enlightenment myth. Galileo appeared as a victim of that medieval obscurantism that persists in the Church. A clear-cut line separates good and evil. On the one hand, we find the Inquisition: the authority that embodies superstition, the adversary of freedom and knowledge. On the other hand—natural science, represented by Galileo; behold the force of progress and of human liberation from the chains of ignorance that keep man powerless against nature. The star of Modernity shines in the dark night of the obscure Middle Ages.[7]

Curiously, Ernst Bloch, of all people, with his romantic Marxism, was one of the first to oppose this myth openly, while offering a new interpretation of what had happened.

According to Bloch, the heliocentric system—like the geocentric one—is based on presuppositions that cannot be proved. Prominent among them is the statement that an absolute space exists—an option that, however, was then ruled out by the theory of relativity. He writes:

> Since, with the abolition of the conjecture of an empty, motionless space, movement no longer occurs with respect to it, but only the movement of bodies relative to each other, and since the measurement of this motion depends on the choice of the body that is taken as the point of reference, therefore—as long as the complexity of the resulting calculations does not make the hypothesis impracticable—now as then one could support the idea of a fixed earth and a movable sun.[8]

[7] See Walter Brandmüller, *Galilei und die Kirche oder das Recht auf Irrtum* (Regensburg, 1982).

[8] Ernst Bloch, *Das Prinzip Hoffnung* (Frankfurt am Main: Suhrkamp, 1959), 920; cf. F. Hartl, *Der Begriff des Schöpferischen: Deutungsversuche der Dialektik durch E. Bloch und F. v. Baader* (Frankfurt am Main: Lang, 1979), 110.

The advantage of the heliocentric system over the geocentric one consists therefore, not in a greater correspondence to objective truth, but only in the fact that it offers us greater ease in calculation. So far Bloch only expounds a modern concept of natural science. The evaluation of it that he makes, however, is surprising:

> Once the relativity of movement is given with certainty, an ancient system of human and Christian reference has no right to interfere in astronomical calculations and in their heliocentric simplification; however, it has the right to remain faithful to its own method of keeping the earth in relation to human dignity and to order the world around what will happen and what has happened in the world.[9]

Although here the two spheres of knowledge are still clearly differentiated from one another with regard to their methodology, acknowledging both their limits and their respective rights, a synthetic judgment by the agnostic-skeptical philosopher Paul Feyerabend seems much more drastic. He writes: "The Church in Galileo's time adhered to reason more than Galileo himself and took into consideration also the ethical and social consequences of Galileo's teaching. Its sentence against Galileo was rational and just, and the revision of it can be legitimized only for reasons of political convenience."[10] From the perspective of the concrete consequences of Galileo's new approach, finally, C. F. von Weizsäcker takes a further step forward when he sees a "very straight line" leading from Galileo to the atomic bomb.

To my great surprise, in a recent interview on the Galileo

[9] Bloch, *Das Prinzip Hoffnung*, 920ff.; Hartl, *Der Begriff des Schöpferischen*, 111.

[10] P. Feyerabend, *Widen den Methodenzwang* (Frankfurt am Main, 1976, 1983), 206.

case, no question of this sort was asked: "Why did the Church claim to obstruct the development of the natural sciences?" but, instead, the exact opposite, namely: "Why did the Church not take a clearer position against the disaster that would necessarily take place once Galileo opened Pandora's box?"

It would be absurd to construct a hasty apologetic on the basis of these statements. Growth in faith starts, not from the resentment and rejection of rationality, but from its fundamental affirmation and from its inclusion in a larger reasonableness. We will return to this point farther on. Here I wanted to recall a symptomatic case that shows the extent to which modernity's doubt about itself has affected science and technology today.

2. *The anxious search for spirituality and ethics*

We must now consider a second aspect: the new search for *ethos* and "spirituality". Just as it is not possible to evaluate as altogether negative or positive the widespread doubt that collides with science and modernity nowadays, so too we cannot present as a monolithic phenomenon the new openness toward the spiritual dimension of the world and of human existence.

Naturally there are clearly positive aspects here. In the culminating period of modernity, the moral dimension was relegated to the subjective sphere, and technological progress was considered a value in itself, which could no longer be called into question in any way. Precisely in these same spheres, though, the ethical question has emerged once again today as a question about the moral criterion for our action.

Thinking about moral norms as limits to our scientific research and our conduct is an attitude that today is no longer branded a priori in any way as a form of obscurantism: first, the atomic bomb and, then, biologically destructive forms of technological production made plain the other face of progress.

To tell the truth, the practical effectiveness of this fundamental observation continues to be limited in most cases, as demonstrated by the discussion about genetic manipulation and about artificial fertilization. Human life—the life of persons, although not yet born—is utilized for the "higher ends" of research, or for other ends that are considered good, and today as in the past it does not seem that there will be any break in that routine. The abuse of man, who is treated like a thing, and casual carelessness with the divine secret of his life do not appear to be on the decrease. But there is opposition to it, and precisely from within the natural sciences themselves.[11]

3. The new religiosity

Finally, there are likewise many aspects to the rediscovery of the religious dimension.

Just as we notice in the most eminent figures of today's natural sciences a new and decisive orientation toward the ethical problem and a rejection of the self-limitation of positivism, so too we confront today the phenomenon of young people who with a new passion are asking themselves questions about God and are willing to let their whole lives, down to their roots, be defined by him. And at the same

[11] Worth reading for its new methodological approach is the study by C. Labrusse-Riou, "L'homme à vif: biotechnologie et droits de l'homme", *Esprit* 156 (November 1989): 60–70. See also the insistent summons of Hans Jonas, "Technik, Ethik und Biogenetische Kunst", *Internationale katholische Zeitschrift Communio* 13 (1984): 501–17. See also R. Löw, ed., *Bioethik* (Cologne: Communio, 1990).

time there is a more resolute generosity in other young people who, no longer satisfied with vague sentiments and half-hearted decisions, aspire to unconditional obedience to the truth.

Besides this, however, we observe the existence of a very widespread and yet rather vague mental disposition that could be described as a sort of nostalgia for spirituality and for religious experience. It would be wrong to underestimate this phenomenon; it would also be insufficient, though, to see in it the beginning of a new orientation toward the Christian faith.

This nostalgia often comes from a disappointment caused by the insufficiency of the world of science and technology; it conceals within it an inclination toward the past and, above all, a deep skepticism about man's vocation to the truth. To this way of thinking, the truth appears historically discredited, precisely by the intolerance of those who believed themselves to be its sure custodians. Moreover: experiencing the limits of science and the fragility of ideologies drives people to skepticism more than it inspires courage in the search for truth. Therefore, they prefer to replace the truth with "values", on which it is possible to find at least a partial agreement. But a choice of this type does not cease to be problematic if the criterion of the truth is beyond human reach.

Above all, though, a religion born of skepticism and disillusionment about the possibilities of knowing cannot help but be a domain of the irrational. It floats in the dimension of non-binding recommendations and easily ends up becoming a sort of pain reliever. New mythologies are taking shape, as manifested quite clearly in the variously changeable phenomena that go by the general description of "New Age". The parallels with ancient gnosis are obvious. Now as then, abstruse mythologies combine into one with the exaggerated pretense of having in our grasp the keys of knowledge and of having found an exhaustive explanation of the realities in which mysteries of the universe are revealed and knowledge becomes redemption.[12] The living God sinks into the spiritual depth of existence; man immerses himself in it and at last is dissolved into it so as to become one with the All from which he comes. The warning of Karl Barth—who says that religion can become a sort of self-satisfaction that reaffirms a human being in himself and shuts him off from God instead of leading to him—has returned with new relevance.

III. The Pathways of Faith Today

The time has now come to ask explicitly the question that has secretly guided our considerations thus far: What must we do, then? What can lead to a future that is worthy of human beings?

Considering summarily the forces that we have spoken about until now, we can trace them back to two fundamental directions: relativism and faith. Relativism allies itself easily with positivism; in reality, it is the true and proper philosophical foundation of the latter. In some situations, a little relativism and a bit of skepticism may be helpful; we do not mean to debate that. But relativism proves to be totally inadequate as a common foundation on which to live. Indeed, if it is conceptualized and implemented in a logically consistent way—without secretly propping it up

[12] Documentation on this subject can be found in *Eine Welt—Eine Religion? Die synkretistische Bedrohung unseres Glaubens im Zeichen von "New Age"*, ed. P. Beyerhaus and L. E. von Padberg (Asslar: Gerth Medien, 1988).

with an ultimate certitude of faith—it either ends up being reduced to nihilism or else sets up a mentality of the positivist, authoritarian sort that controls everything, thus leading once again to totalitarian concepts.

But if, despite their partial usefulness, skepticism and relativism do not offer a globally satisfactory way forward [*itinerario*], then what other possibilities remain? Are we not once again urged to turn our attention to ways in which man can overcome himself, to the path of faith in the living God?

A thousand objections are raised to an answer like that: all the forms of a sad, dead faith that the past has produced and the present continues to produce seem to prove them correct. The courage to believe today, as people once did, cannot be transmitted along purely intellectual paths. First of all, it needs witnesses who verify its truth and human authenticity with their lives and their suffering. In Eastern Europe, the faith became a force that proved more powerful than "scientific socialism", and this is due to the humility and patience of those who suffered; in their testimony a higher hope was visible.

In this sense, our question goes far beyond a purely intellectual discussion, even though the conceptual clarification of it cannot be neglected and has an irreplaceable function.

Therefore, in view of the caricatures and the stunted forms of faith, we must ask ourselves: What is the intrinsic, essential form of faith? Or, to put it differently: How must a faith be configured if it is to respond to the signs of the times and, thus, to show man the way of salvation in this hour? I would like to mention three lines of reflection.

1. Believing is reasonable

Faith is not the surrender of reason faced with the limits of our knowledge; it is not a retreat into the irrational, given the dangers of a purely instrumental [and potentially exploitative] reason. Nor is faith an expression of weariness or flight; rather, it is a courageous affirmation of being and openness to the greatness and complexity of reality. Faith is an act of affirmation; it relies on the strength of a new Yes, which man becomes capable of pronouncing by virtue of the initiative through which God comes to meet him.

Precisely in the current situation of overt and widespread resentment against the rationality of technology, it seems to me important to demonstrate the essential reasonableness of faith. The critical reinterpretation that is now underway can legitimately rebuke modernity, not for its confidence in reason as such, but rather only for its reduction of the concept of reason, seeing that this reduction is what then opened the door to the irrational ideologies. Mystery, however, as faith arrives at it, is not something irrational but, rather, the extreme profundity of the divine reason, which we, with our weak eyesight, are no longer capable of fathoming. The words with which John opens his Gospel, repeating in greater depth the creation account contained in the Old Testament, have always been and continue to be a fundamental affirmation of faith: "In the beginning was the *Logos*", creative reason, the energy of God's intellect, which fills things with significance. We can understand the mystery of Christ correctly only on the basis of this beginning, in which reason is manifested at the same time as love, too.

The first affirmation of faith therefore tells us: everything that exists is thought-that-has-become-reality. The Creator Spirit is the origin and the principle that establishes all things.

All that exists is rational by its origin, because it proceeds from the creative reason.

Once again we are faced with the fundamental opposition between materialism and faith. The creed of materialism postulates that in the beginning was the irrational and that only the laws of chance produced rationality on the basis of irrationality. Reason is therefore a by-product of the absence of reason, and its structures as well as its laws are simply the result of combinations produced by an external authority, devoid of ethical or aesthetic content. Man thus becomes an agent [*addetto*] in the assembly of the world, which he causes to progress in keeping with his own purposes. But the irrational is still the authentic original power.

Faith teaches exactly the opposite: the Spirit is the creative origin of all things, and therefore they bear within themselves a reason that is not derived from themselves and that infinitely surpasses them, although it constitutes their most intrinsic law. Creative reason, which endows things with their objective rationality, a hidden logic, and a proper intrinsic order, is at the same time moral reason, and it is Love. Man is therefore capable of recognizing the traces of that reason and, thus, to make things progress according to their nature. His dominion is service; his freedom is attention [*impegno*] to the intrinsic truth of things and, thus, openness to the love that makes him like God.

The modern era is characterized by an odd hesitation between rationalism and irrationality. Therefore to me it seems important to define clearly the positions that confront each other on this field. The fundamental alternative facing the path traveled by the modern era is the following one: Is there irrationality at the beginning of all things, is the true origin of the world irrational, or does it come from creative reason? To believe means to embrace the second position: it alone is "reasonable", in the sense of the word that is most profound and worthy of a human being.

Given the current crisis of reason, this essential, reasonable nature of faith must start again to shine clearly. Faith preserves reason precisely because it embraces it in all its breadth and depth and protects it against the attempts to reduce it simply to what can be verified experimentally. Mystery is not posited as an enemy of reason; on the contrary, it preserves and defends the intrinsic rationality of being and of man.

2. *The reciprocity of intellect, will and sentiment in the unity of believing*

Let us turn now from the sphere of knowledge to the sphere of will and sentiment. With the reflections explained so far, we have already made here an initial fundamental option about the reasonableness of faith. But let us now take a step back. Given the radical threat represented by the Enlightenment, Schleiermacher sought to preserve religion by defining it as sentiment: "Its essence is not thought or action, but opinion and sentiment."[13] Again: "Praxis is art, speculation—science, while religion is sensibility and a taste for the infinite."[14] The nineteenth century followed him decisively in this way of framing the matter, thus arriving at a characteristic formula of reconciliation between religion and science. Reason was left totally free to conduct itself as it willed; religion, now reduced to pure sentiment, placed no obstacles to it and was for its part free to express itself in

[13] Friedrich Schleiermacher, *Über die Religion: Reden an die Gebildeten unter ihren Verächtern* (Berlin, 1799), cited the edition by H.-J. Rothert (Hamburg: F. Meiner, 1958), 29.

[14] Ibid., 30.

the sphere of sentiment, thus assuring for itself a legitimacy of its own.

The danger of this sort of spiritual peace appears once again today. Yet this is not about peace at all but, rather, about a division of man, in which both reason and sentiment are damaged equally.

It is in fact an abandonment of reason to state that it is capable of "functioning" only in the sphere of what is instrumental, without considering it capable of reaching the truth of being: the truth about us, about creation, and about God. However, today this skepticism almost totally dominates the field. In most cases, we no longer even care to admit the hypothesis that, right in the midst of our questioning, we could discover the truth. This false humility degrades the human being, blinds our behavior, and empties out our sentiment.

Even in the Catholic Church, we can hardly ever observe the claim that in faith the truth about God is revealed to our inspection. Moreover, there is a widespread sense that all religions are groping in the dark and that basically all their statements are nothing but symbols of what is completely unknowable. Religion thus turns into the sphere of the most exalted sentiments. With the propulsive force of the noblest sentiments, religions—which end up being interchangeable—ought to be placed at the service of mankind's highest purposes and be instruments for the building of a "society of universal peace".

Now we all want peace. A return to God should enable us to recognize human beings as brothers and sisters and thus should serve the cause of peace; this imperative is justified. But a religion that is only an instrument with which to attain set objectives is debased inasmuch as it is a religion that cannot act except as pure sentiment.[15] In all errors, some truths are concealed. It is true that religion calls for peace; it is also true that sentiment is part of religion and that reforms that deprive it of the humus of the feelings are miscalculated. But these truths preserve their force only when they do not lose their intrinsically organic character. And this organic character consists in the fact that faith takes up sentiment and rescues it from its indeterminacy, offering an authentic foundation for it. The sentiment of the infinite lies in the truth of the fact that there is an infinite God and that he addresses his word to us finite creatures. The faith is strengthened, not by relegating it to the sphere of the indefinite, but only by considering it in all its greatness.

Faith is not saved by scaling it down; that way you succeed only in selling it off. Only when all its potentialities are acknowledged does it acquire significance. Then we are no longer the ones who save the faith, but rather the faith is what saves us.

3. The personal dimension and the spiritual dimension of faith

The integration of knowledge, will, and sentiment takes place in the person. The Christian faith by its very nature has a personal structure. It is the response of one person to the call of another. It is the meeting of two free wills.

Whereas initially we affirmed that the essence of the Christian faith, as it is described in the Bible, is not irrationalism but, rather, the more decisive recognition of reason as the foundation and destiny of all things, now we can

[15] Concerning these tendencies, see the incisive presentation by Reinhard Slenczka, "Das Forum 'Gerechtigkeit, Frieden und Bewahrung der Schöpfung'", *Kerigma und Dogma*, 35 (1989): 316–35.

add: the Christian faith includes by its nature an overarching philosophy of freedom. Starting from a different perspective, we would have to repeat here what was already said about the fundamental alternatives of thought. We had said that modern rationalism, on the basis of its own methodological self-limitation, situates the irrational at the origin of the rational. In this case, that implies that what remains essentially foreign to freedom must be set down as the foundation of what is free; and that therefore freedom—which came about through reason—is nothing but a byproduct of the world's self-assembly.

Faith, on the contrary, aware that in the beginning is the *Logos*, starts instead from the primacy of freedom. Only the tie with the *Logos* guarantees freedom as a structural principle of reality.

This choice has definite advantages from the theoretical and systematic perspective. Philosophies of necessity assert that they can explain everything. They give the instructions to follow in order to produce in a necessary fashion the best possible world. The philosophy of freedom that springs from faith cannot do that. It possesses no universal formula for a solution; or better, its formula is the freedom of God's love, which calls us in Jesus Christ and unceasingly shows us the way to human freedom.

This has repercussions also on the concrete forms of religiosity. An apersonal religiosity corresponds to an apersonal philosophy. There is no denying that tendencies of this sort exist among Christians, too. The courage of faith in the personal God who listens to us ends up wearing out. Piety is reduced to letting oneself be submerged in the current of being, liberating oneself from the burdens of freedom, the responsibilities of personal dignity, in other words: plunging again into the abyss of nothingness.

Christian prayer, in contrast, is the response of one free will to another free will, an encounter of love. Once again: the tendency to an apersonal religiosity conceals within it a fragment of truth. It aspires to overcome the difference that separates us from the other and from others. But the retreat from being, the surrender that it signifies, does not save. The difference is overcome precisely when the encounter of two freedoms becomes love. Not the negation of the person, but his highest gesture, love, creates the unity for which we creatures of the One and Triune God yearn from the depths of our being.[16]

We can therefore conclude: faith is not a comfortable path. Anyone who presents it that way will fail. It places a human being in the presence of the most exalted aspiration because it knows how much a human being is worth. But precisely because it does this, it is beautiful and well suited to our nature. If our way of seeing is able to accept it in all its greatness and depth, then faith brings in itself the answers for which our era is waiting.

[16] See Congregation for the Doctrine of the Faith, *Letter to the Bishops of the Catholic Church on Certain Aspects of Christian Meditation* (Vatican City, 1989). Still worth reading in this regard is J. A. Cuttat, *Expérience chrétienne et spiritualité orientale* (1965).

9

A Turning Point for Europe?

Let me begin my reflections on the situation of our continent with an image. In Israel's history, the collapse of the walls of Jericho appears initially as the symbol of God's power to shape history but also (and above all) as the sign that the land has been handed over to the people who came from a foreign country and had wandered for forty years in the wilderness. It was not military force that threw down the walls; they collapsed in the presence of a liturgical procession with God's holy ark and in the presence of the music that accompanied this liturgy. Naturally, the triumphal element in this moment, which remained a signal of hope in all subsequent centuries in the midst of innumerable tribulations, became obscured again in the history that followed: life remained exposed and threatened even in the land they had now at last reached. Inner decadence gave ever-new strength to external foes, and the fact that Jericho was finally rebuilt became the sign of a new dispersal, in which the preceding dissolution of the spiritual foundations of freedom now simply became an externally visible event, too (cf. 1 Kgs 16:34).

This complex of fulfillment and responsibility, of gift and task, comes spontaneously to mind when one thinks of the political events in the most recent past in Europe, although we naturally ought not to draw inappropriate parallels between the salvation history related in the Bible and events of our own time, thus attributing a false sacral character to these events. It had long seemed incredible to us, men of the enlightenment, that walls should fall down before a procession of people at prayer and before the blasts of their trumpets. But now we have ourselves experienced, if not exactly the same thing, at least something somehow similar: the ideological wall that divided not only Europe but in an invisible manner the whole world everywhere no longer stands as once it did. And it was not thrown down by the power of weapons. Certainly, it was thrown down, not simply by means of prayers, but through an eruption of the spirit, through processions for freedom that were ultimately de facto stronger than barbed wire and cement. The spirit has shown its power; the trumpet blast of freedom was stronger than the walls that were meant to keep it in check. And even if we ought not to bring God too directly into play here, nevertheless, it remains true that faith in him, or at least the question about God, was not insignificant for the sounding-forth of those liberating trumpet blasts.

The fact that closed doors have opened, that separating walls have collapsed, and that there is more freedom—these are the consoling and encouraging events of the most recent past of which we ought not to lose sight. They are and remain signposts of and a basis for hope. But neither can we disregard what Israel's history tells us about the course of events after the walls fell: namely, that the joy of freedom and of the land possessed in common soon dried up in the troubles of everyday living; that the fact of dwelling in the same land did not in itself knit together a State; and that Israel's growing forgetfulness of God and egotistic misunderstanding of freedom drove it to an inner decadence that ended once again in the loss of freedom (cf. Judg 2:11–23). Freedom is very demanding; it does not keep itself alive, and it ceases to exist precisely when it attempts to be boundless.

In other words: the collapse of Marxism does not of itself bring about a free State and a healthy society. History shows again and again the truth of Jesus' image that in the place of one impure spirit who is driven out, seven much worse spirits come when they find the house empty and swept out (Mt 12:43–45 par.). One who abandons Marxism has not thereby automatically found a new foundation on which to base his life. The loss of a hitherto life-supporting ideology can very easily result in nihilism, and that would truly be the reign of the seven worse spirits. But who could ignore the growing tendency to nihilism on the part of the relativism to which we are all exposed today?

Thus we have an urgent question: With what contents can we fill up the intellectual vacuum that has come into being after the failure of the Marxist experiment? On what intellectual foundations can we build a common future in which East and West are joined in a new unity, but also in which North and South find a common path? When we strive to make a diagnosis of our situation and a prognosis of our future tasks and possibilities, this must be done against the criterion of the world as a whole, because today the destiny of each part of mankind is always dependent on the whole, and the decisions of each part have in turn their effect on the whole, so that the only proper way to speak of what is one's own is to speak of the other person. I should therefore like to begin by looking briefly at three fields of tension in today's world politics and economy but also in intellectual confrontations: at the so-called Western world, which has been connecting and blending more and more with what was Eastern Europe after the ideological dogmatism of the East began to evaporate; it will then be necessary to look at the so-called Third World; and finally, we should not fail to give some thought to the third force of the world politics and of the moral-religious drama of our times, namely, the Islamic world, which is emerging ever more strongly.

1. Diagnosis

a. Germany as an example: The new Western-Eastern world in the process of construction

Let us begin with ourselves. On what political forces can we reckon; what tasks confront us, and what dangers must be heeded? It is in Germany that the common European task of this hour is posed with the greatest concreteness and emphasis: in our country, one state from among the previous Eastern states of Europe and one postwar democracy of Western character must grow together to become one single living-space. This process of growing together must at the same time be a growing into a European community in which the nations are no longer autonomous entities that make claims of hegemony vis-à-vis other states but are elements of a greater polymorphic community in which all are related to each other as givers and receivers. Thus two inherited burdens, nationalism and ideological division, must be overcome simultaneously. It will be possible to overcome the economic and political problems posed by the unification of two spheres that have developed in such different ways if a common will undergirds what is done. This common will will withstand the challenges if it is supported by corresponding common convictions. In this sense, the question of intellectual foundations is also the fundamental political question that confronts us today.

Do such foundations exist? There is no doubt that the constitution of the Federal Republic of Germany gives expression to such foundations; it was upon these foundations that the somewhat artificial construction of postwar history was able to grow and regain strength, despite all the tensions. It would be worth investigating more closely the philosophy that stands behind this constitution. Its aim is a legally structured freedom; it knows that freedom and law are not antitheses but, rather, presuppose each other. It knows that the legislator cannot explain the arbitrary in legal terms and that law is not to be derived simply from statistics. Precisely after the appalling abuse of legal positivism in the Führer's law of the Third Reich, in which injustice had become law and the State had been degraded to the level of a robber band, there existed the awareness that every positive formulation of law must be based on values that elude our manipulation. Only unconditional respect for these values gives the freedom to decide its dignity and its supporting foundations. This is why the Basic Law also knows the limits of the majority principle. And it knows that this inviolability of values, which alone protects the inviolability of the dignity of man and, thus, his freedom, is based on the fact that these values truly exist and that we bear a responsibility in relation to them. This is expressed very clearly in the preamble to the Basic Law, when we read: "In awareness of its responsibility before God and men . . . the German people . . . has resolved upon this Basic Law of the Federal Republic of Germany."[1] All of this naturally implies that the Basic

[1] Cf. E. L. Behrendt, *Gott im Grundgesetz. Der vergessene Grundwert "Verantwortung vor Gott"* (Munich: Meta Verlag, 1980). This remarkable work deserves more attention than it has found hitherto, in my view. A few quotations can serve to indicate the direction of what it says: "That it is the God of the Old and New Testaments to whom our Basic Law appeals as the addressee of responsibility is to be inferred from history, from the ideas of the one who drew up the last constitution . . . from the concept of responsibility . . . but above all from the material structure of the norms of

Law is built on the existence of insights and convictions that themselves do not stand in the law and as such cannot be made into laws but that make laws possible in the first place. The constitution rests on foundations that it cannot prescribe for itself but must presuppose.

This brings us to the critical point of our situation today. To what extent do these foundations still exist? E.-W. Böckenförde has pointed out on occasion that the actual consciousness in society has distanced itself in the intervening period to some extent from these foundations.[2] A new constitutional debate (which is scarcely to be wished for, at least at the moment) would presumably shed a pitiless light on this gradual drying-up of foundations. Even so, what has grown on the basis of the Basic Law is still impressive and strong. Our constitution guarantees a form of life that cannot be condemned as capitalism, since it has produced a social order in which the strong support the weak and in which achievement has its reward but also its responsibility. Accordingly, while our economic order presupposes competition, it does not forget the one who fails to

---

this Basic Law itself. This Christian God, and he alone, makes possible and indeed requires tolerance." Ibid., 318. "Christianity will one day, perhaps soon, have to defend itself and its intellectual foundations courageously. . . . If we lose the adjective 'Christian', then we also lose the God before whom man's responsibility was established and can still be established today. Then it is an unspecific, nonobligatory God that is offered to us. . . . The basis of the responsibility is then an empty shell of a word." Ibid., 321.

[2] "Ist der deutsche Katholizismus systemkonform? Ein Gespräch mit E.-W. Böckenförde", in *Herder-Korrespondenz* 43 (1989): 262–66. Here Böckenförde shows directly only the changed attitude to the Basic Law in the Church, which leads after initial hesitation to an ever-stronger acceptance and use of the Basic Law; but, indirectly, we also see clearly the development of societal awareness in another direction, which tends rather to lead away from the bases in this world view.

succeed here through no fault of his own. With our legal and social order, we can offer the eastern half of Germany an order of values in which each individual has his dignity because responsibility before God and men is the decisive basis.

But, as has already been said, we must not overlook the fact that the foundations—ultimately, the recognition of a responsibility before God and men—are threatened by an insidious erosion and can thereby gradually come to lose their supportive power. A. de Tocqueville pointed out in his studies of democracy in America that the legal forms of this democracy worked because of the unwritten consensus that produced them, that is, on the basis of a Protestant Christian image of man and of the world that stamped the entire structure of life despite or, indeed, precisely because of the strict legal separation between Church and State. He showed that the unwritten foundations are much more essential for the continued existence of this democracy than all written law.[3] The situation in our case is not ultimately different. These supportive convictions do not coincide with the doctrines of one particular Christian church, and even today they surely extend far beyond the circle of those who profess allegiance to the churches. Thus one may hope that, thanks to their human evidential character, they can be imparted to the great majority of the East German citizens, too, who are no longer touched by the Christian tradition.

Nevertheless, the extinction of the churches would signify an intellectual landslide on a scale we cannot yet imagine. In my opinion, the events of 1968 and the subsequent

[3] Cf. Joseph Ratzinger, *Church, Ecumenism, and Politics: New Endeavors in Ecclesiology*, trans. Michael Miller et al. (San Francisco: Ignatius Press, 2008).

development have made clear the direction in which this could go. For the Parisian student revolution, which launched the phenomenon of 1968, did not crash into the Church from outside: rather, it erupted from the postconciliar fermentations of Catholicism and from earlier trends in revolutionary American Protestant theology. The celebration of the Eucharist on the barricades in Paris as the fraternity of those struggling for anarchist freedom and as a sign of hope for the political messianism of a new world giving birth to itself in terror shows the essentially religious—or better, pseudoreligious—character of what was going on.[4] Nor is it possible to overlook this theological implication in the German and Italian terrorism of the 1970s. One cannot understand the form taken by the Italian terrorism of the early 1970s without the inner crises and ferments of postconciliar Catholicism;[5] in Germany, it drew its nourishment especially from the student parishes, here with a more American and Protestant coloring.

The political messianism and the violent zealotry that accompanied it have subsided in the meantime. It had already lost its credibility even before the debacle of real socialism. In the course of its actions, it became obvious that this could be neither the updating of Christianity nor the threshold of a better world; it became clear that the message of Jesus offers no basis for these applications. But the wounds received then have remained; they appear in various forms. The increasing power of drugs is a sign of an emptiness in

[4] The study by M.J. Le Guillou, O. Clément, and J. Bosc, *Évangile et révolution* (Paris: Editions du Centurion, 1968), written directly under the impact of the events, remains still the most impressive contribution to this question.

[5] Cf. M. Cuminetti, *Il dissenso cattolico in Italia* (Milan: Rizzoli, 1983); A. Socci and R. Fontolan, *1947–1987. Tredici anni della nostra storia* (Milan: Socci-Fontolan, 1988).

the soul to which nothing more remains after the loss of ideological promises. Life has become boring and empty. Last autumn, the Italian government began an advertising campaign against the spread of drugs, in which pictures of the cheerful life of young people were shown, followed by the slogan: "This is what life is like. Don't burn it up with drugs." But could these pictures, in which young people laugh and joke, be truly convincing? *Is* life like that? Do not the films that then follow, with images full of cruelty, hatred, anger, and disappointments, show that life is quite different? Is this not real life? We have been told with great thoroughness that the unscathed world does not exist, and modern filmmakers appear to take it as honesty when they show man almost always as base and coarse. But both are distorted images of life. Life is not only happiness and games: it is pain, temptation, and failure. And yet in all this, it is beautiful if it is supported by love and possesses a hope that transcends the present moment. If we cannot show a picture of life in which even pain, hardship, and death are meaningful and belong to a larger whole, then we cannot rehabilitate human existence. This is surely the chief question to which we must give an answer today: Is it really good to be alive and to be a human being? We cannot answer this question unless there is a goodness that is bestowed on each individual and is stronger than all our failure.

The ideological terrorism of the 1970s has divided today in two directions: on the one side, we have the "withdrawal symptoms" caused by the loss of ideology—the desert of nihilism, in which consolation is sought in drugs. On the other side, we can observe the transition from violent activity to criminal organizations, which no longer need any ideology. The drug cartel in Colombia is recruited in part from former ideological combatants. But we must also ask: How are things with religion? Has it regenerated itself? Where does the path lead?

I would say that there are without doubt signs of regeneration that permit us to hope—young movements in which a great power of faith is at work, a convincing ethical seriousness and a readiness to commit one's own life that is admirable. Such movements can be a yeast that gives fresh vital force and authenticity to the humane values of the Gospel that mark our constitution. But we cannot deceive ourselves about the continuing exodus from the churches or about the internal crises that continue to shake them. On the whole, one can observe a progressive dissolution of religion in our society, in a twofold direction. We have already met the first of these directions when we looked at the events of 1968: politics becomes religion, and religion turns into a political passion. Faith in the transcendence and the eternal destiny of man decays: it appears to be without rational foundation and valueless for shaping life in this world. But what remains is the expectation of unconditional salvation. The experience of being unredeemed, of alienation, becomes stronger, and fulfillment—which cannot lie beyond and is not given as a gift of any grace—must now be realized through one's own action in this world. But this ties an expectation to politics that politics cannot satisfy. Religion that has turned into politics makes excessive demands of politics and thereby becomes a source of the disintegration of man and of society.

The other form of the dissolution of religion leads into an area that can be called "gnosticism", in terms of the history of religions, and that is often classed today under the label of esotericism. It covers many varied forms of religious substitutes with often strange mixtures of the rational and the irrational. Occultism and magic become attractive; it is always a matter of a religion that does not demand faith but that leads into deeper strata of existence along the path of rites and psychological practices, conveys the feeling of breaking through barriers and of liberation, and supplies from hidden depths a power against the forces that threaten our life. In the search for a technique of redemption, recourse is had to non-European forms of religion that do not hold man in the tiresome balance of faith but offer him practical forms of self-redemption. Much is said today about the secularization of our society. This is correct in the sense that religion withdraws into the private realm. But it does not disappear: it only changes its form and thereby, of course, its inner essence, too. If one looks at the marketplace of religions spread out before us today, one can clearly observe both their presence in the transformation and the change in the essence of the religious phenomenon. The essence of the Christian faith, considered from the perspective of the phenomenology of religions, consists in its uniting man's primal religious drive in a subtle synthesis with a rationally formed turning to the one God who is seen to be the reason at work in the origin of all things and as creative love. The consequence of this is an ethos that listens to the reason of creation and finds in this an echo of the reason of the Creator. This synthesis of understanding, will, and feeling is not easy; it is always in danger of being dissolved in one direction or the other. Beyond the sphere of Christianity, this same tension also determines the drama of religious history. Almost all religions know the one God, the one origin of the world who imparts meaning, behind the divine powers of the world. Even for polytheism, it is clear in general terms that the gods are not the plural of God, because God does not exist in the plural. He is unique. Although the gods are designated by the same name, they are powers of a lower rank. But, again and again in the history of religions, this one God disappears from worship and from concrete religious conduct. He is too distant, and, above all, he is not dangerous, either because he is only good, the absolutely good one who therefore does evil to no one, or else because one thinks that he is not concerned about what happens to men, who are too lowly for him. Thus worship is directed, not to the only good one, from whom in any case nothing is to be feared, but to the many ambiguous powers who concretely beset our life and with whom one must come to terms.[6] This chronic defection from the one God to the many ambiguous powers in the history of religions I would call paganism in the qualitative sense of the word. In this sense, we are threatened today by a new paganism in the enlightened Western world, but also for this reason in all other cultures, too. The man who excludes the one good foundation of all things as too distant, too uncertain, and too unimportant, so that he may turn instead to the powers that lie closer at hand, abases himself. The decomposition of the Christian synthesis facing us must ultimately also lead to a disintegration of man himself.

b. The "Third World"

Before we draw conclusions from this attempt at a diagnosis of today's Western-Eastern world, we must first look at the two other spheres that are making their mark on world history at present: the so-called Third World and the world of Islam. As far as the Third World is concerned, the fall of the invisible (or sometimes very visible) wall that divided the world everywhere is beyond doubt great progress, since the

[6] I have attempted to describe these connections in my contribution to the Festschrift for Karl Rahner, *Gott in Welt* (Freiburg: Herder, 1964), 2:287–305.

antagonism of East and West had been projected onto the whole rest of the world. Countries lacking the necessities of life were supplied with refined weapons systems and were repeatedly designated as the arena of vicarious wars in which both power blocs strove to assert their relative superiority. A political messianism was taught that tore these countries apart from within and divided them into hostile combat positions; violence was unleashed on all sides, among the defenders of conservative ideologies no less than among the revolutionary groups on the left. These phenomena have not simply disappeared under the sign of the growing reconciliation between East and West through the disintegration of Marxist ideology, especially because their societal causes continue to exist: but there are increasing possibilities of finding rational political solutions. This is an extremely positive process; a politics free of ideology must show itself here to be an ethically responsible politics, demonstrating that the lack of a fully developed ideology does not mean the absence of the ethical values that generate the force to achieve reconciliation and the nonviolent overthrow of the structures of injustice.

The opportunity confronting us makes high demands on our moral and religious strength. Only if we hold firm here will the new Western-Eastern world itself be able to master its fundamental problems. The model of development that has hitherto been practiced in the West is inadequate here.[7]

[7] The interview given by P. Merz to the *Herder-Korrespondenz* is instructive on the present state of the debate about development. "Entwicklungszusammenarbeit nach dem Ende des Ost-Westkonflikts", *Herder-Korrespondenz* 44 (1990): 519–26. Despite all the important acknowledgments and insights here, one is surprised at the continuing almost total failure to take up questions of morals and worldview. When, for example, the achievements and successes up to the present are defended by a reference to the increase in life expectancy from forty-six to sixty-two years, and in literacy from 43 to 60

It was unsatisfactory even without the additional burden of the East-West conflict. Certainly one cannot make the West alone responsible for the fact that the economic distance between North and South did not diminish but rather increased in the last decades. There are also internal causes in the Third World itself, especially the often prevalent corruption and, in not a few places, the lack of a work ethic. But this already brings us to the dubious point of the Western form of aid: namely, the belief that one could prescind altogether from ethical problems and bring about in a purely mechanical fashion the construction of modern economies while bypassing the existing ethical and social systems. Even the churches, who really ought to have known better, often succumbed to this materialistic illusion. Many of their emissaries were of the opinion that one must first spread the blessing of prosperity, and then one could also go on to speak of God. But this is a fundamentally false application of the axiom "*primum vivere, einde philosophari*" (first let us live, then let us philosophize). For the core of faith in God and of its ethical force is not a philosophy that lies within the reach only of those who have enough for their life: rather, it is the precondition of life, it *is* life. The young African intellectuals who studied at European universities acquired for the most part only an academic knowledge completely devoid of the ethical and the religious. All that remained to them was the choice between positivism and Marxism, but neither of these two philosophies is capable of building up a society in which freedom and justice are connected in a meaningful way. Here lie the deepest roots of the anger that is spreading in the Third World today against Europe

---

percent, one must ask what increased life expectancy means when the contents of life are lost, and what literacy means in view of the loss of meaning.

and America in particular. Certainly, this anger is also (and initially) caused by the difference in prosperity between the two halves of the earth. It is clear, however, that the existence of a deeper wound plays a role in the passionate recourse to African culture and religion, to the Latin American or Asian identity, that we observe today: the consciousness that one's own soul has been trampled upon, that one has been hurt in one's inmost depths, and that with all the gifts one received, one has been robbed of one's dignity and of what allows one to live in the deepest sense. In this connection, it is interesting that the rebellion in Latin America today against the European culture and tradition, after the Marxist model ran its course, is orchestrated with two new motifs. The memory of the five hundred years that have elapsed since Europe invaded America should remind one of the oppression of the Indian cultures, which one would now like to discover anew as the true soul of South America. Besides this, there is a passionate turning to the Blacks who were carried off to America and the lamentation over the loss of their cultural and religious identity. Both movements identify Europe with Christianity; to this extent, they are also a rebellion against Christianity as the religion of the overlords and as an alienating power—a rebellion that paradoxically finds its strongest spokesmen among theologians, who attempt in this way to give a new form to the theme of liberation. But in Africa, too, there is an ever-stronger fight not only against Christianity but especially against the inculturation of the Christian faith in African culture as a form of alienation; and there is a new search for their own religious tradition, though this has lost its roots and can continue to exist in a fruitful manner only if it arises anew within the Christian sphere.

Contemporary with these processes, we can observe a

stronger tendency to dissolve the one Church into sects; not only sects with an essentially Christian character, but sects of increasingly syncretistic construction, which blend together elements of very diverse provenance to make new forms. Particularly noticeable is the advance of sects of North American origin throughout Latin America, whose traditional Catholic character has been replaced in many places by a new religious pluralism. The reasons for this revolutionary turn of events are still very far from clear. Many factors work together: the greater mobility and dynamism of the new religious groups; active and sometimes aggressive missionary methods, linked to social and economic advantages; an insufficient evangelization on the Catholic side. Besides this, two reasons are mentioned again and again, whose validity, of course, would have to be investigated in greater depth. On the one hand, a one-sided political pastoral care has created in many places a religious vacuum that is filled by the sects, who respond to the unsatisfied religious hunger precisely of poor people. The latter commonly have no use for the ideology of a better future world and have to suffer the most under the violent actions that supposedly lead to it. On the other hand, one hears again and again the hypothesis that the propaganda of the sects is being promoted by the United States, which supposedly hopes to achieve thereby a structural harmonization of the southern half of America with its own mentality, with favorable repercussions in political and economic structures. Such expectations, of course, could prove to be deceptive, because an opposition against what is foreign is now being aroused against new forms of religious dependency at the same time, and it is not possible to foresee the internal developments of the religious consciousness after the fragmentation of Christianity. This picture would be all too incomplete, however, if one failed to point also to the impressive renaissance of Catholicism in many places, with a rediscovery of both its religious depths and its social responsibility under the challenges of the present day precisely in Latin America, so that it is thereby also able to inspire enthusiasm and give formation.

c. The Islamic world

Finally, we must turn our attention briefly to the Islamic world; naturally, it is not possible here to give even an approximate description of this multi-faceted reality. I should like only to look critically at one of the catchwords in the present debate, which is often offered as a general key to understanding today's course of events: "fundamentalism". If we begin by ascertaining briefly the basis of the contemporary renaissance of the Islamic world, two causes strike us at once. First, there is the economic, and thereby also the political and military, strengthening of the Islamic countries through the importance that oil has attained in international politics. But whereas the economic advance in the West has led in general to a dilution of religious substance, in the Islamic world, the new economic strength is linked to a new religious self-awareness; it is of course true that religion, culture, and politics stand together in Islam in an inseparable unity. This new religious self-awareness and the attitudes resulting from it are often termed "fundamentalism" in the West today. In my view, this is the inappropriate transfer of a concept from American Protestantism into a wholly different world, and this does not help us truly to understand what is going on. Fundamentalism according to the word's original meaning, is a tendency that arose in Protestant America in the nineteenth century as a protest against evolutionism and biblical criticism. It attempted to supply a firm Christian foundation against both of these through the defense of the absolute inerrancy of Scripture.[8] There doubtless exist analogies to this attitude in other spiritual worlds, too, but one falls victim to a false simplification if one changes analogies into an identification. This catchword has been made into an all-too-simple key that permits us to divide the world into two halves, a good half and a bad half. The series of supposed fundamentalisms has in the meantime passed from the Protestant over the Catholic to the Islamic and the Marxist fundamentalisms. The differences in content go utterly unheeded; one is a fundamentalist if one has firm convictions, for this is viewed as something that provokes conflicts and is opposed to progress. In contrast, the "good" is the doubt that takes up the battle against old certainties—that is, every modern undogmatic or antidogmatic movement.

But one cannot truly give an explanation of the world while bypassing the contents so simply, merely using a formal division into categories. In my view, one ought to abandon completely talk of Islamic fundamentalism, because it does more to conceal very different processes under a simplifying label than to shed light on them.[9] It is important that one make a distinction between the *starting point* of the new Islamic awakening and then the different *forms* that this

[8] S. E. Ahlstrom offers precise information and a detailed bibliography. "Fundamentalismus", in *Religion in Geschichte und Gegenwart* (Tübingen: Mohr Siebeck, 2007), 2:1178f. The article "Fundamentalismus" by J. Niewadomski, in *Lexicon der Sekten*, ed. H. Gasper, J. Müller, and F. Valentin (Freiburg: Herder, 1990), 330–36, is rich in materials but yields, in my view, to the temptation to broaden the concept in such a way that it becomes a slogan of ideological conflict, losing its own inherent outlines.

[9] The concept of "Islamic fundamentalism" has been criticized by J. Reissner. "Thus, what we call 'Islamic fundamentalism' is to be interpreted by religious science not as a 'return to the Middle Ages' but as the attempt to confront the questions of the present day while preserving Islam's claim to validity." Presentation by Reissner, in *Jahres- und Tagungsbericht des Römisches Instituts der Görres-Gesellschaft* (Cologne: Görres Gesellschaft, 1990), 177.

takes. As for the starting point, it seems to me very significant that the first indications of the turning point in Iran were attacks on American movies. The Western way of life with its moral permissiveness was felt to be an attack on their own identity and on the dignity of their own way of life. At the height of its power, the Christian world had evoked a sense of underdevelopment and of doubt in the Islamic way, at least in the educated circles of the Islamic world; but now contempt grows at the sight of how morality and religion are relegated to the merely private sphere, at the sight of a public life that is shaped in such a way that only religious and moral agnosticism counts as acceptable. The power with which this way of life was officially forced upon them, above all through American cultural exportation, so that it should appear to be the only normal thing, was experienced more and more as an attack on the depths of their own being. The reason why it was not the atheistic Soviet Union but rather the religiously tolerant America, which has indeed a strongly religious character, that was seen and combatted as the personification of evil is connected with this collision between a morally agnostic culture and a structure of life in which nation, culture, morality, and religion appear as an indivisible totality.

The concrete forms taken by this new self-awareness are varied. An obsession with the letter of religious traditions is often bound to a political and military fanaticism in which religion is seen directly as a path to earthly power. The Islamic tradition itself could easily suggest this instrumentalization of the religious energies for the political field. In connection with the phenomenon of Palestinian opposition, a revolutionary interpretation of Islam has developed that comes very close to Christian theologies of liberation and has facilitated the coalescence of Western European, Marxist-inspired terrorism and Islamic terrorism. What is superficially called Islamic fundamentalism found no difficulty in associating itself with socialist ideas of liberation: Islam is presented as the true bearer of the struggle of oppressed peoples for freedom. It is along this line that R. Garaudy, for example, found his way from Marxism to Islam, in which he sees the bearer of revolutionary forces against the dominant capitalism. In contrast, as deeply religious a ruler as King Hassan of Morocco has recently expressed his profound anxiety about the future of Islam: one understanding of Islam that sees its essence in devotion to God struggles with a political-revolutionary interpretation in which the religious element becomes part of a cultural chauvinism and is thereby ultimately subordinated to the political. The confrontation with this many-faceted phenomenon should not be taken too lightly. The Islam that is sure of itself has to a large extent a greater fascination for the Third World than a Christianity that is in a state of inner decay.

2. The Task

a. State and society

What is the consequence of all this for society and Church here? What must we do? In the case of society, we ought to pay greater attention than hitherto, especially because of the experiences of the last two decades, to what Horkheimer and Adorno have called the dialectics of the Enlightenment. By this is meant the "total self-destruction of the Enlightenment",[10] which occurs where the Enlightenment abso-

[10] M. Horkheimer and T. W. Adorno, *Dialektik der Aufklärung* (Frankfurt am Main: Fischer, 1988). I take this quotation and the following from the noteworthy essay by H. Staudinger, "Christentum und Aufklärung", in *Forum Katholische Theologie* 6 (1990): 199.

lutizes itself and wishes to know only what is calculable and explicable but denies or relegates to the merely private sphere everything that is not readily at its disposal. In other words, no society will long survive if in its public structure it is built agnostically and materialistically and wishes to permit anything else to exist only below the threshold of the public. If we wish to summarize succinctly today's problem and the challenge it poses, I would say that it lies in the double dissolution of the moral realm, which seems to have been making inexorable progress up to now: in the privatization of morality, on the one hand, and in its reduction, on the other hand, to the calculation of what will be successful, of what promises better chances of survival. This makes a society an immoral society in its public and communal essence—or, in other words, a society that attaches no value to what really gives dignity to man and constitutes him as a human person.

Thus, the first and most urgent imperative seems to me the renewed recognition of the place of the moral sphere in its inviolability and dignity. The distinguishing mark of man is that he not only acknowledges his physical inability to do something as a limit but also freely respects the moral prohibition against doing something as an equally binding and real limit. He is free, and he is a human person, when he not only bows to the law of necessity but also acknowledges the law of freedom as the sphere that determines him; then, he can go in the opposite direction, breaking through the limits of what is physically necessary, or attempting to push these limits farther, without imperiling himself or creation. The inherent worth of a society is seen in the values it counts worth protecting. A concern for physical integrity, which sometimes seems quite pathological, is characteristic of our society. There may indeed be something true involved here, but the frantic anxiety and the distortion of perspectives that can be observed here point rather to that "radicalized mythical anxiety" that Horkheimer has shown to be a mark of an Enlightenment that is leading into positivism.[11] Over against this pathological concern for the protection of our physical integrity stands a widely diffused indifference to the moral integrity of the human person, which seems worthy of no praise but is rather scorned as hypocrisy or absurdity by the rationalist turned positivist. But this is actually the negation of man as man, the negation of freedom and of human dignity. We will not long survive like that, and we certainly cannot give effective help to anyone else.

Naturally, there are understandable reasons for the relegation of the moral dimension to the private sphere: fear of moral constraint, of manipulation by the State, of ideological intolerance. But these fears are essential principles for a lawgiver only because of their inherent moral value: the acknowledgment of the conscience and of its own right, the acknowledgment of the limits placed on the State's discretion, and so on. To this extent, a bit of morality has been made a part of the public order, and the State is no longer totally uninvolved in moral-religious issues. But why is it that we can really attach a public obligation only to the setting of these boundary lines? They are important, but they are not the sum total of what a society needs in order to survive. Despite all the Christian self-criticism, which has become ever more intense and radical since the Enlightenment, we ought to find our way back to an awareness of the great moral tradition of Christianity, to the pre- or meta-dogmatic core (so to speak) of its moral constants, and to

[11] Horkheimer and Adorno, *Dialektik*, 13; Staudinger, "Christentum und Aufklärung", 201.

recognize this as our spiritual and intellectual identity, on the basis of which we can live—as this was still presupposed in the Basic Law of 1949. If we do not rediscover a part of our Christian identity, we shall not be able to meet the challenge of this hour.

b. The Church

But what ought the Church or the churches to do in this connection? I would reply: They should, first of all, truly be themselves for once. They must not allow themselves to be downgraded to a mere means for making society moral, as the liberal State wished; still less should they want to justify themselves through the usefulness of their social works. The more the Church aims directly at what in her ought to be something "of itself extraneous", so to speak, the more she will fail in this attempt. It is typical that in the Church today, the more she understands herself first and foremost as an institute for social progress, the more the social vocations dry up—the calls to serve the old, the sick, children, and so forth, vocations that flourished so much when the Church still looked essentially to God. One could say that this is a purely empirical proof of the truth of Jesus' *logion*: "Seek first [God's] kingdom and his righteousness, and all these things shall be yours as well" (Mt 6:33). Horkheimer and Adorno, with the clear sight of the outsider, have denounced the attempt by theologians to sneak past the core of the faith, removing the provocatory character of the Trinity and life beyond death as well as of the biblical narratives by reducing these to the level of symbols. They tell us that when theologians bracket off dogma, what they say has no validity; they bow to that "fear of the truth" in which the spiritual and intellectual decline of the present day has its roots.[12] No, one cannot save the Church in this way. She must first do decisively what is her very own, she must fulfill the task in which her identity is based: to make God known and to proclaim his Kingdom. Precisely thus, and only thus, does that sphere of the soul come into existence in which the moral dimension regains its existence, far beyond the circle of those who believe.

Irrespective of this, the Church must accept her responsibility for society in various ways, not least by attempting to make herself comprehensible; she must give insight into what belongs to God and into the moral sphere that results from this. She must convince, for it is only by convincing that she opens up space for what has been entrusted to her; and this can be made accessible only along the path of freedom, which means via reason, will, and emotion. The Church must be ready to suffer. She must prepare space for the divine, not through power, but through spirit, not through institutional strength, but through witness, through love, life, and suffering: and in this way she must help society to find its moral identity.

Goethe once termed the struggle between belief and unbelief the great theme of world history, picking up a theme of Augustine's philosophy of history. Augustine himself, of course, expressed this differently: he sees in world history the struggle between two kinds of love, love for self, which goes as far as despising God, and love for God, which goes as far as despising oneself. Today, we can perhaps formulate this in still another way: history is marked by the confrontation between love and the inability to love, that devastation of the soul which comes when the only values man is able to

[12] For criticism of theology, see, for example, T. W. Adorno, *Stichworte*, quoted in Staudinger, "Christentum und Aufklärung", 203. On the "fear of the truth", see Horkheimer and Adorno, *Dialektik*, 3.

recognize at all as values and realities are quantifiable values. The capacity to love, that is, the capacity to wait in patience for what is not under one's own control and to let oneself receive this as a gift, is suffocated by the speedy fulfillments in which I am dependent on no one but in which I am never obliged to emerge from my own self and thus never find the path into my own self. This destruction of the capacity to love gives birth to lethal boredom. It is the poisoning of man.[13] If he were to have his way, man would be destroyed, and the world with him. In this drama, we should not hesitate to oppose the omnipotence of the quantitative and to take up our position on the side of love. This is the decision that the present hour demands of us.

[13] Compare with T. Goritschewa's description of the intellectual situation before her conversion: "To be more clever than the others, more capable, stronger—that was my goal. But no one had ever told me that the highest goal lies not in overtaking and beating others but in loving." *Von Gott zu reden ist gefährlich* (Freiburg: Herder, 1984), 21. The antithesis is very finely presented in fiction in Michael Ende's fairytale novel *Momo*. I am thinking of the scene where one of the grey gentlemen offers Momo the whole arsenal of technically perfect dolls. When Momo objects, "I don't believe . . . that anyone can love them", he replies: "The only thing . . . that counts in life is succeeding in something, becoming something, possessing something. If you have more success, if you become more and have more than the others, you get everything else quite automatically: friendship, love, honor and so on." Michael Ende, *Momo* (Stuttgart: Thienemanns, 1973), 93f. Similarly, there is another scene where Master Hora, the mysterious administrator of time, speaks of the dead human time, whose steamy bell-jar makes one sick: "At the beginning, one does not notice much of this. One day, you have no more desire to do anything. Nothing is interesting, you are bored. . . . You become quite indifferent and gray. . . . There is no longer any anger, any enthusiasm. You can no longer rejoice, no longer mourn. . . . Then it has grown cold, and you can no longer love anything or anyone. . . . This sickness is called lethal boredom."

PART THREE

The Church and the Rebirth of Europe: Educational Challenge and New Evangelization

10

The Objection to the Church and the Distortion of the Image of Man

Meeting with the Doctrinal Commissions of Europe, Laxenburg, May 2, 1989

As bishops who bear responsibility for the faith of the Church in our countries, we ask ourselves where especially do the difficulties lie that people have with the faith today, and how can we rightly reply to them.

We need no extensive search in order to answer the first of these questions. There exists something like a litany of objections to the practice and teaching of the Church, and nowadays its regular recitation has become like the performance of a duty for progressive-thinking Catholics. We can ascertain the principal elements of this litany: the rejection of the Church's teaching about contraception, which means the placing upon the same moral level of every kind of means for the prevention of conception upon whose application only individual "conscience" may decide; the rejection of every form of "discrimination" as to homosexuality and the consequent assertion of a moral equivalence for all forms of sexual activity as long as they are motivated by "love" or at least do not hurt anyone; the admission of the divorced who

Published as "Difficulties Confronting the Faith in Europe Today", *Communio: International Catholic Review* 38, no. 4 (2011): 728–37.

remarry to the Church's sacraments; and the ordination of women to the priesthood.

As we can see, there are quite different issues linked together in this litany. The first two claims pertain to the field of sexual morality; the second two to the Church's sacramental order. A closer look makes it clear, however, that these four issues, their differences notwithstanding, are very much linked together. They spring from one and the same vision of mankind within which there operates a particular notion of human freedom. When this background is borne in mind, it becomes evident that the litany of objections goes even deeper than it appears at first glance.

What does this vision of mankind, upon which this litany depends, look like on closer scrutiny? Its fundamental characteristics are as widespread as the claims that derive from it, and so it can be easily traced. We find our starting point in the plausible assertion that modern man would find it difficult to relate to the Church's traditional sexual morality. Instead, it is said, he has come to terms with his sexuality in a differentiated and less confining way and thus urges a revision of standards that are no longer acceptable in the present circumstances, no matter how meaningful they may have been under past historical conditions. The next step, then, consists in showing how we today have finally discovered our rights and the freedom of our conscience and how we are no longer prepared to subordinate it to some external authority. Furthermore, it is now time that the fundamental relationship between man and woman be reordered, that outmoded role expectations be overturned, and that complete equality of opportunity be accorded women on all levels and in all fields. The fact that the Church, as the particularly conservative institution that she is, might not go along with this line of thinking would certainly not be surprising. If the Church, however, would wish to promote human freedom, then ultimately she will be obliged to set aside the theological justification of old social taboos, and the most timely and vital sign of such a desire at the present moment would be her consent to the ordination of women to the priesthood.

The roots of this opposition continue to emerge in various forms and make it clear that what we are dealing with in our imaginary but quite pointed litany is nothing less than a very coherent reorientation.

Its key concepts present themselves in the words "conscience" and "freedom", which are supposed to confer the aura of morality upon changed norms of behavior that at first glance would be plainly labeled as a surrender of moral integrity, the simplifications of a lax conscience.

No longer is conscience understood as that knowledge which derives from a higher form of knowing. It is instead the individual's self-determination that may not be directed by someone else, a determination by which each person decides for himself what is moral in a given situation.

The concept "norm"—or, what is even worse, the moral law itself—takes on negative shades of dark intensity: an external rule may supply models for direction, but it can in no case serve as the ultimate arbiter of one's obligation. Where such thinking holds sway, the relationship of man to his body necessarily changes, too. This change is described as a liberation, when compared to the relationship obtaining until now, like an opening up to a freedom long unknown. The body then comes to be considered as a possession that a person can make use of in whatever way seems to him most helpful in attaining "quality of life". The body is something that one has and that one uses. No longer does man expect to receive a message from his bodiliness as to who he is and what he should do, but definitely, on the basis of his reasonable deliberations and with complete independence, he expects to do with it as he wishes. In consequence, there is indeed no difference whether the body be of the masculine or the feminine sex, the body no longer expresses being at all; on the contrary, it has become a piece of property. It may be that man's temptation has always lain in the direction of such control and the exploitation of goods. At its roots, however, this way of thinking first became an actual possibility through the fundamental separation—not a theoretical, but a practical and constantly practiced separation—of sexuality and procreation. This separation was introduced with the Pill and has been brought to its culmination by genetic engineers so that man can now "make" human beings in the laboratory. The material for doing this has to be procured by actions deliberately carried out for the sake of the planned results, which no longer involve interpersonal human bonds and decisions in any way. Indeed, where this kind of thinking has been completely adopted, the difference between homosexuality and heterosexuality as well as that between sexual relations within or outside marriage have become unimportant.

Likewise divested of every metaphysical symbolism is the distinction between man and woman, which is to be regarded as the product of reinforced role expectations.

It would be interesting to follow in detail this revolutionary vision about man that has appeared behind our rather haphazardly concocted litany of objections to the Church's teaching. Without a doubt, this will be one of the principal challenges for anthropological reflection in coming years. This reflection will have to sort out meticulously where quite meaningful corrections to traditional notions appear and where there begins a truly fundamental opposition to faith's vision of man, an opposition that admits no possibility of compromise but places squarely before us the alternative of believing or not. Such reflection cannot be conducted in a context that is more interested in discerning the questions that we have to pose for ourselves today than in looking for the answers. Let us leave off this dispute for now; our question, instead, must be: How does it happen that values that presuppose such a background have become current among Christians?

It has become quite evident at the present time that our litany of objections does not turn upon a few isolated conflicts over this or that sacramental practice in the Church, nor is it over the extended application of this or that rule. Each of these controversies rests upon a much more far-reaching change of "paradigms", that is, of the basic ideas of being and of human obligation. This is the case even if only a small number of those who mouth the words of our litany would be aware of the change involved.

They all breathe in, so to speak, the atmosphere of this particular vision of man and the world that convinces them of the plausibility of this one opinion while removing other views from consideration. Who would not be for conscience and freedom and against legalism and constraint? Who wishes to be put into the position of defending taboos? If the questions are framed in this way, the faith proclaimed by the Magisterium is already manoeuvred into a hopeless position. It collapses all by itself because it loses its plausibility according to the thought patterns of the modern world and is looked upon by progressive contemporaries as something that has long been superseded.

We can then give a meaningful answer to the questions raised only if we do not permit ourselves to be drawn into the battle over details and are able, instead, to express the logic of the faith in its integrity, the good sense and reasonableness of its view of reality and life. We can give a proper answer to the conflicts in detail only if we keep all the relationships in view. It is their disappearance that has robbed the faith of its reasonableness.

In this context, I would like to list three areas within the world view of the faith that have witnessed a certain kind of reduction in the last centuries, a reduction that has been gradually preparing the way for another "paradigm".

1. In the first place, we have to point out the almost complete disappearance of the doctrine on creation from theology.

As typical instances, we may cite two compendia of modern theology in which the doctrine on creation is eliminated as part of the content of the faith and is replaced by vague considerations from existential philosophy, the 1973 edition of the ecumenical *Neues Glaubensbuch* published by J. Feiner and L. Vischer, and the basic catechetical work published in Paris in 1984, *La foi des catholiques*. In a time when we are experiencing the rebellion of creation against man's work and when the question of the limits and standards of creation upon our activity has become the central problem of our ethical responsibility, this fact must appear quite strange. Notwithstanding all this, it remains always a disagreeable fact that "nature" should be viewed as a moral issue. An anxious and unreasonable reaction against technology is also closely associated with the inability to discern a spiritual message in the material world. Nature still appears as an irrational form even while evincing mathematical structures that we can study technically. That nature has a mathematical intelligibility is to state the obvious; the assertion that it also contains in itself a moral intelligibility, however, is rejected as metaphysical fantasy. The demise of metaphysics goes hand in hand with the displacement of the teaching on creation. Their place has been taken by a philosophy of evolution (which I would like to distinguish from the scientific hypothesis of evolution). This philosophy intends to discard the laws of nature so that the management of its development may make a better life possible. Nature, which ought really to be the teacher along this path, is instead a blind mistress, combining by unwitting chance what man is supposed to simulate now with full consciousness. His relationship to nature (which is, to be sure, no creation) remains that of one who acts upon it; it is in no way that of a learner. It persists as a relationship of domination, then, resting upon the presumption that rational calculation may be as clever as "evolution" and can therefore lift the world to new heights. The process of development up to this point had to struggle along without human intervention.

Conscience, to which appeal is made, is essentially mute, just as nature, the teacher, is blind; it just computes which action holds the best chances for betterment. This can (and should, according to the logic of the point of departure) occur in a collective way, for what is needed is a party which, as the vanguard of history, takes evolution in hand while exacting the absolute subordination of the individual to it. Otherwise, things occur individualistically and conscience then becomes the expression of the subject's autonomy, which, in terms of the grand world picture, can only seem absurd arrogance.

It is quite obvious that none of these solutions is helpful, and this is the basis for the deep desperation of mankind today, a desperation that hides behind an official façade of optimism. Nevertheless, there is still a silent awareness of the need of an alternative to lead us out of the blind alleys of our plausibilities, and perhaps there is also, more than we think, a silent hope that a renewed Christianity may supply the alternative. This can be accomplished, however, only if the teaching on creation is developed anew. Such an undertaking, then, ought to be regarded as one of the most pressing tasks of theology today.

We have to make evident once more what is meant by the world's having been created "in wisdom" and that God's creative act is something quite other than the "bang" of a primeval explosion. Only then can conscience and norm enter again into proper relationship. For then it will become clear that conscience is not some individualistic (or collective) calculation; rather, it is a *consciens*, a "knowing along with" creation and, through creation, with God the Creator. Then, too, it will be rediscovered that man's greatness lies, not in the miserable autonomy of proclaiming himself his one and only master, but in the fact that his being allows the highest wisdom, truth itself, to shine through. Then it will become clear that man is so much the greater the more he is capable of hearing the profound message of creation, the message of the Creator. And then it will be apparent how harmony with creation, whose wisdom becomes our norm, does not mean a limitation upon our freedom but is, rather, an expression of our reason and our dignity. Then the body also is given its due honor: it is no longer something "used", but is the temple of authentic human dignity because it is God's handiwork in the world. Then is the equal dignity of man and woman made manifest precisely in the fact that they are different. One will then begin to understand once again that their bodiliness reaches the metaphysical depths and is the basis of a symbolic metaphysics whose denial or neglect does not ennoble man but destroys him.

2. The decline of the doctrine on creation includes the decline of metaphysics, man's imprisonment in the empirical, as we have said. When this occurs, however, there is also of necessity a weakening of Christology. The Word who was in the beginning quite disappears. Creative wisdom is no longer a theme for reflection. Inevitably, the figure of Jesus Christ, deprived of its metaphysical dimension, is reduced to a purely historical Jesus, to an "empirical" Jesus, who, like every empirical fact, contains only what is capable of happening. The central title of his dignity, "Son", becomes void where the path to the metaphysical is cut off. Even this title becomes meaningless since there is no longer a theology of being sons of God, for it is replaced by the notion of autonomy.

The relationship of Jesus with God is now expressed in terms such as "representative" or the like, but as to what this means, one must seek an answer by the reconstruction of the "historical Jesus".

There are today two principal models for the alleged figure of the historical Jesus: the bourgeois-liberal and the Marxist-revolutionary. Jesus was either the herald of a liberal morality, struggling against every kind of "legalism" and its representatives; or he was a subversive who can be considered as the deification of the class struggle and its religious symbolic figure.

Evident in the background are the two aspects of the modern notion of freedom that are seen embodied in Jesus; this is what makes him God's representative. The unmistakable symptom of the present decline of Christology is the disappearance of the Cross and, consequently, the meaninglessness of the Resurrection, of the Paschal Mystery. In the liberal model, the Cross is an accident, a mistake, the result of shortsighted legalism. It cannot, therefore, be made the subject of theological speculation; indeed, it really should not have occurred, and a proper liberalism makes it in any event superfluous.

In the second model, Jesus is the failed revolutionary. He can now symbolize the suffering of the oppressed class and, thus, foster the growth of class consciousness. From this viewpoint, the Cross can, in a certain sense, even be given an important meaning, but one that is radically opposed to the witness of the New Testament.

Now in both these versions there runs a common thread, namely, that we must be saved, not through the Cross, but from the Cross. Atonement and forgiveness are misunderstandings from which Christianity has to be freed. The two fundamental points of the Christian faith of the New Testament writers and of the Church in every age (the divine sonship understood in a metaphysical sense and the Paschal Mystery) are eliminated or at least bereft of any function. It is obvious that with such a basic reinterpretation, all the rest of Christianity is likewise altered—the understanding of what the Church is, the liturgy, spirituality, etc.

Naturally these crude denials, which I have described here with all the severity of their consequences, are seldom spoken of so openly. The movements, however, are clear, and they do not confine themselves to the realm of theology alone. For quite some time, they have entered into preaching and catechesis; on account of the ease of their transmission, they are even more pronounced in these fields than in strictly theological literature. Quite clearly, then, the real decisions today fall once again in the field of Christology; everything else follows from that.

3. Finally, I should like to refer briefly to a third field of theological reflection that is threatened by a thoroughgoing

reduction of the contents of faith, namely, eschatology. Belief in eternal life has hardly any role to play in preaching today. A friend of mine, recently deceased, an exegete of note, once told me of some Lenten sermons he had heard at the beginning of the 1970s. In the first sermon, the preacher explained to the faithful that hell does not exist; in the second, purgatory went the same way; in the third, he eventually undertook the difficult task of trying to convince his hearers that even heaven does not exist and that we should seek our paradise here on earth. To be sure, it is seldom as drastic as that, but diffidence in speaking about the hereafter has become commonplace.

The Marxist accusation that Christians justified the injustices of this world with the consolation of the world to come is deeply rooted, and the present social problems are now, indeed, so serious that they require all the powers of moral commitment. This moral requirement will not at all be called into question by the one who views the Christian life in the perspective of eternity, for eternal life cannot be prepared for otherwise than in our present existence. Nicholas Cabasilas, for example, expressed this truth in a wonderful reflection in the fourteenth century. Only those attain to it (that is, the future life) who already are its friends and have ears to hear. For it is not there that friendship is begun, that the ear is opened, that the wedding garment is readied and all else prepared; it is, rather, this present life that is the workplace where all this is fashioned. For just as nature prepares the embryo, even while it leads a dark and confined existence, for living in the light and forms it, as it were, according to the pattern of the life that is to come, just so does it happen with the saints. Only the exigency of eternal life confers its absolute urgency on the moral duty of this life. If, however, heaven is only something "ahead" of us and no longer "above" us, then the interior tension of human existence and its communal responsibility are slackened. For we indeed are not "ahead", and whether this prospect of what is ahead is a heaven for those others who appear to us to have gone "ahead", we are not in a position to determine, since they are as free and as subject to temptation as we are ourselves.

Here we find the deception inherent in the idea of the "better world", which, nonetheless, appears today even among Christians as the true goal of our hope and the genuine standard of morality. The "Kingdom of God" has been almost completely substituted in the general awareness, as far as I can see, by the utopia of a better future world for which we labor and which becomes the true reference point of morality—a morality that thus blends again with a philosophy of evolution and history and creates norms for itself by calculating what can offer better conditions of life.

I do not deny that it is in just this way that the idealistic energies of young people are unleashed and that the results are fruitful in terms of new aspirations to selfless activity. As an all-embracing norm for human endeavor, however, the future does not suffice. Where the Kingdom of God is reduced to the "better world" of tomorrow, the present will ultimately assert its rights against some imaginary future. The escape into the world of drugs is the logical consequence of the idolizing of utopia. Since this has difficulty in arriving, man draws it to himself or throws himself headlong into it. It is dangerous, therefore, if the better world terminology predominates in prayers and sermons and inadvertently replaces the faith with a placebo.

All that has been said here may appear to many to be all too negative. It was not intended, of course, to describe the situation of the Church as a whole, with all her positive and negative elements. It was rather a case of setting out the obstacles to the faith in the European context.

Within this limited theme, I have not claimed to present an exhaustive analysis. My sole intention was to examine, beyond the individual problems that are constantly surfacing, the deepest motives that give rise to the individual difficulties in ever-changing forms.

Only by learning to understand that fundamental trait of modern existence which refuses to accept the faith before discussing all its contents will we be able to regain the initiative instead of simply responding to the questions raised. Only then can we reveal the faith as the alternative that the world awaits after the failure of the liberalistic and Marxist experiments. This is today's challenge to Christianity; herein lies our great responsibility as Christians at the present time.

11

The Church's Faith and the New World's Utopia

Intervention at the Special Assembly for Europe of the Synod of Bishops (November 28–December 14, 1991)

We are here to interpret the signs of the time. And we have seen that at this moment of world history, our first duty is to proclaim the Gospel of Christ. For the Gospel is the true source of freedom and humanity. The Lord himself outlined the core of this proclamation in very brief words when, at the beginning of his public ministry, he summarized the essentials of his Gospel as follows: "The time is fulfilled, and the kingdom of God is at hand; repent, and believe in the gospel" (Mk 1:15). These words must constitute the centerpiece of all evangelization.

But the Kingdom of God is neither a place nor a time nor a structure within the world that we have to devise and set up for ourselves. The Kingdom of God is God himself, who comes closer to us, communicates himself to us, unites himself with us, so as to rule in us. To proclaim the Kingdom of God is nothing other than to proclaim the living, true God. Someone who does not know God does not know man, and someone who forgets God destroys human existence itself because he ignores the true dignity and greatness of the human being.

In this sense, Saint Irenaeus says: "If man were completely

separated from God, he would cease to be." With that, Irenaeus introduced the famous definition of Christian humanism, which, however, is often quoted only in an incomplete form: "The glory of God is man fully alive, but the life of man is to see God" (*Adversus Haereses*, IV, 20, 7). To see God means to perceive his existence with the eyes of the heart and to open the ears of the heart for his word. But that means to align one's own existence entirely toward God.

If our heart does not perceive and accept God's existence, our real living stops. The heart becomes empty and then tries to draw life from other sources, but in doing so it sets out on the path of self-destruction. This is demonstrated by the many signs of our time in which the tragic consequences of the absence of God become visible in an obvious way.

If in the new proclamation of the faith we must speak above all about God in order to be able really to speak about man, it is good to examine our conscience. A not inconsiderable part of our catechesis and our proclamation seems to be defined by the conviction that above all else we must first solve the most urgent problems in the economic, social, and political spheres, so as then to be able to speak in tranquility and peace about God, too. In this way, though, the truth of the matter is turned upside down. We then proclaim our wisdom and a human kingdom, whereby we hide behind the veil of our ideas and initiatives the true light on which everything depends.

Perhaps we must even admit that today the Church herself in some cases speaks too much about herself, revolves too much around herself and her structures, which are always in need of improvement, so that the profession of faith in the living God who gives us the Way and the Life is not adequately reflected in her and by her. To this case we can apply what the Lord says symbolically about the eye as the light of the body: whether the whole body is light or dark depends on this light (Mt 6:22ff.).

The Church is called to be the eye in the body of mankind, through which people see the divine light and through which this light enters into the world. An eye that tries to see itself is blind. The Church is not made for herself. She exists in order to be the eye through which God's light reaches us and to be the tongue that speaks about God.

It is true about the Church, too, that whoever seeks himself will lose himself. The Church finds herself when she calls people to God's Kingdom by making them belong to the living God. Therefore, she must be very careful about creating new structures of human law. The criterion for the Church must always be to see herself in such a way that she becomes ever freer and better suited to proclaiming the Gospel.

I would like to add two remarks. If the Church proclaims God above all, she does not speak about an unknown God but, rather, about a God who in his Son took flesh and revealed to us his heart, which loves us to the end, even to death on the Cross. In the Christian proclamation, everything can be traced back to God, but God is in Christ the true Emmanuel. He became "God with us", as Saint Matthew says in the first chapter of the Gospel of Matthew (Mt 1:23) and as it is fulfilled in the last chapter of the Gospel of Matthew: "I am with you always, to the close of the age" (Mt 28:20). The Church does not proclaim an accumulation of dogmas and commandments, the yoke of which is too heavy for human beings, but rather she proclaims an "easy yoke": God, who in Christ is with us, who leads us and carries us with his love.

The second remark is this: Someone who speaks about God speaks about man's eternal life, for God is not a God of the dead, but a God of the living (Mk 12:27). Here, too, we must examine our conscience. For fear of the accusation that we alienate man from his worldly duties if we speak about eternal life, our proclamation of eternal life has often become too faint and lukewarm.

But a human being who has been robbed of the hope for eternal life is very seriously maimed. The certainty given to a human being that he can live in eternity with God but can also be eternally lost does not diminish the obligation to apply oneself to earthly tasks but, rather, gives them their true weight and their true meaning.

For this reason, we must speak with great confidence about the immortality of the soul and also about the resurrection of the body. This is our joy: the Lord went "to prepare a place" for us, for in his Father's house "there are many rooms" (Jn 14:1–2). The Lord himself is our place; he himself is our abode. This is our joy, the joy of the Gospel, that no one will take from us (Jn 16:22). We must proclaim this joy in the New Evangelization.

12

The Educational Challenge

In this paper I have been asked to speak about the present-day crisis of peace and justice and to indicate the contribution religion can make to the resolution of the problem. Now there is no such thing as religion in the abstract; it always has a concrete historical form. So my starting point will not be a general concept of religion. Instead, I shall direct my questions concretely to my own faith as a Christian and a Catholic. What can our faith, in its true and original character, do to help us resolve these problems? Perhaps also, what can and must it not do if it is to remain true to what it is? To make the first half of the discussion more manageable, I would like to define the issue somewhat more narrowly and precisely. I do not intend to offer an empirical analysis of today's crisis of peace and justice in all its different facets. Given the scale of the thing, it would fill a whole book and is perhaps an impossible undertaking for one person on his own, even supposing he has more specialized knowledge and opportunities for research than I have. My intention is not descriptive but, in the broad sense of the term, normative. In other words, by looking at the actual phenomena, I want to see what peace is, what justice is, and how the two are connected, in order to understand our ethical task. However, such an analysis takes place, not "within the limits of reason alone" (to use the words of Kant), but in the light of what the Christian faith can tell us about the two themes, that is to say, in an openness of reason to knowledge. Reason does not itself simply produce knowledge, and yet the knowledge, once given, is real knowledge. In this respect, religion has a contribution to make in the analysis of the phenomena as well as in the highlighting of the ethical imperatives.

1. Threats to Peace—Loss of the Criteria for Justice and Injustice

Our theme links peace and justice. The crisis of the one is the crisis of the other, and vice versa. When justice begins to falter, peace falters, too. In fact, one might say that wars always break out when there is no clear or compelling criterion of justice. I think this becomes evident when we consider the four ways in which peace is actually threatened in today's world.

The first threat to peace, the one that most preoccupies public awareness, is the danger of world war, the danger that the great power blocs, into which the world is divided, would unleash against each other those weapons of mass destruction that in all probability would bring about the destruction of the human race.

The second way in which peace is endangered and destroyed consists in the so-called "classical" wars. In the last forty years, in different parts of the world, these have taken place in unending succession: wars in the Middle East, in Africa, in Southeast Asia, the war between Argentina and Great Britain, and so on.

The third form might be called the State's loss of internal peace. This takes two distinct and yet interrelated forms:

The so-called liberation movements struggle for power when they regard the State's legal power as one of injustice.

They see rebellion against the order of the State, a rebellion in itself destructive of peace, as a commitment to justice and, thus, the only way to establish peace, in fact, a duty in the cause of true peace. Interestingly, a large number of those people who consider themselves to be pacifists with regard to the first type of war (world war) look upon this other form of struggle, often very cruel and bloody, as something really sacred, a higher form of the *bellum justum*, an active form of peace. At the same time, the heart of the modern crisis becomes clear—the loss of a common criterion of justice.

During the Middle Ages, after years of multifarious feuding between families and towns, after an era of widespread arbitrary justice, a general peace broke out when the individual legal persons renounced their power. These worked out their relationships with each other within a commonly accepted law of the land (*Landrecht*) and transferred the protection of that law to central authorities—the "judiciary" and its various organs.[1] The result of this was a clear separation of two essentially different kinds of power: the State's organs of law have means of implementation that are accepted, within the framework of the peace thus created, as the force of law. They are no longer the "power" that for one person is the means by which he tries to safeguard his rights but for another is an act of injustice to be resisted. Instead, they protect the rights of all. They constitute "legal power", something fundamentally different from the law-breaking power of violence. Today a process is under way that may amount to the reversal of the medieval renunciation of power. The reversal could have various causes. Per-

[1] Cf. H. Maier, *Worauf Frieden beruht* (Freiburg: Herder, 1981), 20ff.; U. Duchrow, *Christenheit und Weltverantwortung* (Stuttgart: Klett-Cotta, 1970), 533ff.

haps the state has ceased to defend justice and is palming off arbitrary whim in the guise of justice. On the other hand, it may be that ideological groups are creating their own partial ideas of justice, thereby breaking away from the universality of justice, in order to achieve their own ends. What underlies both is an ethical and religious revolution. On the question of what is right and wrong, consensus has collapsed.

We have just said that the reversal of the renunciation of power may be the fault of the State when it passes off injustice as law. Or it may be caused by the law-breaking partiality of a group bent on making its own rights the only law, which means that it, too, legitimizes injustice. Depending on which of the two it is, people will talk of a liberation movement or of terrorism. Of course, every form of terrorism will present itself as a liberation movement, and when there is no clear criterion of justice, it can do that very easily.

It is worth remembering that, in the first phase of German terrorism, when the phenomenon had hardly affected other Western countries, there was a widespread tendency in the West to regard the terrorists as true freedom-fighters, victims of a newly emerging state of totalitarianism. Only when the phenomenon became international and people had the chance to see the "freedom struggle" at close quarters did it become indisputably clear that here was a brutal violence, contemptuous of humanity, and that its idealized, anarchic freedom was conceived chiefly as a freedom to be violent and a freedom from law. On the other hand, people in Europe are always enthusiastically ready to celebrate every kind of terrorism in the Third World as a liberation movement. For more than twenty years, Helmut Kuhn has been sharp-sightedly explaining the reason for this:

> As order divorced from justice becomes terrible, so unjust prosperity, obtained by exploitation and the suffering of others, becomes offensive. This is the reason for the bad conscience that spoils the Western world's enjoyment of its postwar prosperity and finds no solace in the thought of giving foreign aid.[2]

What is more, though the initial phase of European terrorism may be credited, despite everything, with a certain idealism, at least an idea of something, today the disintegration of justice, and with it the unleashing of violence, is proceeding apace. The worldwide network of drug-trafficking, coupled with prostitution, the arms traffic, and the old criminal syndicates is gradually becoming a threat to humanity. The loss of justice, without a great open war, is destroying peace from the inside and more effectively than the classic wars were ever able to do. It may be that, from an unexpected quarter and in an unusual form, something of the dimensions of a world war is developing.

The fourth way in which peace is destroyed has already been hinted at above; in fact, it is closely connected with what we have just said. It can happen that a State falls into the hands of groups that palm off injustice as justice, destroying justice from top to bottom, and thereby, in their own way, creating a peace that in reality is dictatorship. Such a State, by the methods of modern mass-domination, can produce total subjugation and so give an impression of order and tranquility, while people of uncompromising conscience are thrown into jail, forced into exile, or murdered. As Augustine asserted emphatically, a State without justice

[2] H. Kuhn, *Der Staat: Eine philosophische Darstellung* (Munich: Kösel, 1967), 193.

is a great robber band.[3] Hitler's *Reich* was such a robber state. Outwardly, it may look as if there is peace, but it is the peace of the graveyard. The tragedy is that, under total tyranny, there is no possibility at all of a war of liberation. Dictatorship quietly sets itself up as the triumph of peace. This is what the New Testament means when it predicts that the Antichrist will appear as the harbinger of "peace and security".[4] Here we confront the paradoxical aspect of our subject. What poses as definitive peace may well be the total destruction of peace.

2. The Foundation and Form of Justice

The heart of our contemporary problems can be seen in the third aspect of the crisis. Here again it becomes clear how closely connected religion is with peace and justice. We have shown that today peace is breaking up *within* nations, that agreement about what is right and wrong has collapsed. Now, what holds a society together and gives it peace is law. The fact that peace between nations has constantly

[3] *De civitate Dei,* bk. 4, chap. 4: "Remota itaque iustitia quid sunt regna nisi magna latrocinia? quia et latrocinia quid sunt nisi parva regna?"

[4] 1 Thessalonians 5:3 presents the reign of the slogan "peace and security" as a sign of the imminent end of the world, but it does not link it with the figure of the Antichrist. Later reflection does make the connection, absolutely correctly in my opinion. Soloviev does it in a very penetrating way in his story about the Antichrist. Soloviev's Antichrist is the author of a book that has aroused worldwide attention. Its title is *The Open Way to Peace and Prosperity in the World.* In the manifesto that he issues after his proclamation as world ruler, he says: "Peoples of the world! The promises have been fulfilled! World peace is ensured forever. . . ." Also important is the penetrating interpretation of the Antichrist traditions in Josef Pieper, *The End of Time: A Meditation on the Philosophy of History*, trans. Michael Bullock (San Francisco: Ignatius Press, 1999), 119–44.

been wrecked by war is connected with the lack of an effective international law, a law that not only orders a society on the inside but is also commonly recognized among the nations as their binding norm; they submit to it, whether or not it be to their advantage. Now if law ceases to have a commonly accepted content, it becomes powerless, and the distinction between legal power and wrongful power is blurred. The representatives of legal power become "pigs", and the representatives of wrongful power the champions of liberty. Law without proof of identity looks like arbitrary whim, and all that is left is power: *Homo homini lupus*.

And so the question of peace is in practice identical with the question of law, and the real question for the survival of the human race is, therefore, the question of what constitutes the foundations and unalterable content of law. But where and how can an answer be found to the question? Or rather let us put it the other way round: Why has the distinction between right and wrong ceased to be obvious to us? Why can we not differentiate them? These questions require us to consider the foundation and fashioning of law in the modern world. Of course, once again this cannot take the form of a historical analysis. Instead, I shall try to focus on a few decisive points. As far as I can see, there are three.

a. Authoritas—Utilitas

First, there are the famous words of Thomas Hobbes: *Authoritas, non veritas facit legem.*[5] The Socratic question about what right and wrong really are, in themselves and according

[5] M. Mettner, "Friede", in *Neues Handbuch theologischer Grundbegriffe*, vol. 1, ed. P. Eicher (Munich: Kösel, 1981), 421. On Hobbes, compare H. Maier, "Hobbes", in *Klassiker des politischen Denkens*, ed. H. Maier and H. Denzer I (Munich: C. H. Beck, 1969), 351–75.

to the inner truth of things, independently of all traditions and enactments of law, is dismissed as impractical.[6] The law is based, not on the discernible reality of right and wrong, but on the authority of the person with the power to enact it. It comes about through legislation, and in no other way. Its inner protection is thus the power to push it through, not the truth of being. This thesis enabled various things to happen. First of all, it helped political rule to become independent of the various other powers in medieval society. It was used to support the claims of absolute monarchies. But it also became the axiom of legal positivism, which has been able to establish itself widely since the nineteenth century. The consequences are far-reaching. Now one government can declare to be legal what its neighbor makes illegal. At the same time, in the minds of a large number of politicians today (in other words, the legislative *authoritas*), this is modified to mean that the law has to mirror, and to translate into norms, the value judgments actually found in society. When majority opinion becomes in this way the only real source of law and the essential criterion of *authoritas*, the paradox is not in any way diminished. The man condemned today may see himself as the pioneer of the law of tomorrow and so feel justified to use every means at his disposal to usher in the future, of which he regards himself as the custodian. If truth is as inaccessible as is here supposed, then there is no distinction in reality between right and wrong, no distinction between rightful and wrongful power, but only the pressure of the momentarily stronger group, the supremacy of the majority.

[6] Romano Guardini's *Der Tod des Sokrates* (Berlin, 1943; new impression Mainz-Paderborn: Grünewald, 1987) is still important for what it says about the nature and permanent validity of the Socratic question. Cf. also Kuhn, *Der Staat*, 24ff.

This notion of law is matched by an idea of peace that one might sum up as follows: *Utilitas, non veritas facit pacem.* In similar fashion to Adam Smith, Immanuel Kant developed his doctrine of perpetual peace largely along these lines:

> The spirit of commerce sooner or later takes hold of every people, and it cannot exist side by side with war. And of all the powers (or means) at the disposal of the power of the state, financial power can probably be relied on most. Thus states find themselves compelled to promote the noble cause of peace. . . . And wherever in the world there is a threat of war breaking out, they will try to prevent it by mediation, just as if they had entered into a permanent league for this purpose.[7]

In other words, it is a question of making egotism, man's strongest and most reliable power and the source of his conflicts, into a real instrument of peace, because it is precisely egotism that makes peace seem more useful than war. Realistic politics will doubtless take account of this view and see it as an element in the peacemaking process. But on its own, as history since Kant adequately proves, it is insufficient for the building of perpetual peace.

b. Three fundamental rights—The ambivalence of the rights of man doctrine

The two ideas just mentioned (*authoritas* and *utilitas*) present themselves in our post-metaphysical age. In a situation in

[7] *Zum ewigen Frieden.* The edition I consulted was that of the Wissenschaftliche Buchgesellschaft, vol. 6 (Darmstadt, 1964), 226. [For an English translation, see H. Reiss, ed., *Kant's Political Writings* (Cambridge: Cambridge University Press, 1970), 114.] Cf. Kuhn, *Der Staat*, 351ff.; Mettner, "Friede", 422. Obviously, this citation is not intended as a presentation or evaluation of the entire thought of this Königsberg philosopher on the subject of peace, which is much richer and more profound than this.

which the unknowability of the true and man's incapacity for the good seem to have become absolute certainties, the attempt is made to build justice and peace on the foundation of authority and utility. Opposed to these two post-metaphysical ideas, the political effects of which are obvious, is a more strongly metaphysical current of thought. I am thinking of the three fundamental rights laid down by John Locke in his *Second Treatise of Government* (1690): life, freedom, property. The background to this is the *Magna Carta*, the *Bill of Rights*, and ultimately the natural law tradition.[8] Here is a quite explicit claim that the rights of the person precede the State's enactments of law. Locke's way of expressing the rights of man doctrine is clearly directed against the State. It is of revolutionary significance. Not surprisingly, long before Marx, the Enlightenment developed a revolutionary tradition of its own. The old doctrine of the just war turned into the doctrine of a struggle for perpetual peace to be conducted in the form of worldwide civil war.[9] This gives an inkling of the ambivalence of the rights of man doctrine. When the concept of freedom is hypertrophied and the State is regarded essentially as an enemy, peace does not have a chance. But there is a sound core to the idea of human rights, and so it continues to be a guide to the truth and a protective barrier against positivism. There is something that is right in itself, and this constitutes the true bond among men because it stems from our common nature.

[8] Important on this point and what follows is Kuhn, *Der Staat*, 262–66. See also E.-W. Böckenförde and R. Spaemann, eds., *Menschenrechte und Menschenwürde* (Stuttgart: Klett-Cotta, 1987), especially the contribution of G. Stourzh, "Die Begründung der Menschenrechte im englischen und amerikanischen Verfassungsdenken des 17. und 18. Jahrhunderts", 78–90.

[9] Cf. Mettner, "Friede", 422–23.

Attempting to uncover the roots of the crisis of justice and peace shows us what can heal it. Law can be the effective power of peace only when the yardstick for measuring it is not in our hands. The law is molded, not created, by us. In other words, there can be no foundation for law without transcendence. When God and the basic pattern of human existence laid down by him are ousted from public consciousness and relegated to the private, merely subjective realm, the concept of law dissolves into thin air and, with it, the foundation of peace.

3. What the Church Can and Must Do— What She Neither Can nor Should Do

This brings us to the third part of our discussion, the contribution that religion can and should make to peace. I have already indicated above why I am taking religion concretely to mean Church. I think it is necessary to distinguish between what the Church must do for peace and what she must not and cannot do.

a. The tradition and protection of the basic criterion

The Church's first task in this area is to keep alive, in fidelity to her holy tradition, the basic criterion of justice and to detach it from the arbitrariness of power. What her great founders have seen and said, what Jesus and his witnesses saw and said, the Church must carry through the years as a great light for the human race. In each generation, she must shine that light on present-day questions and offer the Word given to her as the answer to the problems of the age. She must carry conviction and help men to see with and through Jesus what they cannot see by their own powers. She must ensure that in the conflict between *utilitas* and *veritas*, between *authoritas* and *veritas*, truth does not founder. Man has been given an organ for apprehending truth as well as an organ for determining utility. There is nothing wrong with utility, but when it is made absolute, it becomes a force for evil. Utility destroys itself when it disregards truth. The same is true of *authoritas*. The trouble is that the organ of utility and the organ of power are more palpable and more immediate in their effects than the organ of truth. That is why the organ of truth needs assistance, needs support. This is what the Church's task ought to be: to give this otherwise all too easily suppressed faculty the strength it needs.

The task of the Church in this area is, therefore, first and foremost "education", taking that word in the great sense it had for the Greek philosophers. She must break open the prison of positivism and awaken man's receptivity to the truth, to God, and thus to the power of conscience. She must give men the courage to live according to conscience and so keep open the narrow pass between anarchy and tyranny, which is none other than the narrow way of peace. In society she must create the conviction that can support good law. For, though we just now rejected the idea of majority opinion as the source of law, it is also clear that law cannot be permanently effective unless it has some kind of public credibility. In this consideration, it must appear as a highly questionable development that the modern administration of justice has quite publicly ceased to regard moral and religious values as goods deserving of legal protection; it seems to think that only material goods and the libertarian freedom of the individual need defense. In this consideration, it must appear as a highly questionable development that the same holds true in the Church. Hardly anyone looks upon faith as a good deserving of protection, at least not when it is in conflict with individual freedom or public opinion.

b. The renunciation of direct political action

Alongside this primary task of creating conviction, forming conscience, and fashioning community as a space for peace is the mission of the Church's office-bearers, supported by the conviction of the faithful, to speak out publicly on questions of the moment and to be advocates of peace. In our own times this has been taken up with great passion. In addition to the classical channels of communication in the Church, many kinds of commissions and institutions are developing that dedicate themselves passionately to the question of peace and try to come up with the right words in reply. Not everything that comes to light by this means is enlightened. But the concern itself is, without doubt, a proper part of one of the Church's real tasks. What the Church has to remember is that, though the sources of law have been entrusted to her safekeeping, she does not have any specific answers to concrete political questions. She must not make herself out to be the sole possessor of political reason. She points out paths for reason to follow, and yet reason's own responsibilities remain.

All this comes together in the Church's most interior and yet also most human task: the task of making, not just talking about, peace, in deeds of love. No social service of the State can replace Christian love in both its spontaneous and organized forms. In fact, social service totally disintegrates when it loses the inspiration of the love that comes from faith. The Church's fidelity to her true nature is shown in her ability to support human beings in the vocation to love, to bring the vocation of love to maturity, and to give it concrete form in the life of the community. Through the power of love, the Church must serve the poor, the sick, the lost, the oppressed. She must go into prison, into the suffering of mind and body, as far as the dark way of death. In areas torn by the strife the human race always has experienced and always will experience, the Church must give men the strength to survive and, with the power of forgiveness, awaken the capacity to make a new start. Only the man who can forgive can build and preserve peace.[10]

All this goes to show the limits of the Church's task and powers. She cannot enforce peace. She could not do it in the past, and she cannot do it in the future. She must not be transformed into a kind of political peace movement, whose only *raison d'être* would be the attaining of perpetual world peace. The planned "peace council" of religions is, therefore, because of the nature of the Church, an impossibility. The leaders of the Church have no authority to take direct political action. They have not received a mandate for it from the faithful, certainly not from the Lord himself. In fact, one ought rather to say that the attempt to bring about a worldwide empire of peace through a worldwide union of religions is perilously close to the third temptation of Jesus: "All [the kingdoms of the world] I will give you, if you will fall down and worship me" (cf. Mt 4:9).[11] In this way of

[10] On the connection between peace and forgiveness, see H. Schlier, *Der Geist und die Kirche* (Freiburg: Herder, 1980), 133.

[11] In *The End of Time*, Pieper quotes from *The Era of Atomic Power* (London: Student Christian Movement Press, 1946), 44: "[A] world organization might become the most deadly and impregnable of tyrannies, the final establishment of the reign of anti-Christ." *The End of Time*, 129. Pieper continues,

thinking, world peace almost inevitably becomes the *Summum bonum*, to which everyone submits and for whose attainment all other religious acts and values are mere means. But a God who becomes the means to supposedly higher ends is no longer God; in fact, he has given away his divinity to something higher, whose cause he must serve. It is obvious that peace established in this way is, of its very nature, in danger of turning into either the totalitarianism that allows only one way of thinking or worldwide civil war.

c. *Witness and ministry of love*

Consequently, the Church does less, not more, for peace if she abandons her own sphere of faith, education, witness, counsel, prayer, and serving love and changes into an organization for direct political action. In so doing, she blocks access to the wellsprings from which the powers of peace and reconciliation continually flow. Precisely because the utmost must be done for peace, the Church must remain true to her real nature. Only when she respects her limits is she limitless, and only then can her ministry of love and witness become a call to all men. What the Church ultimately has to contribute to peace has been persuasively summed up, I think, in some words of Metropolitan Damaskinos. I endorse them without qualification and so would like to conclude by quoting them:

"The Kantian ideal of the abolition of truly 'external' wars, which would be attained in a World State, has its reverse side: the place of external wars would be taken by internal 'police actions' the character of which would approximate very closely the extermination of pests." Ibid., 130–31. Cf. Kuhn, *Der Staat*, 355: "It is as martyr that the Church is most truly herself. But as an organization for creating fraternity among men, she founders on the earthly supremacy of politics."

It is my considered opinion that, over and above her social service, the contribution of the Orthodox Church to peace, freedom, justice, and brotherhood among the nations consists in a witness of love. . . . The Church's role cannot be identified with any kind of political strategy or with the political expediency of the authorities of governments among which her peoples live. In this context the Orthodox Churches' scope for initiative and action is restricted. Her witness and presence bring with them dangers which may lead her leaders to martyrdom, . . . but it is precisely this love that is ready for martyrdom which ultimately strengthens the will of the Orthodox Churches. It enables them, in collaboration with their brethren in the other Christian Churches and confessions, to bear witness—the witness of faith and love—in a world that perhaps has more need of it than ever.[12]

[12] Metropolitan Damaskinos Papandreous, "Contribution de l'Église orthodoxe à la réalisation des idéaux chrétiens de paix, de liberté, de fraternité et d'amour entre les peuples, et la suppression des discriminations raciales", in *Weisheit Gottes—Weisheit der Welt*, ed. W. Baier et al. (St. Ottilien: EOS Verlag, 1987) 1342f.

13

The Responsibility of Faith to Society and to the World

Prefatory Note: The award of the great Leopold Kunschak Prize, which was bestowed on me, to my surprise and joy, on March 9, 1991, gave me the opportunity to give an account of my own relationship to the questions of Catholic social doctrine and at the same time to attempt a statement of principle about the connection between faith and social responsibility. My own theological starting point was indeed obviously far removed from the questions posed here; but it has become clearer to me, in retrospect, that this distance was only apparent.

1. The Basis of Faith and the Social Relevance of Faith

When I began my theological studies, just after the end of the Second World War, the decisive motivating factor for me was the question of the *ratio spei*, the question of the reason for our hope, as the First Letter of Peter puts it (3:15), in a phrase that was rightly understood in the Middle Ages as the basis for all theology. According to the Apostle, we must bear in ourselves the reason for our hope in such a way that this *logos* can become *apologia:* the word of hope wishes to become the answer to the question of the man who seeks to discover where hope is and who wishes to understand the reason why one is permitted to hope. This New Testament phrase, heavy with substance, is a description of the essential process of all theology, but it applies in a particular manner to that section of the theological endeavor which desires to investigate the basis, the foundation of faith and its hope, wishing to give an account of faith—a discipline that was first called apologetics (from *apologia*, the Greek word for "answer") and then also fundamental theology (because it asks the question about the foundation).

The reason for our faith and the communicability of its hope and of the meaning it gives to our life: these were the questions I wished above all to address when I began my studies, and this is why I decided to specialize in the area of fundamental theology. The question thus posed goes to the root of faith. But it is not in the least divorced from the world. For the chief objection to Christianity appeared to me to be its apparent failure to transform the world and man. In the twentieth century after Christ, National Socialism and Communism had come to power. While the testimony they gave against the Redeemer of the world did not appear to me for one moment to be convincing, let alone alluring, in its negative way it did put faith to a harsh test: It was obvious that the world had not become better in twenty centuries of Christian proclamation, for the horrors that were now taking place were at least the equal of those that had occurred in pre-Christian times. Was it still really possible to call the years after Christ "years of salvation"? Were not the years on which we looked back terrible years of "un-salvation", and must we not indeed expect perhaps even worse years in the future?

Forty years later, I found the questions that had moved me at that period formulated with utter clarity by Julien Green, although, naturally, the answer he gives is one I cannot share. At the end of his book on Saint Francis, this great author writes:

> World War II shook my soul the way one shakes somebody by the shoulders. . . . The world at war struck me as one vast atrocity. My mind gradually came to the conclusion that the Gospel was a failure. Christ himself had wondered about the faith he would find on earth at his second coming. The souls he had touched and drawn to him seemed isolated in the storm unleashed by madmen. Almost at the midpoint between the first Christmas and the hell humanity was writhing in, a man had appeared on earth, another Christ, the Francis of my childhood, but he too had failed. Failed? Apparently. . . . He was convinced that salvation would come through the Gospel. The Gospel was eternity, the Gospel had only just begun. What were twenty centuries in the eyes of God?[1]

2. The Two Paths Taken by Theology after the Second World War

a. Faith as desecularization

I have never believed for one moment that the *apologia* of the Gospel could consist in pointing to the effect it would have at some future time. On the contrary, one would truly have to concede the validity of Karl Marx's objection that the Gospel has had time enough to prove its possibilities. But the question of what kind of promise the Gospel has for this history of ours, what it promises us and what it does not—this question was and remains unavoidable: it had to stand at the center of an "*apologia* of hope". In this way, the problem

[1] J. Green, *God's Fool: The Life and Times of Francis of Assisi*, trans. Peter Heinegg (San Francisco: Harper & Row, 1985), 273.

of the social responsibility of faith belongs to the center of fundamental theology's task. It is, of course, true that this problem was curiously defused in the theological context of the period just after the war. The political Catholicism of the period between the world wars had collapsed with the appearance of the Third Reich, and it was not possible for it to return. The spirit of the Youth Movement nourished skepticism against all kinds of groups and organizations. After faith was forcibly deprived of all political responsibility in 1933, it had received new power and depth precisely by being compelled to find a purely religious form. The loss of power had been an advantage for it. It had become purer. Its own hope, for which there is no substitute, had emerged in its indestructible greatness precisely in the places of earthly hopelessness, in the grayness of the concentration camps and in the courts of those who held power. Thus, there was a desire to avoid every new amalgamation of faith with the political level. The desire for a purely religious realization of the Gospel determined the direction of theology, while of course—as we shall soon see—there was certainly a vigilant awareness in the political sphere of the secular responsibility of faith.

The confrontation between Romano Guardini and Carl Sonnenschein in the Berlin of the 1920s seems to me characteristic of the experience people had had in those years, the experience that now indicated the path ahead. In his memoirs, Guardini gives this description of Sonnenschein's position:

> Sonnenschein had stood deep in the modernist movement. When the crisis came for him, he had not only separated himself from this movement: he must also have dismissed theological problems as a whole. His standpoint in Berlin was: "We are in a besieged city in which there are no

> problems but only slogans." This formula may be impressive, but it is false. . . . Genuine praxis . . . that is, correct conduct, comes from the truth. And one must struggle to find the truth.[2]

Guardini goes on to formulate his own position, which is thereby outlined in its essence:

> As time passed, I became less and less concerned . . . with immediate effect. What I had wanted from the outset, first instinctively and then more and more consciously, was to bring the truth to light. Truth is a power, but only when one does not demand that it have any immediate effect.[3]

These sentences of this great teacher seem to be a completely appropriate indication of the true essence of a new distinction between the secular order and faith, as well as the essence of a correct praxeology, a correct statement of the relationship between faith and praxis. But the positions taken in the period shortly after the war moved on and at first scarcely developed at all the tendency to take concrete responsibility for the world that is undeniably contained in Guardini's position (as the further development of his thought showed). The new slogan was supplied by Bultmann, who attempted here to adopt Heidegger as an instrument for the interpretation of biblical revelation: this slogan was "desecularization". A strangely dualistic position, which continues to have its effect today, developed from this program: the Christian faith, which itself is interpreted as desecularization, aims, not at the sanctification of the world, but at its secularization.

It is the release of the world into its secular character,

[2] R. Guardini, *Berichte über mein Leben: Autobiographische Aufzeichnungen* (Düsseldorf: Patmos, 1984), 111.

[3] Ibid., 109.

an intentional desacralization. The inherent line of development of Christianity itself is realized precisely in the increasing emancipation of the world from the religious dimension. Thus there would be no greater error than the desire to create a Christian society. The more radically secular the world becomes, the better it is. Christian action in the world could not consist of communicating to society Christian patterns of order. It is seen, on the contrary, in the renunciation of such confusions between faith and world. We can find one of the most recent examples of the continued effect of such positions in the book *Le Rêve de Compostelle*, in which a group of French theologians reacts to the youth meeting at Santiago de Compostela by accusing the pope of a backward-looking romanticism that aims at a reestablishing of Christendom: one ought to want the opposite of this.[4] In this conception, desecularization and secularization go hand in hand and produce strange paradoxes. It is precisely representatives of the purely religious path who tend to become actively involved in Marxist parties, clearly in order to push Christianity aside into pure unworldliness. Paradoxically, this political neutrality turned into a new form of political activity.

Of course in those early days after the war, one could as yet scarcely foresee these dialectical leaps of a new turning to the religious center. On the contrary, this was the great hour of Christian politicians, after the collapse of the anti-Christian madness. The new construction was based very consciously on the ethical principles of Christianity, and thus there was a conscious linkage to the spiritual center of faith itself, while there was independence from ecclesiastical

[4] R. Luneau and P. Ladrière, eds., *Le Rêve de Compostelle: Vers la restauration d'une Europe chrétienne?* (Paris: Centurion, 1989).

directives, in the appropriate autonomy of the State. The social responsibility of faith was the decisive directive to the conscience of a generation of politicians whom we can but name with gratitude as the fathers of a new Europe: Adenauer, Schuman, de Gasperi, de Gaulle, but also men such as Raab, Figl, and Kunschak.

b. Faith as politics

The concept of the secular world, which I should wish to call a Manichaean error, was bound sooner or later to call forth an opposite effect, which emerged as early as the 1960s, first in the form of political theology and then in the shape of liberation theology with its many variants. The phenomenon is so well known that I need not give any further description of it. One brief reference to a central concept must suffice. Exegesis had long noted that the "Kingdom of God" was the central concept of Jesus' proclamation. In the radical-eschatological interpretation of the figure of Jesus, which began with Albert Schweitzer and was then deepened philosophically and theologically by Bultmann, this meant that Jesus had nothing to say that was inner-worldly: he pointed only to that which was "wholly other". The program of desecularization and secularization corresponded to this view. But now, in the face of growing social distress and inescapable Christian responsibility, this interpretation changed into its own opposite. Today, the "kingdom" is the central slogan of all the forms of liberation theology. It is characteristic that one now speaks simply of the "kingdom"—without mentioning God—and that this is understood now as the ideal human society. It is the aim of faith and the task of all theology to work to bring about the "kingdom". The central word of faith becomes a political concept, an expression of the goal of all good politics. Faith itself thereby becomes political ideology. Politics has absorbed faith into itself.

3. The Social Responsibility of Faith

Between these two extremes, which have in many cases united to form a strange alliance, there stands today the question of the social and political responsibility of faith. In this constellation, this question has in fact become the central point of all fundamental theology's endeavors; what is at stake here is nothing more and nothing less than the question of whether we as believers are permitted to hope and what the genuine contents of our faith are. In the final section of my reflections, I should like to sketch only briefly the outline of an answer.

Here, I shall tackle the question of the social responsibility of faith paradigmatically on the basis of a text from the Old Testament that became a central Christological text in the New Testament and teaches us to understand the unity of the Testaments correctly. It seems to me that the correct understanding of our problem, indeed, the appropriate understanding of the Christian faith as a whole, depends on the correct understanding of the relationship between Old and New Testaments. The opposing positions I have attempted to sketch in my historical review are based on a misunderstanding of this relationship. Harnack, who categorized Christ's message as strictly individualistic and thereby reduced it to an "ethics of attitude" in the sense of Max Weber, had demanded that Marcion's legacy finally be executed and the New Testament separated from the Old. Bultmann's position of desecularization is based on the same hermeneutical starting point. Bultmann, too, is unable to recognize any unity between the Testaments; for him, the only way in which the Old Testament leads over into the New is through its failure. A New Testament torn away from the Old Testament is necessarily without a world; a Jesus torn away from the life context of the Old Testament is merely a moralist who can inspire attitudes; the "salvation of the world" does not stand within his horizon.

In the case of the radicalized political theologians, on the other hand, the relationship between Old and New Testaments is just the reverse: the New Testament is taken back into the Old; redemption becomes the Exodus, interpreted in a political way, as the secular act of liberation, and thus the Kingdom of God becomes the product of the human act of liberation. In this process, it is not only Christology that totally loses its own features; the Old Testament itself is deprived of its dynamic that points ahead and upward, and it is turned around even in its own direction of movement.

But let us look at a text that will demonstrate this in an exemplary manner: the first of the Servant Songs, Isaiah 42:1–4 (5–9). We are told here three times in four verses that the Servant, the one whom God has chosen, brings "justice" to the peoples, establishes it on earth, genuinely gives justice. The Hebrew word *mishpat*, translated here as "justice", is one of the more commonly used words of the Old Testament, appearing no less than 425 times in the Hebrew Bible.[5] The nuances of its meaning can be extremely variable in individual cases, but all move within the sphere of justice, righteousness, law, judgment, so that P. Uys can define *mishpat* simply as "the God-given norm to ensure a

[5] Cf. B. Johnson, "Mishpat", in *Theologisches Wörterbuch zum Alten Testament*, ed. Botterweck, Ringgren, and Fabry (Stuttgart: Kohlhammer, 1973), 5:95.

well-ordered society".[6] The fact that it is set in parallelism three times to *sedaqah*, "righteousness", points in the same direction. It seems, therefore, that the task of the Servant of the Lord, this mysterious messianic figure, is to give justice to the world. It is not surprising that liberation theology's interpretation of Scripture has believed it could use this to build a bridge between Marx and the Bible, since here the *mishpat* of the poor, the action to establish right order, appears as the central messianic task.[7]

We must therefore look a little more closely, in order to understand what we learn in this text about the figure of Christ and about the hope that has its origin in him and about the commission he gives. The as yet unknown Servant stands in a clear parallel to the figure of Moses, indeed precisely as the fulfillment of the promise: "The LORD your God will raise up for you a prophet like me among you, among your brethren—him you shall heed. You are to listen to him. . . . I will put my words in his mouth, and he shall speak to them all that I command him" (Dt 18:15, 18).[8] In the Old Testament tradition, the decisive action in Moses' activity as mediator is not the act of leading the people out of Egypt but the act of handing on the Law at Mount Sinai. It is only through this that the Exodus from the foreign land takes on meaning and stability. For the people is set free and becomes a free nation of its own only by becoming a legal community. Lack of freedom is the condition of being without law. This is why the gift of the Law is the real establishment of liberation—and of a Law

[6] Quoted by Johnson, "Mishpat", 101.

[7] José Miranda, *Marx and the Bible* (New York: Orbis, 1974), esp. 109ff.

[8] For the parallel to Moses, see the exemplary exposition by C. Westermann, *Das Buch Jesaja. Kapitel 40–66* (Göttingen: Vandenhoeck & Ruprecht, 1966), 77–81.

that is truly justice, namely, right order in relationship to one another, in relationship to creation, and in relationship to the Creator. Man's freedom can exist only in the correct mutual allocation of these freedoms, and this is possible only if they all take the freedom of God and his truth as their criterion. True justice, just justice, can come into existence only when the true God is recognized aright, so that man, too, recognizes himself aright and orders his existence in a life with others on the basis of God. This is why Sinai was for Israel the criterion and the foundation of its freedom; it always lost its freedom to the extent that it departed from justice, returning to a condition without law and thereby falling back into servitude.

At this point, we must pause for a moment. If one identifies liberation with the victorious Exodus, one looks on it as an event of power whose success, as it were, automatically transposes the individual and the entire people into the condition of freedom. But if one recognizes that the essence of the liberation lies in the gift of the Law bestowed by God, then one sees that liberation is always linked to freedom and can be communicated only through freedom. More precisely, it is linked to a double mediation: the mediation through reason that opens itself, that makes itself accessible to God, and that thus becomes able to discern justice and injustice; and it is linked to the mediation through will that puts into action what has been recognized. Since man in his historical existence always retains the freedom to refuse these mediations, freedom never attains complete perfection within history.[9]

This permits us now to understand the figure of the new

[9] I have set out these connections in greater detail in my book *Church, Ecumenism, and Politics: New Endeavors in Ecclesiology*, trans. Michael Miller et al. (San Francisco: Ignatius Press, 2008), 247ff.

Moses whom the prophet describes under the title "Servant of the Lord". Unlike the first Moses, he no longer merely communicates justice to Israel alone but "will bring out justice to the nations" (Is 42:1) and establishes it on earth (42:4). The previously isolated individual event becomes universal; salvation now is for the whole world, which is gathered together and reconciled in the common justice of the one God. But this does not take place by means of conquest and subjection. The prophet says that the Servant of God "does not cry out" in order to distinguish him from the type of "liberators" who declare the establishment of their own power to be liberation and redemption. A trait that had already been increasingly emphasized by tradition in the figure of Moses now emerges with complete clarity in the Servant of God: he suffers for justice. He does not meet injustice with new injustice: he endures injustice in suffering and thereby sets limits to it; he transforms it from within. If one adds up all these elements, it becomes clear that Law and prophets flow together in the figure of the Servant of God to form a new unity: the Servant does what Moses did. He gives *mishpat*, he gives the justice that comes from God and thereby brings about the reconciliation of freedoms, which is the only true form of human freedom. But this justice is now no longer Torah but is precisely *mishpat*; it is no longer a firmly defined national body of laws but is an open form of law that must attain ever anew the synthesis of universality and particularity, so that it remains open to future history and its challenges, while yet opposing every arbitrariness with the immovable criterion of the truth.

The Servant of the Lord in Isaiah remains expectation; he takes up the promise of the "other prophet" from Deuteronomy 18 and develops it. Those who encountered Jesus could not avoid seeing in him the fulfillment of this hope. Thus the introductory words from the Song of the Servant (Is 42:1) stand over his baptism—like a title set over the entire activity of Jesus that explains in advance who and what he is (Mk 1:11). Jesus' claim on the Old Testament is clearly presented precisely through this connection and also the extent of its substance specified. In him, Law and prophets now truly flow together in the way we have just suggested. But this implies that any reduction of his message to an ethics of attitude and any individualistic or existentialistic interpretation in the sense of the ideology of desecularization miss the essence of his figure. It also means that a political interpretation of Jesus that makes him a failed rebel paints a totally false picture of him. Jesus was not Barabbas or Spartacus, but precisely Jesus. He possesses the entire concreteness of all the social and legal directives of the prophets and also, therefore, the entire Law, as this is illuminated and universalized by the prophets. Faith in him goes beyond the social and political realm, but, precisely in this, it is a faith in social responsibility. The social dimension is included in faith—not in the form of a ready-made party program or a ready-made order for the structure of the world. It is contained in faith precisely in the mode of responsibility, and this means that it requires mediation through reason and will. Reason and will must attempt to make concrete and to put into practice the criterion of God's *mishpat*, set up by faith, in changing historical situations, always in the essential imperfectibility of man's action within history. It is not permitted to man to set up the "Kingdom", but he is charged to go toward the Kingdom through justice and love. The necessary mediation contained in the concept of *mishpat* indicates at the same time the precisely theological and methodological *locus* of Catholic (Christian) social doctrine. Faith's hope always goes infinitely farther than all our realizations, reaching into the realm of the eternal; but precisely the fact that this hope is given to us gives us the courage to take up again and again, despite all inadequacy, the struggle for a just order that is the form of freedom and builds up a dam against the tyranny of injustice.

14

The Church and Europe

In order to make clear the specific character of my book, its purposes and its limits, I would like, first of all, to say a few words about the way in which it came about. The prefect of a congregation, who day after day from morning until evening is absorbed in demanding tasks of the most varied sorts, does not have the opportunity to develop major topics mentally in tranquil reflection so as then to give them an adequate literary presentation. None of my books in recent years had the opportunity to take shape according to this classic procedure of academic work.

On the other hand, however, it would be rather serious if a mission ordered to the spiritual foundations of our existence were tackled only in a bureaucratic way with the help of modern administrative techniques. Then Drewermann's reproach would be basically right, that the Church's claim to truth is in reality only a way of managing power. Of course, one safeguard against this is the mere fact—to speak only humanly—that the prefect is only one among equals and that the decisions of the meeting of cardinals, which the "congregation" *is* in the strict and proper sense of the word, are preceded by long and complex consultative procedures and by multiple studies by experts of the first rank.

But, finally, those who have responsibility must still accept the thought content of this process, and ultimately they can decide only to the extent to which they themselves become involved in the reflection. So it happens that daily work continually becomes a challenge to enter into the cultural debate of our time and to seek our own place in it, based on the faith.

I view in this context the many, many invitations that I receive every day to give conferences and introductions; naturally, only a very small number of them can be accepted. Someone who wants to participate as a man of the Church—and therefore on the basis of the faith and reason that are intrinsic to her—in reflection and action concerning the major tasks of the Church and of the world must also continually be exposed to the public debate and seek to be present in this debate as one who gives but also as one who receives.

In this way, this book took shape, as my other books in recent years did, too: it is a collection of texts that came about through public participation in the reflection on present-day problems and the dialogue with them. The topics were not chosen by me but were proposed to me. They are therefore different, like the individual occasions from which they were born. In retrospect, however, it becomes evident that they are internally linked and can be arranged in a book according to an order that is not merely external.

At the beginning, there are questions of principle about the moral and religious foundations of our political action. After the fall of the Berlin Wall, which had divided Europe into an Atlantic sector and a Soviet one, the problem of our part of the earth emerges in a new way: what was separated wants to be once again a united whole, and therefore, after the failure of the utopian theories, it is searching in a renewed way for a connection with its own history.

At first glance, it is quite obvious that "Europe" is not a

geographic concept but, rather, a historical and moral quantity. In the upheavals of recent years, it has become extremely clear that political, social, and economic action is not conducted simply in a technocratic way but, rather, is basically a moral and religious problem.

Naturally in today's complicated world, a number of specialized technical skills are necessary that cannot be replaced with moralistic axioms. From this perspective, a theologian's competence in political problems is limited; the Instructions by the Congregation for the Doctrine of the Faith on liberation theology intended precisely to recall this limit, given the wrong-headed attempts to mix faith and politics. But, on the other hand, there is no such thing as neutral politics, either. The student revolt in 1968 was right in trying to point out the impossibility of a neutral science; the same is true of politics.

In the topics proposed to me, which this book deals with, I sought to satisfy these two aspects of the problem: on the one hand, not to avoid the questions that people like to describe as "worldly" problems and, on the other hand, not to give the illusion that theology has an answer to everything.

Objections to the Topic of Europe

Permit me now to go a little more concretely into the topic of Europe. Everyone agrees that the East and the West have to find a new unity and that this problem is posed in a decisive way on the continent of Europe, which was divided before. In this sense, it is difficult to deny that today this characteristic structure that we call Europe has become in a new way a problem and a task. But this consensus ends when the concrete problems start.

I see three contrasting fears that are expressed with regard to the ideal of Europe and that therefore make action for a renewed European community appear problematic. In the first place, I mention the fear that the program Europe might promote the "restoration tendency" of the Catholic Church. Supposedly hidden under the slogan "the new evangelization" is the objective of turning back the Reformation and the Enlightenment and, assisted by the favorable circumstances of the present hour, of rebuilding a Europe dominated by the Catholics under the pope's guidance. Supposedly the desire is finally to return to a time before the modern era and to revive the dream of a Catholic world. Against this, it is said, we ought to defend progress, freedom of thought, laicism [i.e., a non-confessional state], and worldliness.

A second fear of a rather contrasting nature has been expressed recently, echoing many authors, by the Hungarian philosopher Thomas Molnar, in exile in America, where he teaches: he fears the Europe of the economic bureaucracy in Brussels; he is afraid of the reduction of reality to the market and merchandise. For him, the fundamental line of current European politics runs toward a submission to the "American way of life", whereby Europe would dissolve by itself and would become an appendage of North America: he sees signs of the assimilation of this way of life, from fast food to language and city planning, and is frightened by its interior emptiness—futurologists anticipate that both Venice and Rome (to take just two nearby examples) will be surrounded by a belt of satellite cities, which will lead to the decadence of the ancient *urbs* [city] as a living space.

Thus, there is a growing fear that the unification of Europe will ultimately be dominated solely by the criteria of a culture that is purely quantitative in character, in which bigger is better and more is all that matters, while at the same time what is authentically human is lost. Universal tolerance here becomes at the same time universal intolerance: only what allows itself to be fit into the quantitative criterion can have any value; if truth and ethics emerge from the purely private sphere and aspire to some claim of public value, they go beyond the bounds of permissible pluralism and appear as a totalitarian claim that is trying to subject man to a yoke. Therefore they cannot pretend to practice tolerance.

Given these phenomena, the discussion about a new world order may have a not very consoling aspect; it is no accident that in recent years the memory of Benson's book *Lord of the World* (1907) has reawakened; it describes his vision of a similar unified civilization and of its destructive power for the human spirit; the Antichrist is represented as the great peacemaker of a similar new order of the world. Moreover, a new edition of the book was published in Germany in 1990—obviously based on the conviction that this kind of assimilation should be considered a real danger that must be resisted.

Finally, there is the fear of Eurocentrism and the memory that European history is not quite the story of a whole world, to which we could now return again after all the horrors of the modern ideologies. The new insurgency of nationalisms with all their destructive cruelty and narrow-mindedness, which we are experiencing today, can only confirm the relevance of those warnings about a backward-looking romanticism.

What is to be said with regard to these fears, which seem to rule out both building on the history of Europe and emerging from it into an ahistorical-quantitative civilization? First of all, it is clear that it would make no sense to seek to return to the past. There is no way back. An idea of Europe that did not manage to integrate the heritage of the modern era, too, would have no future; it would rely, moreover, on an abstract concept of history.

But I see no one who has that sort of thing in mind. The new evangelization does not mean reissuing what already was. It has its origin in the awareness that the Gospel of Jesus Christ, precisely because it comes from eternity, bears within it not only a yesterday and a today but, most importantly a tomorrow also. Every era will experience this and will live it out in a new way; only insofar as it reaches not only the geographical ends of the earth but also the temporal ends of the earth and of its history will it be able to develop completely and to show its true greatness. The new evangelization means that the wellsprings of man's identity are revealed to him and that in precisely this way he is made capable of developing all the fullness of his being.

Directions for a Journey

This already gives in a nutshell the answer to the second and the third questions that I tried to present earlier. The knowledge and the discoveries of science and of modern technology must not be annulled; even though many doubts have arisen among us in this regard, nevertheless, everything that is true knowledge, and the human utilization of this knowledge, remain valid and appreciable.

Today we have more critical ideas about technological progress because we are beginning to see the threat to the earth resulting from its indiscriminate advance. In this sense, we must find lines of discernment and criteria that can promote a more nuanced relation with our science and our practical possibilities; if we were to limit ourselves to resisting and rejecting them, it would do no good at all.

There is a sort of resentment against the modern world

that can combine with the most diverse ideologies and hence become decidedly dangerous. It bears repeating that the idea of a new evangelization does not belong to this type of negative thinking. Instead, it urgently exhorts us to see the one-sidedness of the modern era, the one-sidedness of a civilization still oriented toward quantity alone; it offers us criteria for discernment, which we urgently need.

I am convinced that there is no denying that until now work for the unification of Europe has been done one-sidedly under the banner of economics and quantity, while paying no attention to history and to ahistorical factors. Proceeding farther along this path without corrective interventions would offer no true hope to Europe. The homogenization of life in all of its spheres, from clothing to food, buildings and language, brings with it a flattening of spirits, within which the continual change of external forms is experienced as utter tedium. The man becomes soulless; he becomes in the true sense of the word foreign to himself, alienated. Where morality and religion are relegated to the exclusively private sphere, they come to lack the strength that alone can form a community and hold it together.

Here we face a very serious problem: the antithesis between tolerance and truth, which is increasingly becoming the dilemma of our time. This problem is decisive for the survival of Europe and of the democracies that sprang from European culture, but despite several valuable essays, a well-founded philosophical discussion of it is still lacking, although the dilemma is a matter of common knowledge, at least in terms of the radical formulation of the positivistic concept of the State in the writings of [the Austrian political philosopher] Kelsen. It is true that the State as such is not a source of truth and hence cannot impose any definite worldview or religion; it must guarantee freedom of religion and of thought.

But if the consequence drawn from this is the complete moral and religious neutrality of the State, then this canonizes the principle of might makes right: the majority becomes the sole source of law, and statistics is the legislator. This would be tantamount to the self-elimination of Europe, because then logically we would have to reopen a debate about human rights, as has already been shown in the debate over abortion. Here, exactly what Adorno and Horkheimer said about the dialectic of the Enlightenment and about its incessant self-destruction is coming true. The survival of liberty is at stake, and precisely in order to defend it, we must succeed in rediscovering the way to return to the Aristotelian insight of some fundamental truths and values of human existence that are self-evident and inviolable.

Liberty without moral foundations becomes anarchy, and anarchy inevitably leads to totalitarianism—indeed, it is already a manifestation of the totalitarian spirit. The self-evident character of what is moral and holy has in fact been lost for us in general skepticism and in the disputation of every certainty that cannot be proved in a laboratory. Nevertheless, even today a person can know that fidelity is good and not infidelity, that respect for values is good and not cynicism, that care for the other and not violence befits man; that we are in the presence of the mystery of divinity and receive our dignity from it.

I would like to express this even more concretely. Aristotle is not enough; Europe found in the Christian faith the values that sustain it and that, beyond our particular European history, provide a foundation for the human dignity of all men and women.

Today Europe is making an attempt to divest itself of its own history and to declare itself neutral with regard to the Christian faith, indeed, with regard to faith in God, in order to arrive finally at a tolerance without borders.

Pitting thought and behavior against history in this way is self-destructive.

The State cannot impose a specific religion on anyone; Vatican II correctly taught this in its Decree on Religious Liberty. But this does not mean that it should consider the majority alone as creating values and deprive itself of all cultural foundations.

The State does no one an injustice but, on the contrary, lays down the prerequisites for law when it sets the great human choices of the Christian worldview as the foundation for its framework of law.

Complementary Problems

In conclusion, I would also like to take a position briefly on two questions that are posed in this context. The concrete face of Europe is characterized by two major schisms of the modern era: the Reformation of the sixteenth century and the laicism that proceeded from the Enlightenment. Vatican Council II boldly sought to break down the walls of both divisions, or at least to open doors and passageways between the separate worlds, which for many reasons are hostile to one another.

In the Decree on Ecumenism and in the Pastoral Constitution on the Church in the Modern World, the council undertook these two dialogues and thus set out on the path toward what is held in common and has not completely disappeared, not even in the divisions.

The path of encounter is obviously more difficult than could have been imagined in the initial enthusiasm; the different basic choices are situated too deep. As a positive result, we can note the fact that today there is collaboration between Christians in responding to the fundamental problems of our time and that even the lines dividing so-called laicism and the Church have started to fluctuate: along with the concept of democracy, the Church has accepted the principles of tolerance and pluralism and has experienced precisely in recent decades in a sufficiently obvious way that she has only to gain from the establishment of religious liberty, since in fact she must continually operate in states and societies in which she is in a minority or her spiritual foundations are threatened outright.

On the other side, the old liberalistic dogmatism has liberated itself in many ways from its rigid, anti-ecclesial position and has learned to view as an error the limitation of the Church to the private sphere and to understand better her claim to a public space. This balance attained by the two parties during the postwar period through painful experiences is threatened once again today by the radicalizations of the Enlightenment about which we spoke before.

We cannot reasonably expect that the three faces of modern Europe—Catholicism, Protestantism, laicism—will unite together in a not-too-distant future But it is necessary to work tirelessly for their mutual understanding and for encounters between them. The marginalization of faith and the radicalization of liberty that leads to anarchy would be the end of Europe and also the end of the great European heritage of human dignity and human rights, which are founded on respect for man's likeness with God and for the inviolability of the image of God.

At this point, the second problem arises, which I would like to address again: given the emigrations of peoples that we are witnessing, are we not heading for a multicultural society? Does it make sense to remain attached to Christian foundations when Islam and the Asiatic religions, as well as post-Christian modern religious formations, are rapidly making the previous Europe simply disappear? Should we not, instead, prepare for a coexistence of completely different value systems?

Here certainly we are confronting open-ended questions, the breadth of which we can scarcely survey yet. The impending danger is that the disappearance of religious and moral certainties in Europe might lead by an intrinsic logic to hostility toward the future, even precisely where the utopia of the future, better world is eagerly cherished.

Depopulation is certainly the plainest sign of this No to the future; drug abuse points in the same direction. But this retreat from history has nothing to do with hospitality toward the foreigner. True hospitality and true openness to the other consist, rather, in overcoming first of all the concentration of wealth in some countries and in making sure from now on that every part of the globe and every country remains habitable or becomes increasingly so and, thus, the whole earth is a home for mankind.

On the other hand, we must show hospitality to all those who are threatened by persecution or are otherwise deprived of the conditions for a dignified life. Certainly this will include for the future a greater cultural plurality than the one to which we have been accustomed. But an unlimited multiculturality, in which the Christian foundations of Europe would have to be dissolved, cannot and must not necessarily follow as a logical consequence. In that case, for example, polygamy would have to be reintroduced as a legal form, and customs depriving women of their rights, which we have overcome, would once again have to be declared legal, along with many other things. Here, too, a false tolerance would end up contradicting itself.

The book, which I now hand over to public opinion, deals

with these fundamental problems; above all, I would like to clarify the relation between tolerance and the ineradicable foundations of European identity, which in all its breadth and in its deepest part is a Christian identity. All that I have at heart in these modest essays I find summed up in a passage from the speech that the Holy Father gave on October 11, 1988, to the European Parliament in Strasbourg; I want to conclude with this citation:

> It is also my duty to emphasize strongly that if the religious and Christian foundation of this continent in its role as the inspiration of ethics and in its social effectiveness is ever marginalized, not only will the heritage of the European past be denied, but also a future worthy of the individual European—and, indeed, all Europeans, believers and non-believers alike—will be seriously compromised.

PART FOUR

The True Europe and Its Mission

15

Reflections on the Ideals of Tomorrow's Europe

What is Europe? What can and should it be in the total context of the historical movement in which we are involved at the beginning of the third Christian millennium? After the Second World War, the search for a common identity and a common will in Europe entered a new phase. After two suicidal wars had devastated Europe in the first half of the twentieth century and inflicted terrible suffering on the whole world, it had become clear that all the European states were the losers in this cruel drama and that everything must be done to prevent its recurrence.

Instead of Divisive Nationalisms, One Common Identity

Europe has always been a continent of contrasts, shaken to its core by many conflicts. In the nineteenth century, the national states had come into being, and their competing interests had given a new dimension to destructive hostility. The work of European unification was guided basically by two motivations. In response to the divisive nationalisms and the hegemonistic ideologies that had given the old hostilities a radical form in the Second World War, it was intended that the common cultural, moral, and religious inheritance of Europe should shape the awareness of its nations. This common identity of all the European peoples was to open up a path of peace, a path into the future that all could take together. The search was for a European identity that would not extinguish or deny the individual national identities but would bind them together in a higher fellowship to form one single community of peoples. The shared history was to be activated as a force for peace. There can be no doubt that the founding fathers of European unification regarded the Christian heritage as the core of this historical identity, though naturally not in its confessional forms. That which is common to all Christians, transcending denominational borders, seemed to them to supply a force strong enough to harmonize political conduct in the world. And this did not appear incompatible with the great moral impulses of the Enlightenment, which had displayed the rational side of Christianity, so to speak, and which seemed compatible with the essential impulses derived from the Christian history of Europe, despite all the antitheses that had existed in the past. This overarching conviction never completely clarified a number of individual points in the drama of the confessional divisions and in the battles fought by the pioneers of the Enlightenment, and this means that questions were left open that still await a proper examination. In the first phase of European unification, however, the conviction that the great building blocks of the European heritage were compatible was stronger than the questions that this process necessarily posed.

At the outset of European unification, a second motivation accompanied this historical and moral element. With the end of the Second World War, European dominance of the world, which had been expressed above all in the colonial system with its interlocking economic and political networks, had collapsed once and for all. In this sense,

Europe as a whole had lost the war. America was now the dominant power on the stage of world history. But Japan, although defeated, also became an economic power along-side the United States, and the Soviet Union with its satellite states formed an *imperium* to which states in the Third World looked for support against America and Western Europe.

In this new situation, the individual European states could no longer act as equal partners with the superpowers. It was necessary to bind together their interests in one common European structure if Europe was to retain any importance at all in world politics. National interests had to be integrated into a common European interest. In addition to the search for a common identity generated by history that could promote peace, there was also the defense of common interests and, therefore, the intention to exercise that economic power which is a precondition of political power. In the course of the last fifty years, this second aspect of European unification has become ever more predominant. Indeed, it is this aspect alone that determines virtually every question. The euro, the common European currency, is the clearest expression of what the work of European unification means from this second perspective: Europe presents itself as an economic and monetary totality that as such takes part in shaping history and defends its own place.

Karl Marx maintained that religions and philosophies were merely ideological superstructures concealing the true realities of an economic situation. This is certainly not correct. One ought in fact to reverse this proposition and say that intellectual attitudes determine economic conduct and that economic situations then, in turn, have a decisive influence on religious and moral perspectives. After the initial phase in which ethical and religious considerations played a decisive role, economic considerations came to be the dominant factor in the development of Europe as an economic power.

Shared Criteria for Action

Now, however, we can see with increasing clarity that the development of economic structures and activity go hand in hand with intellectual decisions. At first, very little explicit reflection on these decisions takes place, but they come to demand a greater measure of clarification. Great international conferences like those held in Cairo (1994) and Beijing (1995) articulate the search for shared criteria for action, but these are more than merely the expression of questions. One could call them a kind of council of the world spirit, at which shared certainties are formulated and declared to be normative for human existence. The policy of granting or withholding economic aid is one way of enforcing such norms, which deal primarily with the control of population growth in the world and the universal obligation to employ particular means to achieve this goal.

The old ethical norms governing the relationship between men and women took the form of tribal traditions in Africa. In the great Asiatic cultures, they were derived from the regulations of the cosmic order. In the monotheistic cultures, they were an appropriate application of the model supplied by the Ten Commandments. They are being replaced today by a system of norms that presupposes a total sexual freedom. At the same time, its primary concern is to lay down the maximum size for the world's population and to prescribe the technical means that must be made available. A similar tendency presides at the great conferences on world climate. In both cases, the search for norms is prompted by fear that world reserves will be pressed beyond their limits. In both cases, the participants desire to defend the freedom of human dealings with reality while also reducing the consequences of an unlimited exercise of this freedom.

The third type of large-scale international conferences, the summits at which the leading economic powers try to regulate the globalized economy, has become the ideological battlefield of the post-Communist period. On the one hand, technology and economics present themselves as vehicles that facilitate the radical freedom of man. On the other, their omnipresence, with their inherent norms, is now seen as a global dictatorship. And those who fight against this globalization employ an anarchic wildness that would almost suggest that they see the freedom to destroy as an essential part of human freedom as a whole.

The Task Facing Us

What does all this mean for the question about Europe? It means that a construction that aimed one-sidedly at the consolidation of economic power is now giving birth to a new kind of system of values, and we must examine to what extent this will serve our needs in the present and the future. The European Charter that was recently published could be called an attempt to find a middle path between this new canon of values and the classical values of European tradition. It will certainly prove helpful as an initial indication of the direction to be taken, although ambiguities on important points make it impossible to overlook the problems inherent in this kind of attempt at mediation between differing perspectives. We must carry out an examination of the urgent questions on the level of basic principles, but it is obvious that space does not permit me to do this here. All I wish to do is to try to formulate more precisely the issue at stake.

As we have seen, the fathers of European unification in the aftermath of the Second World War agreed that there was a basic compatibility between the moral heritage of Christianity and the moral heritage of the European Enlightenment. In the Enlightenment, the idea of autonomous reason led to a transformation of the biblical concept of God in another direction: God the Creator and Sustainer, who continuously maintains and guides the world, had become merely the initiator who "kicked off" the universe. The concept of revelation was eliminated. In many ways, Spinoza's formula *Deus sive natura* (God or nature") can be called characteristic of the Enlightenment vision. But this means that there was indeed faith in a kind of nature that bore the divine imprint and in the capacity of man to understand this nature and to evaluate it as making a rational claim upon him.

Marxism made a radical break with this faith. The world that exists is a product of evolution in which reason plays no role, and it is only man who can bring forth the rational world from the irrational raw material of reality. This, united to Hegel's philosophy of history, to the liberal dogma of progress, and to the socioeconomic interpretation generated by this dogma, led to the expectation of a classless society that would appear in the course of historical progress as the final product of the class struggle. This became ultimately the only normative moral idea: whatever serves to bring closer this state of salvation is good, and whatever opposes it is evil. Today, a second Enlightenment has not only moved on from the *Deus sive natura* but has also seen through the irrationality of the Marxist ideology of hope.

Instead of this, it postulates a rational future goal that bears the title "new world order" and is now meant to become the basic ethical norm. It shares with Marxism the evolutionistic idea that the world we encounter is the product of irrational chance and of its own inherent regular processes, which means that the world cannot bear any ethical directives in itself as the old idea of nature envisaged. The attempt to deduce rules for human conduct from the rules of evolution is widespread, but scarcely convincing. An increasing number of philosophers, such as Singer, Rorty, and Sloterdijk, are raising their voices to tell us that man has the right and the duty to construct the world anew in a rational manner. Hardly anyone questions the need for a new world order, which must be a world order of rationality. So far, so good. But what is "rational"?

The criterion of rationality is taken exclusively from the experience of technological production based on science. Rationality is oriented to functionality, to effectiveness, and to an increase in the quality of life for all. This entails a use —indeed a domination—of nature that is problematic in view of the dramatic environmental problems our world now faces. But man's domination of his own self nonchalantly takes ever greater steps toward the realization of Aldous Huxley's vision. Man is no longer to be born in an irrational manner but is to be produced rationally. Man as a product is subject to the control of man. Imperfect individuals must be weeded out; the path of planning and production must aim at the perfect man. Suffering must disappear, and life is to consist of pleasure alone.

Such radical visions remain rare and are mostly presented in milder forms. But more and more people agree with the maxim for conduct that says that man is permitted to do whatever he is able to do. When the world is understood in evolutionary terms, it is obvious that there cannot be absolute values; nothing is always bad, and nothing is always good. The only way to discern moral norms is to evaluate the various goods involved in a particular question. This, however, means that higher goals, such as the expectation of success in curing diseases, would justify even the abuse of man, provided only that the good one hopes for appears sufficiently great.

This leads to new forms of coercion and the emergence of a new ruling class. In the final analysis, it is those who possess the professional know-how and those who control the purse strings and the technical equipment who decide the fate of others. When scientists are told that they must not let their competitors get ahead of them in research, this itself becomes a coercive force from which there is no escape, and this coercion now dictates the direction of scientific research. In this situation, what advice can one give Europe and the world? The departure from every ethical tradition and the insistence that all that counts is technological rationality and the possibilities it opens up to us appear specifically European in this situation. But will not a world order with such foundations turn out to be a utopia of terror? Does not Europe—does not the world—need corrective elements drawn from its own tradition and from the great ethical traditions of mankind?

The inviolability of man ought to be an unassailed pillar of ethical regulations. We cannot trust one another and live together in peace unless man recognizes that he is an ultimate end, not a means to some other end, and unless we consequently regard other persons as sacred and inviolable. There is no evaluation of goods that could justify treating man as experimental material for higher purposes. We act ethically—not on the basis of calculations—only when we see this as an absolute principle that stands higher than all evaluations of goods. The inviolability of human dignity also entails that this dignity belongs to every man, to each individual who has a human face and belongs biologically to the human species. Functional criteria cannot possess any validity here: the suffering, handicapped, or unborn human being is a human being. I should like to add that this must be linked to respect for the origin of man in the sexual union of man and woman: man may not become a product. He may not be produced, but only begotten. And this is why one of the constant elements of every humane society is the protection of the special dignity of the fellowship of man and woman on which the future of the human race depends.

All this is possible only if we acquire a new sensitivity to the dignity of suffering. Learning to live also means learning to suffer. This is why reverence for that which is holy is also essential. Faith in the Creator God is the surest guarantee of human dignity. Faith cannot be imposed on anyone, but since it represents a great good for society, it is entitled to claim reverence even on the part of nonbelievers.

It is correct to affirm that rationality is a basic characteristic of the European spirit, thanks to which this spirit has conquered the world—for it is the form of rationality that first emerged in Europe that influences life on all the continents today. But this rationality can turn destructive if it cuts itself off from its roots and makes technological ability the only criterion of conduct. It is vital that it remain connected to the two great sources of knowledge, nature and history. Neither realm simply imparts information, but both can suggest directions. Nature resists unbridled consumption, and this is why the state of the environment has prompted new reflections on the direction that nature itself indicates. The lordship over nature of which the biblical creation narrative speaks does not mean a violent exploitation of nature but, rather, an understanding of nature's inherent possibilities. This suggests a caution in the way in which we serve nature and nature serves us.

The beginning of human life is both a natural and a human process. In the sexual union of man and woman, the natural and the intellectual elements unite to form that which is specifically human, and one ignores this at one's peril. The historical experiences of man, which have been reflected in the great religions, are an abiding source of knowledge and provide directives for reason that apply even to those who do not identify with any one of these traditions. The attempt to think and to live without any contact with these great traditions would be an arrogance that ultimately leaves man helpless and empty.

My remarks do not amount to a conclusive answer to the question of the foundations on which Europe is to be built. All I have sought to do is to sketch the task that faces us. We must not delay in getting to work on it.

16

Why Europe Exists: Secularity and Secularism Yesterday, Today, Tomorrow

Europe—what is it exactly? This question was asked again and again, expressly, by Józef Cardinal Glemp in one of the language circles of the Synod of Bishops on Europe: Where does Europe begin, and where does it end? Why, for example, does Siberia not belong to Europe, even though it, too, is inhabited by Europeans, whose way of thinking and living is, furthermore, quite European? And where do the frontiers of Europe disappear to the south of the community of peoples called Russia? And along what line of demarcation does its boundary run in the Atlantic Ocean? Which islands are Europe, and which ones are not, and why not? In those meetings it became perfectly clear that *Europe* is a geographical concept only in a way that is entirely secondary. Europe is not a continent that can be comprehended neatly in geographical terms; rather, it is a cultural and historical concept.

1. The Rise of Europe

This becomes quite clear if we try to go back to the origins of Europe. Those who speak about the origin of Europe usually cite Herodotus (ca. 484–425 B.C.), who is no doubt the first to be acquainted with Europe as a geographical concept; he defines it as follows: "For Asia, with all the various tribes of barbarians that inhabit it, is regarded by the Persians as their own; but Europe and the Greek race they look on as distinct and separate."[1] The boundaries of Europe itself are not specified, but it is clear that lands that today are the nucleus of modern Europe lay entirely outside of the area considered by the ancient historian. Indeed, with the establishment of the Hellenistic states and the Roman Empire, a *continent* had been formed which became the basis for later Europe, although it displayed entirely different boundaries: these were the lands surrounding the Mediterranean, which by virtue of their cultural ties, by dint of trade and commerce, and by reason of their common political system formed all together a true and proper *continent*. Only the triumphant advance of Islam in the seventh and at the beginning of the eighth century drew a boundary across the Mediterranean and, so to speak, cut it in half, so that all that had been one continent until then was thenceforward subdivided into three continents: Asia, Africa, and Europe.

In the East, the transformation of the world of antiquity took place more slowly than in the West: the Roman Empire with Constantinople as its center held out there—although under increasing pressure on its frontiers—until the fifteenth century.[2] Whereas around the year 700 the southern part of the Mediterranean fell completely outside of what had hitherto been a cultural continent, one notes at the same time an ever more vigorous extension toward the north. The *limes*, which until then had been a continental

[1] Herodotus, *History*, bk. 1, chap. 4, quoted from *The History of Herodotus*, trans. George Rawlinson, in *Brittanica Great Books*, vol. 5 (Chicago: Encyclopaedia Britannica, 1990), 2.

[2] An incisive and wide-ranging look at the formation of Europe, both in the geographic sense and as a system of values, is found in *Divergent Christendoms: The Emergence of a Christian Europe, 200–1000 A.D.*, 8th ed. (Oxford: Wiley-Blackwell, 1995).

boundary line, disappears and opens up toward a new historical space that embraces Gaul, Germany, Britain as lands forming a true and proper nucleus, and it extends ever farther toward Scandinavia. In this process of displacing boundaries, the conceptual continuity with the preceding Mediterranean continent, although measured geographically in different terms, was assured by a theological interpretation of history: in connection with the Book of Daniel, the Roman Empire—renewed and transformed by the Christian faith—was considered to be the final and permanent kingdom in the history of the world in general, and therefore the association of peoples and states that was taking shape was defined as the permanent *Sacrum Imperium Romanum* [Holy Roman Empire].

This process of a new historical and cultural definition was completed quite deliberately during the reign of Charlemagne, and here the ancient name of Europe emerged once again, in a significant variation: this term was now used precisely to designate the kingdom of Charlemagne, and it expressed simultaneously the awareness of the novelty and the continuity with which the new association of states presented itself as the political power in charge of the future. In charge of the future because it considered itself to be in continuity with the history of the world thus far and ultimately to be rooted in what lasts forever [3]

Expressed in the self-understanding that was developing in this way was an awareness of being definitive and at the same time an awareness of having a mission.

It is true that the concept of Europe almost disappeared again after the end of the Carolingian rule and was preserved

[3] Cf. H. Gollwitzer, "Europa, Abendland", in *Historisches Wörterbuch der Philosophie*, ed. J. Ritter, vol. 2 (Basel: Schwabe, 1971), 824–26; F. Prinz, *Von Konstantin zu Karl dem Grossen* (Düsseldorf: Artemis und Winkler, 2000).

only in the language of the learned; it passed into the popular language only at the beginning of the modern era—no doubt in connection with the threat from the Turks, as a means of self-identification—and it became generally accepted in the eighteenth century. Independently of this history of the term "Europe", the establishment of the kingdom of the Franks, as the Roman Empire that had declined and was now reborn, signifies, indeed, a decisive step toward what we mean today when we speak of Europe.[4]

Of course we cannot deny that there is also a second root of Europe, of a non-Western Europe: as already noted, the Roman Empire in Byzantium had effectively resisted the storms of migrating peoples and of Islamic invasion. Byzantium always understood itself to be the true Rome; here, in fact, the Empire had never declined, which was why it continued to assert a claim in its disputes with the other, western half of the empire. This eastern Roman Empire, too, extended farther to the north, until it reached the Slavic world, and it created its own Greco-Roman world, which differs from the Latin Europe of the West in its liturgy, its ecclesiastical constitution, its alphabet, and by its renunciation of Latin as the language of the learned.

To be sure, there are still sufficient unifying elements to make one continent out of these two worlds: in the first place, their common heritage of the Bible and of the early Church, which in both worlds, furthermore, refers beyond itself to a place of origin that now lay outside of Europe, namely, in Palestine; then the same idea of empire, their common basic understanding of the Church, and hence also the common fund of ideas concerning law and legal instruments; finally, I should mention also monasticism, which among

[4] Cf. Gollwitzer, "Europa, Abendland", 826.

the great movements of history had remained the essential guarantor not only of cultural continuity, but above all of fundamental religious and moral values, of man's awareness of his ultimate destiny; and as a force prior and superior to political authority, it became the source of the rebirths that were necessary again and again.[5]

At the very heart of this common and essential ecclesial heritage, there was nevertheless a profound difference between the two Europes. Endre von Ivánka in particular has underscored its importance: in Byzantium the empire and the Church appear to be identified with each other; the emperor is the head of the Church as well. He understood himself as the representative of Christ, and in connection with the figure of Melchizedek, who was at the same time a king and a priest (Gen 14:18), he bore the official title of "king and priest" from the sixth century on.[6] Due to the fact that, starting with Constantine, the emperor had departed from Rome, it was possible in the old capital of the empire for the bishop of Rome to develop an autonomous position as the successor of Peter and supreme pastor of the Church. As early as the beginning of the Constantinian era, a duality of powers was taught there: in fact, the emperor and the pope had separate powers; neither one had complete authority. Pope Gelasius I (492–496) formulated the Western view in his famous letter to Emperor Anastasius and even more clearly in his fourth treatise, in which, contrary to the Byzantine typology of Melchizedek, he emphasizes that the

[5] From the wealth of literature on monasticism, I cite here only these: H. Fischer, *Die Geburt der westlichen Zivilisation aus dem Geist des romanischen Mönchtums* (Munich: Kösel, 1969); F. Prinz, *Askese und Kultur. Vor- und frühbenediktinisches Mönchtum an der Wiege Europas* (Munich: Beck, 1980).

[6] E. von Ivánka, *Rhomäerreich und Gottesvolk* (Freiburg-Munich: K. Alber, 1968).

union of the powers was found exclusively in Christ: "He, indeed, because of human weakness (pride!), separated the two ministries for the following ages, so that no one might become proud" (chap. 11). For matters concerning eternal life the Christian emperors needed the priests (*pontifices*), and the latter, in turn, abided by the imperial ordinances in the course of temporal affairs. In worldly matters, the priests had to follow the laws of the emperor who has been placed in office by a divine decree, whereas he must submit to the priest in sacred matters.[7] Thereby a separation and distinction of powers was introduced, which became extremely important in the subsequent development of Europe and which laid the foundations, so to speak, for what is distinctively typical of the West.

Since the totalitarian impulse always remained alive in both parties, despite this distinction, along with the desire to place one's own power above the other, this principle of

[7] Primary sources and secondary literature can be found in U. Duchrow, *Christenheit und Weltverantwortung* (Stuttgart: Klett, 1970), 328ff. There is a wealth of material on this subject in Hugo Rahner, *Church and State in Early Christianity*, trans. Leo Donald David (San Francisco: Ignatius Press, 1992). Stephan Horn brought to my attention an important passage by Leo the Great contained in a letter dated May 22, 452, from the pope to the emperor, in which he refutes the famous canon 28 of Chalcedon (concerning the primatial position of Constantinople vis-à-vis Rome, based on the presence of the seat of the Empire in the former city): "Habeat sicut optamus Constantinopolitana civitas gloriam suam, et protegente Dei dextera diuturno clementiae vestrae fruatur imperio, alia tamen ratio est rerum saecularium alia divinarum, nec praeter illam petram quam Dominus in fundamento posuit stabilis erit ulla constructio." ["We wish that the city of Constantinople may have its proper glory and, under the protection of God's right hand, might enjoy the perpetual rule of your clemency; nevertheless the scheme of worldly things is different from that of things divine, nor will there be any lasting building apart from that rock which the Lord placed as the foundation."] On this problem see also A. Grillmeier and H. Bacht, ed., *Das Konzil von Chalkedon*, vol. 2, *Entscheidung um Chalkedon* (Würzburg: Echter, 1953), 433–58, 491–562.

separation also became the source of infinite sufferings. The correct way of seeing and applying it, politically and from a religious perspective, still remains a fundamental problem for the Europe of today and tomorrow.

2. At the Turn of the Modern Era

If on the basis of what has been said here we can consider the rise of the Carolingian Empire, on the one hand, and the continuation of the Roman Empire in Byzantium and its mission to the Slavic people, on the other, as the true and proper birth of the *continent* of Europe, the beginning of the modern era meant a turning point for both Europes, a radical change that concerns both the nature of this continent and its geographic contours.

In 1453 Constantinople was conquered by the Turks. O. Hiltbrunner comments laconically on this event: "The last . . . scholars emigrated . . . to Italy and transmitted to the humanists of the Renaissance their knowledge of the original Greek texts; but the East sank into an absence of culture."[8] This statement is formulated in a way that is a bit too harsh, for in fact even the reign of the Ottoman dynasty had its culture; but it is true that the Greco-Christian, *European* culture of Byzantium came to an end. Thus one of the two wings of Europe was in danger of disappearing as a result, but the Byzantine heritage was not dead. Moscow declared itself to be the Third Rome and now founded its own patriarchate based on the notion of a second *translatio imperii* [transfer of the seat of the empire], thus presenting itself as a new metamorphosis of the *Sacrum Imperium* [Holy

[8] O. Hiltbrunner, *Kleines Lexikon der Antike* (Bern-Munich: Francke, 1950), 102.

Empire], as a distinct form of Europe, which nonetheless remained united with the West and was increasingly oriented to it, until Peter the Great attempted to turn it into a Western country. This displacement of Byzantine Europe toward the north brought with it the development that now the boundaries of the continent, too, began to move extensively toward the east. Determining the Ural Mountains as the boundary is completely arbitrary; in any case, the region to the east of them became more and more a sort of substructure of Europe, being neither Asia nor Europe, substantially shaped by the acting subject Europe, without participating itself, however, in its subject character; instead, it was an object and not responsible for its own history. Perhaps that describes, in summary form, the nature of a colonial state.

With regard to Byzantine (not Western) Europe at the beginning of the modern era, therefore, we can speak of a twofold development: on the one hand, there was the dissolution of ancient Byzantium in its historical continuity with the Roman Empire; on the other hand this second Europe obtained in Moscow a new center and expanded its borders to the east, so as to set up finally in Siberia a sort of preliminary colonial structure.

During that same period, we can note in the West also a twofold process with a remarkable historic significance. A large part of the Germanic world separated itself from Rome; a new, *enlightened* form of Christianity arose, so that henceforth a line of demarcation ran through the *West*, which clearly formed another cultural *limes*, a *boundary* between two different ways of thinking and interrelating. Of course, within the Protestant world there was a break, in the first place between Lutherans and the Reformed churches (which includes Methodists and Presbyterians), while the Church of England attempted to devise a middle way between Catholics and Evangelicals; to this was added later the difference between Christianity in the form of a State church, which became typical of Europe, and the free churches that found refuge in North America—a subject to which we will have to return in our discussion.

For now, let us examine the second event, which is essential to the character of the modern era, as opposed to the situation in what at one time was Latin [that is, Western] Europe: the discovery of America. To the expansion of Europe toward the east, thanks to the progressive extension of Russia toward Asia corresponds the transplanting of Europe outside of its geographical boundaries in the world beyond the Atlantic Ocean, which is now called America. The subdivision of Europe into a Latin-Catholic half and a Germanic-Protestant half was transferred to this part of the earth occupied by Europe and had its repercussions there. America, too, became at first an extension of Europe, a *colony*, but it established its own character as an acting subject at the time of the uprising in Europe that resulted from the French Revolution. From the nineteenth century on, America, although profoundly shaped by its European origins, nevertheless has stood opposite Europe as a distinct subject.

In our attempt to discover the deeper, more interior identity of Europe through this historical survey, we have looked now at two fundamental turning points in history: first, the disintegration of the old Mediterranean continent under the influence of the continent of the *Sacrum Imperium*, located farther to the north, in which *Europe* took shape beginning with the Carolingian period as a Latin and Western world; alongside this was the continuation of the old Rome in Byzantium, with its extension toward the Slavic world. The second transition that we have observed was the fall of Byzantium and, on the one hand, the subsequent movement of the Christian idea of empire toward the north and the east and, on the other hand, the internal division of Europe into two worlds, one Germanic and Protestant and the other Latin and Catholic, and furthermore the emigration to America, to which this division was transferred and which ultimately established itself as an independent historical subject that stood opposite Europe. Now we must take into consideration a third turning point, for which the French Revolution was the signal light seen around the world. It is true that the Holy Roman Empire, as a political reality, was already thought to be falling apart from the late medieval period on and had become increasingly fragile, even as a valid and unquestionable interpretation of history, but only now [in the late eighteenth century] did this spiritual framework go to pieces formally as well—that spiritual framework without which Europe could not have been formed. This was a process of considerable importance, both from the political and from the conceptual point of view. In the realm of ideas, this meant that the sacred foundation for history and for the existence of the State was rejected; history was no longer gauged on the basis of an idea of a pre-existent God who shaped it; the State was henceforth considered in purely secular terms, founded on reason and on the will of the citizens.

For the very first time in history, a purely secular State arose, which abandoned and set aside the divine guarantee and the divine ordering of the political sector, considering them a mythological world view, and it declared God himself to be a private affair that did not play a role in public life or the formation of the popular will. The latter was seen now solely as a matter of reason, by which God did not appear to be clearly knowable; religion and faith in God belonged to the realm of feelings and not to that of reason. God and his will ceased to be relevant in public life.

In this way, a new type of schism arose at the end of the eighteenth and the beginning of the nineteenth century, the seriousness of which we now perceive more and more clearly. There is no German word for it, because in that part of Europe it spread more slowly. In the Romance languages, it is described as a division between *Christians* and *secular persons* [Italian, *laici*, French, *laïcs*: "laymen"]. This rift ran through the Latin nations during the last two centuries as a deep breach, whereas Protestant Christianity at first had no trouble allowing room within itself for liberal and Enlightenment ideas, without that necessarily destroying the framework of a broad, basic Christian consensus. The former idea of power disappeared, yielding to a political realism consisting of a recognition of the fact that now nations and states had become identifiable as such through the formation of uniform linguistic regions and that these appeared as the unique and true subjects of history and therefore attained a status higher than they had had previously. The subject of history was now plural, and the explosive and dramatic consequences of this are evident in the fact that the great European nations considered themselves entrusted with a universal mission, which necessarily led to conflicts among them, the deadly impact of which we have painfully experienced in the century that just ended.

3. The Universalization of European Culture and Its Crises

Finally, we must also consider here a later process by which the history of the last several centuries clearly crossed over into a new world. Whereas the two halves of the old Europe, before the modern era, had known essentially only one opponent that it had to confront in a life-or-death battle, namely, the Islamic world, and whereas the advent of the modern era had brought the expansion toward America and toward parts of Asia that did not have their own large autonomous cultural units, now emigration began toward the two continents that until then had been only marginally affected: Africa and Asia, and now there was likewise an attempt to turn them into annexes of Europe, into *colonies*. To a certain extent this, too, was successful, inasmuch as Asia and Africa today follow the ideal of a world shaped by technology and material comforts, so that there, too, the ancient religious traditions are facing a crisis, and strains of purely secular thought are dominating public life more and more.

But there is also a contrary effect: the rebirth of Islam is not only connected with the new material wealth of Islamic countries; it is also nourished by the awareness that Islam is capable of offering a valid spiritual basis for the life of the peoples, a basis that seems to have slipped out of the hands of old Europe, which thus, notwithstanding its continued political and economic power, is increasingly viewed as a declining culture condemned to fade away.

The great religious traditions of Asia, too, especially its mystical element, which finds expression in Buddhism, are rising as spiritual powers in contrast to a Europe that is denying its religious and moral foundations. The optimism concerning the triumph of the European way that Arnold Toynbee was still able to maintain at the beginning of the 1960s today seems strangely outdated: "Of the twenty-eight cultures that we have identified . . . eighteen are dead and nine of the ten left—i.e., all except our own—appear to be mortally wounded."[9] Who would repeat those same words today? And what, in the first place, *is* this culture of ours that has remained? Is European culture perhaps the civilization of technology and commerce that has spread victoriously through the entire world? Or maybe that was born, instead, from the end of that ancient European culture as a post-European phenomenon. I see here a paradoxical coincidence: with the triumph of the post-European technological-secular world, with the globalization of its way of life and its manner of thinking, one gets the impression everywhere in the world, but especially in the strictly non-European worlds of Asia and Africa, that the very world of European values—the things upon which Europe bases its identity, its culture and its faith—has arrived at its end and has actually already left the scene; that now the hour has come for the value systems of other worlds, of pre-Columbian America, of Islam, of Asian mysticism.

Europe, precisely in this hour of its greatest success, seems to have become hollowed out, paralyzed in a certain sense by a crisis of its circulatory system, a crisis that endangers its life, which depends, so to speak, on transplants, which then, however, cannot help undermining its identity. This interior dwindling of the spiritual strength that once supported it is accompanied by the fact that Europe appears to be on the way out ethnically as well.

There is a strange lack of will for the future. Children, who are the future, are seen as a threat to the present; it is thought that they take away something of our life. They are

[9] Arnold Joseph Toynbee, *A Study of History*, vol. 2, *Geneses of Civilizations* (London: Oxford University Press, 1954), quoted in *Hugo Rahner: Sein geschichtstheologisches Denken*, by J. Holdt (Paderborn: Schöningh, 1997), 53. In particular Holdt's section entitled "Philosophical Meditation on the West" (52–61) furnishes important materials for the question concerning Europe.

perceived, not as a hope, but rather as a limitation on the present. This invites a comparison with the decline of the Roman Empire: it was still functioning as a great historical context, but in practice it was already living off of those who would eventually break it up, because it no longer had any vital energy of its own.

With that we have arrived at the problems of the present day. Concerning the possible future of Europe there are two contrasting diagnoses. On the one hand, there is the thesis of Oswald Spengler, who thought that he could ascertain among the great civilizations a sort of natural law: there is the moment of birth, the gradual growth, then the flowering of a culture, its slow decline, aging, and death. Spengler illustrates his thesis in an impressive manner, with documentation taken from the history of various cultures in which one can glimpse this law of natural development. His thesis was that the West has arrived at its final epoch, which runs inexorably toward the death of this cultural continent, despite all efforts to avert it. Naturally Europe can hand on its gifts to a new, emerging culture, as has already happened in preceding instances of the decline of a culture, but as a subject with its own identity, its heyday is already past.

This thesis, which was labeled "biologistic", met with impassioned opposition in the period between the two world wars, especially in Catholic circles; it was impressively countered by Arnold Toynbee, who relied, however, on presuppositions that do not find much of a hearing today.[10] Toyn-

[10] O. Spengler, *The Decline of the West*, trans. Charles Francis Atkinson (New York: Knopf, 1939). On the debate surrounding his thesis, see Holdt, *Hugo Rahner*, 13–17. Confronting Spengler's thought was also a recurring theme in the work of fundamental moral philosophy written during the period between the two wars by T. Steinbüchel, *Die philosophische Grundlegung der katholischen Sittenlehre*, 3rd ed. (Düsseldorf: Schwamm, 1947).

bee highlights the difference between material and technological progress, on the one hand, and real progress, on the other, which he defines as spiritualization. He admits that the West—the *Western world*—is in the midst of a crisis, the cause of which he sees in the fact that it has fallen from religion to the worship of technology, of the nation, of militarism. Ultimately the crisis for him is one of secularism.

If we know the cause of the crisis, it is possible also to show the way to a cure: we have to reintroduce the religious factor, which comprises, in his opinion, the religious heritage of all cultures, but especially "what has remained of Western Christianity".[11] In contrast to the biologistic view, he proposes a voluntaristic view that places its bets on the powers of creative minorities and on exceptional individuals.

The question that arises is: Is this diagnosis correct? And if so, is it within our power to reintroduce the religious element, in a synthesis of residual Christianity and the religious heritage of mankind? Ultimately the question of who was right—Spengler or Toynbee—remains open, because we cannot see into the future. But independently of that debate, we are obliged to ask ourselves what can guarantee the future and what is capable of keeping alive the intrinsic identity of Europe through all the historical metamorphoses. Or to put it even more simply: What is there, today and tomorrow, that promises human dignity and a life in conformity with it?

To find an answer, we must turn our attention once again to the present day and at the same time keep in mind its historical roots. In the preceding discussion, we stopped at the French Revolution and the nineteenth century. At that

[11] Cf. Holdt, *Hugo Rahner*, 54.

time, two new *European* models in particular had developed. In the Latin nations [that is, where the Romance languages were spoken] there was the laicist model: the State was quite distinct from the religious organizations, which were relegated to the private sphere. The State itself renounced any religious basis and claimed to be founded solely on reason and on its own intuitions. When confronted with the frailty of reason, these systems have proved to be fragile and have easily fallen victim to dictatorships; they survive, actually, only because parts of the old moral consciousness continue to exist, even without the previous social foundations, making possible a basic moral consensus. On the other hand, in the Germanic [and Anglo-Saxon] world, there are different models of Church and State, derived from liberal Protestantism; in them an enlightened Christian religion, essentially understood as morality—together with forms of worship guaranteed by the State—assured a moral consensus and a broad religious foundation, to which the faiths other than the State religion had to conform. This model in Great Britain, in the Scandinavian states, and at first even in Germany ruled by the Prussians, for a long time assured national and social cohesiveness. In Germany, however, the collapse of the Christianity of the Prussian State created a void, which then also left room for a dictatorship. Today State churches everywhere have suffered from attrition: religious bodies derived from the State no longer provide any moral force, whereas the State itself cannot create moral force but, rather, must presuppose it and build upon it.

Somewhere between these two models we find the United States of America, which, on the one hand—formed on the basis of free churches—started out from a rigid dogma of [Church-State] separation. On the other hand, beyond the particular denominations, the nation was shaped nonetheless by a basic Protestant Christian consensus that was not hammered out in doctrinal-confessional terms, but was associated with a special awareness of its mission, in its dealings with the rest of the world, as a religious example and thus gave significant public weight to the religious factor, which as a prepolitical and suprapolitical force managed to have influence on political life. Of course we cannot overlook here the fact that in the United States, too, the disintegration of the Christian heritage advances unceasingly, while at the same time the rapid increase of the Hispanic population and the presence of traditional religions from all parts of the world complete the picture. Perhaps we should observe here, too, that certain circles in the United States are giving plenty of support to the Protestantization of Latin America and thus promoting the break-up of the Catholic Church by means of free church structures; they are convinced that the Catholic Church is not in a position to guarantee a stable political and economic system and hence is incapable of functioning as a teacher of nations, whereas it is expected that the model of the free churches will make possible a moral consensus and a democratic formation of the public will, similar to those found in the United States. To complicate the picture further, it must be admitted that today the Catholic Church constitutes the largest religious community in the United States and that in her life of faith she stands up resolutely for her Catholic identity; yet with regard to the relationship between Church and politics, American Catholics have accepted the traditions of the free churches, in the sense that it is precisely a Church unaffiliated with the State that best guarantees the moral foundations of the whole society, so that promoting the democratic ideal appears to be a moral duty that is profoundly in keeping with the faith. In such a position we have good reason to see a continuation, adapted to the times, of the model of Pope Gelasius, of whom I spoke earlier.

Let us turn to Europe. To the two models about which I spoke before, a third was added in the nineteenth century, namely, socialism, which soon subdivided into two different paths, the totalitarian and the democratic. Starting from its initial premise, democratic socialism was able to become part of the two existing models, as a salutary counterbalance to the radical liberal positions, enriching and correcting them. It proved, furthermore, to be something that transcended denominational affiliations: in England, it was the party of the Catholics, who could not feel at home either in the Protestant-conservative camp or among the liberals. In Germany under Kaiser Wilhelm, too, many Catholic centrists felt closer to democratic socialism than to the rigidly Prussian and Protestant conservative forces. In many respects, democratic socialism was and is close to Catholic social doctrine; in any case, it contributed considerably toward the formation of a social consciousness.

The totalitarian model, in contrast, was associated with a rigidly materialistic and atheistic philosophy of history: history was understood deterministically as a process of advancement that passed through a religious and then a liberal phase so as to arrive at the absolute and definitive society, in which religion becomes a superfluous relic from the past and the business of material production and trade is able to guarantee happiness for all. The scientific appearance of this theory conceals an intolerant dogmatism: spirit is the product of matter; morals are the product of circumstances and must be defined and practiced, according to the goals of society: everything that fosters the coming of that final state of happiness and morality. Here the values that had built Europe are completely overturned. Even worse, there is a rupture here with the complex moral tradition of mankind: there are no longer any values apart from the goals of progress; at a given moment, everything can be permitted and even necessary, can be "moral" in a new sense of the word. Even man can become an instrument; the individual does not matter. The future alone becomes the terrible deity that rules over everyone and everything.

Meanwhile, the Communist systems have foundered, above all because of their false economic dogmatism. But too often people ignore the fact that the more fundamental reason for their shipwreck was their contempt for human rights, their subjection of morality to the demands of the system and to their promises for the future. The real catastrophe they left behind is not of an economic sort; it consists, rather, in the drying up of souls, in the destruction of moral conscience. I see as an essential problem in our day, for Europe and for the world, the fact that the economic failure is never disputed, and therefore the former Communists have become economic liberals almost without hesitation, whereas the moral and religious problem, which was really at stake, is almost completely dismissed. Nevertheless, the complex problems left behind by Marxism continue to exist today. The loss of man's primordial certainties about God, about himself, and about the universe—the loss of an awareness of intangible moral values—is still our problem, especially today, and it can lead to the self-destruction of the European consciousness, which we must begin to consider—independently of Spengler's vision of decline—as a real danger.[12]

[12] In this regard, we must cite the following words by E. Chargaff: "Where everyone is free to take the lion's share, for example in the free market, the result is the society of Marsia, a society of bloody corpses." E. Chargaff, *Ein zweites Leben. Autobiographische und andere Texte* (Stuttgart: Klett-Cotta, 1955), 168.

4. What Point Have We Reached Today?

Thus we find ourselves facing the question: Where do we go from here? In the violent upheavals of our time is there a European identity that has a future and to which we can commit ourselves with all our might? I am not prepared to enter into a detailed discussion of the future European Constitution. I would just like to note briefly the foundational moral elements that in my opinion should not be missing from it.

The first element is the "unconditional character" of human dignity and human rights, which must be presented as values that are prior to any governmental jurisdiction. These fundamental rights are not created by the legislator or conferred upon the citizens, "but rather they exist in their own right; they must always be respected by the legislator and are given to him previously as values of a higher order."[13] This validity of human dignity, prior to any political action or decision, is ultimately derived from the Creator: only God can establish values that are based on the nature of man and are inviolable. The fact that there are values that cannot be manipulated by anyone is the real guarantee of our liberty and of human greatness: Christian faith sees in this the mystery of the Creator and of the status that he has conferred upon man as the image of God.

Now today almost nobody will deny outright the precedence of human dignity and fundamental human rights over any political decision; the horrors of Nazism and of its racist theory are still too recent. But within the pragmatic sphere of so-called progress in medicine, there are very real threats to

[13] G. Hirsch, "Ein Bekenntnis zu den Grundwerten", *Frankfurter Allgemeine Zeitung*, October 12, 2000.

these values: whether we think of cloning or of the preservation of human fetuses for the purpose of research and organ donation or of the whole field of genetic manipulation—no one can mistake the gradual atrophy of respect for human dignity that threatens us here. Added to this is a burgeoning traffic in human persons, new forms of slavery, and trafficking in human organs for transplantation. *Good ends* are always adduced to justify the unjustifiable.

In summary: to establish in writing the value and dignity of man, of liberty, equality, and solidarity, along with the fundamental declarations of democracy and of a State governed by law, implies an image of man, a moral option, and a concept of law that are by no means obvious but that are actually fundamental factors in the identity of Europe. These constitutive elements, along with their concrete consequences, ought to be guaranteed in the future European Constitution; certainly they can be defended only if a corresponding moral consciousness is continually formed anew.

A second area in which the European identity appears is marriage and the family. Monogamous marriage, as a fundamental structure of the relation between man and woman and at the same time as the basic cell in the formation of the larger community, was modeled on the basis of biblical faith. This gave Europe, both in the West and in the East, its particular face and its particular humanity, also and especially because the pattern of fidelity and self-denial depicted there had to be won again and again, by many toils and sufferings. Europe would no longer be Europe if this fundamental cell of its social edifice were to disappear or if its nature were to be changed. We all know how marriage and the family are threatened—on the one hand, by the voiding of its indissolubility as a result of increasingly easy forms of divorce, and, on the other hand, through a new kind of behavior that is becoming ever more widespread: the cohabitation of a man and a woman without the legal form of marriage. In tawdry contrast with all that is the demand for domestic partnerships between homosexuals, who now paradoxically are demanding a legal form that would have to be equated more or less with marriage. This trend departs completely from the moral history of mankind, which, despite all the diversity in the legal form of marriage, nevertheless always recognized that said marriage, by its very nature, is the exclusive association of a man and a woman that is open to children and thus to the family. Here we are dealing, not with discrimination, but with the question of what the human person is, as man or as woman, and of how the common life of man and woman can acquire a legal form. If, on the one hand, their living together becomes increasingly detached from juridical forms and, on the other hand, homosexual unions are seen more and more as having the same status as marriage, then we are confronted with a disintegration of the image of man, which can only have extremely serious consequences.

My final point is the religious question. I do not wish to enter here into the complex discussions of the last few years. I would like, instead, to highlight just one aspect that is fundamental to all cultures: respect for what is sacred to someone else and, in particular, respect for the sacred in the more exalted sense, for God, something that we are allowed to expect even in a person who is not disposed to believe in God. Where this respect is violated, something essential in a society is lost. In our society today, thank God, anyone who dishonors the faith of Israel, its image of God, or its great personages is censured. Anyone who insults the Qur'an and the fundamental beliefs of Islam is censured, too. On the other hand, where Christ and what is sacred to Christians are concerned, suddenly freedom of opinion appears to be the highest good, and to limit it would be to endanger tolerance and freedom in general or to destroy them outright. Freedom of opinion, however, discovers its limit in the fact that it cannot destroy the honor and the dignity of someone else; denying or destroying human rights is not freedom.

Here we notice a self-hatred in the Western world that is strange and that can be considered pathological; yes, the West is making a praiseworthy attempt to be completely open to understanding foreign values, but it no longer loves itself; from now on it sees in its own history only what is blameworthy and destructive, whereas it is no longer capable of perceiving what is great and pure. In order to survive, Europe needs a new—and certainly a critical and humble—acceptance of itself, that is, if it *wants* to survive. Multiculturalism, which is continually and passionately encouraged and promoted, is sometimes little more than the abandonment and denial of what is one's own, flight from one's own heritage. But multiculturalism cannot exist without shared constants, without points of reference based on one's own values. It surely cannot exist without respect for what is sacred. Part of it is approaching respectfully the things that are sacred to others, but we can do this only if what is sacred, God himself, is not foreign to us. Of course, we can and must learn from what is sacred to others, but given this encounter with others and precisely for those others it is our duty to nourish within ourselves a respect in the presence of what is sacred and to manifest the face of God who has appeared to us: the God who has compassion on the poor and the weak, on the widows and the orphans, on the stranger; the God who is so humane that he himself became man, a suffering man, who by suffering together with us gives dignity and hope to pain.

If we do not do this, we not only deny the identity of Europe, but we also deprive others of a service to which they have a right. For the cultures of the world, the absolute secularity that has been taking shape in the West is something profoundly foreign. They are convinced that a world without God has no future. And so multiculturalism itself calls us to come to our senses and to look deep within ourselves again.

We do not know how things will go in Europe in the future. The Charter of Fundamental Rights [of the European Union] may be a first step, a sign that Europe is consciously looking again for its soul. In this regard, we must say that Toynbee was correct, that the destiny of a society always depends on creative minorities. Believing Christians should think of themselves as one such creative minority and contribute to Europe's recovery of the best of its heritage and thus to the service of all mankind.

17

Europe in the Crisis of Cultures

Conferral of the "Saint Benedict Prize"
Saint Scholastica Monastery,
Subiaco, April 1, 2005

We are experiencing a moment of great dangers and great opportunities for mankind and for the world, which is also a moment of great responsibility for all of us. During the past century, man's possibilities and his dominion over matter grew to a truly unthinkable extent. But his power to control the world also meant that his power of destruction had reached dimensions that sometimes make us shudder in horror. In this connection, the threat of terrorism spontaneously comes to mind: this new war without limits and without fronts. The fear that it may soon take possession of nuclear and biological weapons is not unfounded, and, as a result, constitutional states have had to resort to security systems similar to those that previously existed in dictatorships; yet the feeling remains that, in reality, all these precautions can never be enough, since global surveillance is neither possible nor desirable. Less visible but no less disturbing are the potentials for self-manipulation that man has acquired. He has probed the innermost recesses of being, has deciphered the components of the human body, and now is capable, so to speak, of "constructing" a human being by himself, which then *comes into the world*, no longer as a gift of the Creator but, rather, as a product of our action, a product that, therefore, can also be selected according to requirements that we ourselves set. This man, therefore, reflects no longer the splendor of being an image of God—which is what confers on him his dignity and inviolability—but only the power of human capabilities. Now he is no more than the image of man—of what man? Then there are the major global problems: the inequality in the distribution of the goods of the earth, the growing poverty, or rather impoverishment, the exploitation of the earth and of its resources, hunger, the sicknesses that threaten everyone, the clash of cultures. All this shows that the growth of our potentials does not correspond to an equal development of our moral strength. Moral fortitude has not increased together with the development of science but, rather, has diminished, because the technological mentality confines morality to the subjective sphere, while we need precisely a public morality, a morality that is able to respond to the threats that weigh on the existence of us all. The real, most serious danger of this moment lies precisely in this imbalance between technological potential and moral strength. The security that we need as a prerequisite for our freedom and dignity cannot come in the final analysis, from technological systems of control but can spring only and precisely from man's moral fortitude: where this is lacking or insufficient, the power that man has will be transformed more and more into a power of destruction.

It is true that today there is a new moralism whose key words are justice, peace, conservation of the environment—words that recall essential moral values that we truly need. But this moralism remains vague and thus slips almost inevitably into the political-partisan sphere. It is, above all, a demand addressed to others and too little a personal duty of our everyday life. Indeed, what does justice mean? Who defines it? What serves the cause of peace? In recent decades, we have seen extensively in our streets and on our squares how pacifism can veer off toward destructive anarchism and terrorism. The political moralism of the 1970s, the roots of which are not entirely dead, was a moralism that succeeded in fascinating even young people who were full of ideals. But it was a misdirected moralism, inasmuch as it was devoid of serene rationality and because, in the final analysis, it put the political utopia above the dignity of the individual human being, showing also that it could go so far as to despise man in the name of great objectives. Political moralism, as we experienced it and are still experiencing it, not only opens the path to regeneration but also blocks the way. The same is true, consequently, about a form of Christianity and a theology that reduce the core of Jesus' message, the "Kingdom of God", to "values of the Kingdom", identifying these values with the great watchwords of political moralism and proclaiming them, at the same time, as a synthesis of all religions. In this way, however, they forget God, even though he is precisely the subject and the cause of the Kingdom of God. In his place remain the great words (and values), which lend themselves to any sort of abuse whatsoever.

This brief look at the situation in the world leads us to reflect on the current situation of Christianity and, therefore, also on the foundations of Europe, the Europe that once was, we can say, the Christian continent, but has also been the point of departure for that new scientific rationality which has bestowed on us great opportunities and likewise great threats. Christianity certainly did not start from Europe, and therefore neither can it be classified as a European religion, the religion of the European cultural sphere. But precisely in Europe, it received its historically most effective cultural and intellectual stamp, and, therefore, it remains intertwined in a special way with Europe. On the other hand, it is also true that since the Renaissance period, and in a completed form since the days of the Enlightenment, this Europe developed precisely that scientific rationality which not only led to the geographical unity of the world and to the meeting of continents and of cultures during the age of discoveries, but now, much more profoundly, thanks to the technological culture made possible by science, truly leaves its imprint on the whole world, indeed, in a certain sense makes it uniform. And in the wake of this form of rationality, Europe has developed a culture that, in a way unknown to mankind before now, excludes God from public awareness, either because he is altogether denied or because his existence is deemed indemonstrable, uncertain, and therefore belonging to the sphere of subjective choices, something irrelevant to public life, however. This purely functional rationality, so to speak, has allowed an upheaval of the moral conscience that is likewise new for the cultures that have existed until now, since it maintains that only what can be proved experimentally is rational. Since morality belongs to an altogether different sphere, as a separate category, it vanishes and must be sought out some other way, insofar as it is necessary to admit that we need morality in some way. In a world based on calculation, the calculation of the consequences is what determines whether or not something should be considered moral. And thus the category of good disappears, as Kant had clearly pointed out. Nothing is good or bad in itself; everything depends on the foreseeable consequences of an action. Although Christianity, on the one hand, found its most effective form in Europe, we must also say, on the other hand, that in Europe a culture developed that is in absolute terms the most radical contradiction not only of Christianity but of the religious and moral traditions of mankind. This makes it clear that Europe is experiencing a true and proper "tension test"; it makes clear also the radical character of the tensions that our continent must confront. But this shows also and above all the responsibility that we Europeans must assume in this historical moment: at stake in the debate about the definition of Europe and its new political form is not some nostalgic "rearguard" battle of history, but rather a great responsibility for mankind today.

Let us take a more careful look at this antithesis between the two cultures that have marked Europe. In the debate over the Preamble of the European Constitution, this antithesis manifested itself in two controversial points: the question about referring to God in the constitution and the one about mentioning the Christian roots of Europe. Given that Article 52 of the constitution guarantees the institutional rights of the Churches, we have no reason to worry, they say. But this means that in the life of Europe, the Churches find a place in the sphere of political compromise, while in the sphere of the foundations of Europe, the mark left by their content finds no space at all. The reasons given in the public debate for this clear "no" are superficial, and it is obvious that rather than indicate the true motivation, they conceal it. The statement that any mention of the Christian roots of Europe hurts the feelings of the many non-Christians who are in Europe is not very convincing, given that we are talking primarily about a historical fact that no one can seriously deny. Naturally this historical mention contains also a reference to the present day, since, in mentioning the roots, we indicate the residual sources of moral orientation, and this is a factor in the identity of this structure that is Europe. Who would be offended? Whose identity would be threatened? The Muslims, whom commentators often like to bring into play in this regard, feel threatened, not by our Christian moral foundations, but by the cynicism of a secularized culture that denies its own foundations. And our Jewish fellow citizens, too, are not offended by the reference to the Christian roots of Europe, inasmuch as these roots go back as far as Mount Sinai: they bear the imprint of the voice that made itself heard on the mountain of God and unite us in the great fundamental orientations that the Decalogue gave to mankind. The same is true about the reference to God: the mention of God does not offend those who belong to other religions are offended, not by the mention of God, but rather by the attempt to construct the human community absolutely without God.

The motives for this twofold "no" are deeper than the alleged motives lead the public to think. They presuppose the idea that only the radical Enlightenment culture, which has reached its full development in our time, could be constitutive for European identity. Therefore, different religious cultures with their respective rights can coexist alongside it, provided and to the extent that they respect the criteria of the Enlightenment culture and subordinate themselves to it. This Enlightenment culture is essentially defined by liberty rights; it starts from freedom as a fundamental value that measures everything: freedom of religious choice, which includes the religious neutrality of the State; freedom to express one's own opinion, provided it does not call this same canon into question; the democratic ordering of the State, namely, parliamentary control over the state institutions; the freedom to form parties; an independent judiciary; and finally, protection of human rights and the prohibition of various forms of discrimination.

Here the canon is still being formed, since there are also

conflicting human rights, for example, in the case of the conflict between a woman's desire for freedom and the preborn child's right to life. The concept of discrimination is constantly being broadened, and thus the prohibition against discrimination can be transformed more and more into a limitation of freedom of opinion and of religious freedom. Very soon we will no longer be able to say, as the Catholic Church teaches, that homosexuality is an objective disorder in the development of a human life. And the fact that the Church is convinced that she has no right to confer priestly ordination on women is considered by some people until now irreconcilable with the spirit of the European Constitution. Obviously this canon of the Enlightenment culture, which is anything but definitive, contains important values that we, precisely as Christians, will not and cannot do without; yet it is likewise obvious that the ill-defined or not-at-all-defined concept of freedom that is at the basis of this culture inevitably involves contradictions; and it is obvious that, precisely on account of the use of this freedom (a use that seems radical), the concept involves limitations of freedom that we could not even have imagined a generation ago. A confused ideology of freedom leads to a dogmatism that is proving to be increasingly hostile toward freedom.

No doubt we will have to return again to the question of the internal contradictions in the current form of Enlightenment culture. But first we must finish describing it. Part of its nature, as a culture of reason that finally has a complete consciousness of itself, is to boast of a universal claim and to think of itself as complete in itself, not needing to be complemented in any way by other cultural factors. Both of these characteristics are clearly seen when one asks the question about who can become a member of the European

Community and, above all, in the debate about the entrance of Turkey into this community. We are talking about a State, or perhaps, rather, about a cultural sphere that does not have Christian roots but was influenced by Islamic culture. Ataturk then sought to transform Turkey into a laicist [secular, non-confessional] State, attempting to transplant the laicism that developed in the Christian world of Europe on a Muslim terrain. We might wonder whether this is possible; according to the thesis of the Enlightenment, laicist culture of Europe, only the norms and the contents of that same Enlightenment culture can determine the identity of Europe, and, consequently, any State that adopts these criteria can belong to Europe. It does not matter, ultimately, into what tangle of roots this culture of freedom and democracy is implanted. And for this very reason, it is declared that the roots cannot enter into the definition of the foundations of Europe, since we are talking about dead roots that are not part of its current identity. Consequently, this new identity that is determined exclusively by the Enlightenment culture also implies that God has nothing to do with the public life and with the foundations of the State.

So it all becomes logical, and even plausible in a way. Indeed, what better can we hope for if not that democracy and human rights will be respected everywhere? The question arises here, however, whether this laicist, Enlightenment culture really is the culture of a reason shared by all mankind, a culture that has been discovered to be finally universal, a culture that ought to have access everywhere, even on a soil that is historically and culturally different. And one wonders also whether it is truly complete in itself, so much so that it has no need of any root outside of itself.

Meaning and Limits of the Current Rationalist Culture

We must now address these last two questions. To the first—namely, to the question of whether mankind has reached a universally valid philosophy that has finally become altogether scientific, in which the reason common to all human beings is expressed—it is necessary to answer that no doubt we have arrived at important achievements that can claim some general validity: the achievement that religion cannot be imposed by the State, but that it can be accepted only in freedom; respect for fundamental human rights that are equal for all; the separation of powers and checks and balances on power. We cannot suppose, however, that these fundamental values, which we acknowledge as generally valid, can be put into practice in the same way in every historical context. Not all societies have the sociological prerequisites for a democracy based on political parties, as is the case in the West; thus, the complete religious neutrality of the State, in most historical contexts, should be considered an illusion. And with that we come to the problems raised by the second question. But let us clarify first the question of whether modern Enlightenment philosophies, considered as a whole, can claim to be the last word of the reason common to all mankind. These philosophies are characterized by the fact that they are positivistic and, therefore, anti-metaphysical, so much so that ultimately God can have no place in them. They are based on a self-limitation of positive reason, which is adequate in the technological sphere, although when it is generalized it involves a mutilation of man. It follows that man no longer admits any moral authority outside of his own calculations and, as we saw, even the concept of freedom, which at first might seem to expand in an unlimited way, finally leads to the self-destruction of freedom. It is true that the positivistic philosophies contain important elements of truth. These, however, are based on a self-limitation of reason typical of a definite cultural situation—that of the modern West—and as such certainly cannot be the last word of reason. Even though they seem totally rational, they are not the voice of reason itself, but, rather, they too are culturally conditioned, that is, bound up with the current situation in the West. Therefore, they are not quite the philosophy that one day should be valid throughout the world. But, above all, it is necessary to say that this Enlightenment philosophy and its respective culture are incomplete. They deliberately cut off their own historical roots, thus depriving themselves of the original forces from which they sprang, that fundamental memory of mankind, so to speak, without which reason loses its orientation. Indeed, now the principle holds that man's ability is the measure of his action. Whatever he knows how to do he can do, also. Nowadays, there is no such thing as know-how separated from capability, because that would be against freedom, which is absolutely the supreme value. But man knows how to do so much, and he knows how to do more and more; and if this know-how does not find its measure in a moral norm, it becomes a power for destruction, as we can already see. Man knows how to clone human beings and, therefore, does it. Man knows how to use human beings by "harvesting" their organs for other human beings and, therefore, does it; he does it because this would seem to be a requirement of his freedom. Man knows how to build atomic bombs and, therefore, does it, while in principle being ready to use them, too. Even terrorism, at bottom, is based on this kind of human "self-authorization" and not on the teachings of the Quran. The radical detachment of Enlightenment philosophy from its roots becomes, in the final analysis, a diminution of man. Man, basically, has no freedom, the spokesmen of the natural sciences tell us, diametrically contradicting the point of departure of the whole question. He must not believe that he is something different compared with all the other living beings, and therefore he, too, should be treated like them—so say the most avant-garde spokesmen of a philosophy that is clearly separated from the roots of mankind's historical memory.

We had asked ourselves two questions: whether rationalist (positivistic) philosophy is strictly rational and, consequently, universally valid, and whether it is complete. Is it self-sufficient? Can it or must it consign its historical roots to the past and, hence, to the sphere of what can be only subjectively valid? We must answer all these questions with a clear "no". This philosophy expresses human reason, not as a whole, but only a part of it, and by way of this mutilation of reason we cannot consider it entirely rational. Therefore, it is also incomplete and can be cured only by reestablishing once again its contact with its roots. A tree without roots withers. . . .

To state this is not to deny everything positive and important that this philosophy says, but rather it affirms its need for completeness, its profound incompleteness. And so once again we find ourselves talking about the two controversial points in the Preamble of the European Constitution. The setting aside of the Christian roots proves to be, not an expression of a superior tolerance that respects all cultures in the same way, unwilling to privilege any one of them, but rather an absolute insistence on one way of thinking and living that, among other things, is radically antithetical to all the other historical cultures of mankind. The real antithesis that characterizes today's world is not the one between various religious cultures, but the one between the radical emancipation of man from God, from the roots of life, on the one hand, and the major religious cultures, on the other. If it comes to a clash of cultures, it will not be because of the clash of the major religions—which have always struggled against one another but which, ultimately, have also always been able to live with one another—but it will be because of the clash between this radical emancipation of man and the great historical cultures. Thus, even the rejection of the reference to God is not an expression of a tolerance that is trying to protect the non-theistic religions and the dignity of atheists and agnostics but, rather, an expression of a conscience that would like to see God cancelled definitively from the public life of mankind and sequestered in the subjective sphere of cultures left over from the past. Relativism, which is the point of departure for all this, thus becomes a dogmatism that believes that it possesses the definitive knowledge of reason and has the right to consider all the rest as only a stage of humanity that has basically been surpassed and that can be suitably relativized. In reality this means that we need roots in order to survive and that we must not lose sight of God if we do not want human dignity to disappear.

The Lasting Significance of the Christian Faith

Is this a simple rejection of the Enlightenment and of modernity? Absolutely not. Christianity, from the beginning, has understood itself as the religion of the *logos*, as the religion according to reason. It did not primarily identify other religions as its precursors but, rather, that philosophical enlightenment which swept the path clear of the traditions so as to turn to the search for the truth and to the good, to the one God who is above all the gods. As a religion of the persecuted, as a universal religion, beyond the various states and peoples, it denied the State the right to consider religion as a part of the governmental order, thus claiming the freedom of the faith. It always defined men, all human beings without distinction, as creatures of God and the image of God, proclaiming that they had in principle the same dignity, although within the inescapable limits of the social orders [in which Christians lived]. In this sense, the Enlightenment is of Christian origin and by no accident arose precisely and exclusively within the sphere of the Christian faith. Whereas Christianity, against its nature, had unfortunately become a tradition and religion of the State. Even though philosophy, as the search for rationality—of our faith, also—had always been a prerogative of Christianity, the voice of reason had been domesticated too much. It was and is to the credit of the Enlightenment that it proposed again these original values of Christianity and restored to reason its own voice. Vatican Council II, in its Constitution on the Church in the Modern World, once again testified to this profound correspondence between Christianity and the Enlightenment, seeking to arrive at a true reconciliation between Church and modernity, which is the great heritage to be preserved by both parties.

In all this, both parties need to reflect on themselves and to be ready to correct themselves. Christianity must always remember that it is the religion of the *logos*. It is faith in the *Creator Spiritus*, in the Creator Spirit, from which all reality comes. This very tenet should be today its philosophical strength, inasmuch as the problem is whether the world comes from irrationality, and reason therefore is nothing but a "byproduct"—maybe even a harmful one—of its development, or whether the world comes from reason, and this is consequently its criterion and its goal. The Christian faith depends on this second thesis, thus having, from the purely philosophical perspective, truly good cards to play, even though the first thesis is considered today by many people the only "rational" and modern one. But a reason that sprang from the irrational and that, when all is said and done, is itself irrational is no solution to our problems. Only creative reason, which manifested itself as love in God crucified, can truly show us the way.

In the very necessary dialogue between secularists and Catholics, we Christians must take great care to remain faithful to this basic line: to live a faith that comes from the *Logos*, from creative reason, and that is therefore also open to everything that is truly rational. But at this point, in my capacity as a believer, I would like to make a proposal to the secularists. During the Enlightenment era an attempt was made to understand and define the essential moral norms by saying that they would be valid *etsi Deus non daretur*, even if God did not exist. Amid conflicting confessions and in the looming crisis of the image of God, this was an attempt to keep the essential values of morality separate from the contradictions and to seek for them an evident character that would make them independent of the multiple divisions and uncertainties of the various philosophies and confessions. Thus they tried to assure the foundations for coexistence and, more generally, the foundations of mankind. In that era this seemed possible, inasmuch as the great fundamental convictions created by Christianity for the most part endured and seemed undeniable. But that is no longer the case. The search for such a reassuring certainty, which could remain undisputed beyond all the differences, has failed. Not even the truly grandiose effort of Kant was capable of creating the necessary shared certainty. Kant had denied that God could be knowable in the sphere of pure reason but, at the same time, had presented God, freedom, and immortality as postulates of practical reason, without which (consistently enough) no moral action was possible in his opinion. Might the current situation of the world give us reason to think once more that he might have been right? I would like to make this point in different words: the attempt, taken to extremes, to shape human affairs by doing completely without God leads us more and more to the brink of the abyss, toward the total abolition of man. We ought, therefore, to turn the axiom of the Enlightenment thinkers on its head and say: even if we do not succeed in finding the way to accept God, we still ought to seek to live and to direct our lives *veluti si Deus daretur*, as though God existed. This is the advice that Pascal had already given to his non-believing friends; it is the advice that we would like to give today as well to our friends who do not believe. Thus no one is limited in his freedom, but all our affairs find a support and a criterion that they urgently need.

What we need above all at this moment in history are men and women who, through a faith that is enlightened and lived out, make God believable in this world. The negative testimony of Christians who spoke about God and lived contrary to him obscured the image of God and opened the door to disbelief. We need men and women who fix their sights on God, learning true humanity from that [*da lì*]. We need men and women whose intellects are enlightened by the light of God and to whom God opens his heart, so that their intellects can speak to the intellects of others and their hearts can open the hearts of others. Only through people who have been touched by God can God make a comeback among people. We need men like Benedict of Nursia who, in a time of dissipation and decadence, buried himself in the most extreme solitude and succeeded, after all the purifications that he had to undergo, in rising again to the light of day, returning and founding Montecassino, the city on the hill that, in the midst of so many ruins, put together the forces from which a new world was formed. Thus Benedict, like Abraham, became the father of many nations. The recommendations to his monks placed at the end of his Rule are directions that show us, too, the way that leads upward, away from the crises and the wreckage.

> Just as there is an evil zeal of bitterness that separates from God and leads to hell, so there is a good zeal that separates from vices and leads to God and to life eternal. By most fervent love, therefore, let monks exercise this zeal, that is, let them see to it that in honour they prefer one another. Let them most patiently tolerate their infirmities whether physical or of character . . . ; in chaste love let them exercise fraternal charity; let them fear God . . . ; on no account let them exalt anything above Christ; and may he bring us all alike to eternal life. (Chapter 72)

18

A New Europe: Address to the Participants in the Congress

Sponsored by the Commission of the Bishops' Conferences of the European Community (COMECE) Clementine Hall, March 24, 2007

Members of the College of Cardinals,
Venerable Brothers in the Episcopate,
Honorable Parliamentarians,
Ladies and Gentlemen!

I am happy to receive such a large number of persons at this particular audience taking place on the eve of the Fiftieth Anniversary of the Treaty of Rome, signed on 25 March 1957. This was an important step for Europe, exhausted by the Second World War and eager to build a future of peace and greater economic and social well-being without suppressing or denying its various national identities. I welcome the Most Reverend Adrianus Herman van Luyn, Bishop of Rotterdam, President of the Commission of the Bishops' Conferences of the European Community, and I express to him my gratitude for his kind words. I also offer greetings to the other prelates, to the distinguished authorities, and to all those taking part in this Convention organized by the COMECE as an invitation to reflect on Europe.

Since March 1957, this Continent has traveled a long road, which has led to the reconciliation of its two "lungs"—the

East and the West—linked by a common history, but arbitrarily separated by a curtain of injustice. Economic integration has stimulated political unification and encouraged the continuing and strenuous search for an institutional structure adequate for a European Union that already numbers 27 nations and aspires to become a global actor on the world scene.

During these years there has emerged an increasing awareness of the need to establish a healthy balance between the economic and social dimensions, through policies capable of producing wealth and increasing competitiveness, while not neglecting the legitimate expectations of the poor and the marginalized. Unfortunately, from a demographic point of view, one must note that Europe seems to be following a path that could lead to its departure from history. This not only places economic growth at risk; it could also create enormous difficulties for social cohesion and, above all, favor a dangerous form of individualism inattentive to future consequences. One could almost think that the European continent is in fact losing faith in its own future. As regards, for example, respect for the environment or the structured access to energy resources and investments, incentives for solidarity are slow in coming, not only in the international sphere but also in the national one. The process of European unification itself is evidently not shared by all, due to the prevailing impression that various "chapters" in the European project have been "written" without taking into account the aspirations of its citizens.

From all this it clearly emerges that an authentic European "common home" cannot be built without considering the identity of the people of this Continent of ours. It is a question of a historical, cultural, and moral identity before being a geographic, economic, or political one; an identity comprised of a set of universal values that Christianity helped forge, thus giving Christianity not only a historical but a foundational role vis-à-vis Europe. These values, which make up the soul of the Continent, must remain in the Europe of the third millennium as a "ferment" of civilization. If these values were to disappear, how could the "old" Continent continue to function as a "leaven" for the entire world? If, for the Fiftieth Anniversary of the Treaty of Rome, the Governments of the Union wish to "get nearer" to their citizens, how can they exclude an element essential to European identity such as Christianity, with which a vast majority of citizens continue to identify? Is it not surprising that today's Europe, while aspiring to be regarded as a community of values, seems ever more often to deny the very existence of universal and absolute values? Does not this unique form of "apostasy" from itself, even more than its apostasy from God, lead Europe to doubt its own identity? And so the opinion prevails that an "evaluation of the benefits" is the only way to moral discernment and that the common good is synonymous with compromise. In reality, if compromise can constitute a legitimate balance between different particular interests, it becomes a common evil whenever it involves agreements that dishonor human nature.

A community built without respect for the true dignity of the human being, disregarding the fact that every person is created in the image of God, ends up doing no good to anyone. For this reason it seems ever more important that Europe be on guard against the pragmatic attitude, widespread today, that systematically justifies compromise on essential human values, as if it were the inevitable acceptance of a lesser evil. This kind of pragmatism, even when presented as balanced and realistic, is in reality neither, since it denies the dimension of values and ideals inherent in human nature. When non-religious and relativistic tendencies are woven into this pragmatism, Christians as such are eventually denied the very right to enter into the public discussion, or their contribution is discredited as an attempt to preserve unjustified privileges. In this historical hour and faced with the many challenges that confront it, the European Union, in order to be a valid guarantor of the rule of law and an efficient promoter of universal values, cannot but recognize clearly the certain existence of a stable and permanent human nature, source of common rights for all individuals, including those who deny them. In this context, the right to conscientious objection should be protected every time fundamental human rights are violated.

Dear friends, I know how difficult it is for Christians to defend this truth of the human person. Nevertheless, do not give in to fatigue or discouragement! You know that it is your duty, with God's help, to contribute to the consolidation of a new Europe that will be realistic but not cynical, rich in ideals and free from naïve illusions, inspired by the perennial and life-giving truth of the Gospel. Therefore, be actively present in the public debate on a European level, knowing that this discussion is now an integral part of the national debate. And to this commitment add effective cultural action. Do not bend to the logic of power as an end in itself! May Christ's admonition be a constant stimulus and support for you: "If the salt loses its flavor it is no longer good for anything, except to be thrown out and trampled by men" (cf. Mt 5:13). May the Lord make all your efforts fruitful and help you to recognize and use properly what is positive in today's civilization, while denouncing with courage all that is contrary to human dignity.

I am certain that God will bless the generous efforts of

all who, in a spirit of service, work to build a common European home where every cultural, social, and political contribution is directed toward the common good. To you, already involved in different ways in this important human and evangelical undertaking, I express my support and my most fervent encouragement. Above all, I assure you of a place in my prayers. Invoking upon you the maternal protection of Mary, Mother of the Word made Flesh, I cordially bless you and your families and communities.

19

Non-negotiable Principles: Address to the Members of the European People's Party on the Occasion of the Study Days on Europe

Hall of Blessing, March 30, 2006

Honorable Parliamentarians,
Distinguished Ladies and Gentlemen,

I am pleased to receive you on the occasion of the Study Days on Europe, organized by your Parliamentary Group. The Roman Pontiffs have always devoted particular attention to this continent; today's audience is a case in point, and it takes its place in the long series of meetings between my predecessors and political movements of Christian inspiration. I thank the Honorable Mr. Pöttering for his words addressed to me in your name, and I extend to him and to all of you my cordial greetings.

At present, Europe has to address complex issues of great importance, such as the growth and development of European integration, the increasingly precise definition of neighborhood policy within the Union and the debate over its social model. In order to attain these goals, it will be important to draw inspiration, with creative fidelity, from the Christian heritage that has made such a particular contribution to forging the identity of this continent. By valuing its Christian roots, Europe will be able to give a secure direction to the choices of its citizens and peoples, it will strengthen their awareness of belonging to a common civilization, and it will nourish the commitment of all to address the challenges of the present for the sake of a better future. I therefore appreciate your Group's recognition of Europe's Christian heritage, which offers valuable ethical guidelines in the search for a social model that responds adequately to the demands of an already globalized economy and to demographic changes, assuring growth and employment, protection of the family, equal opportunities for education of the young, and solicitude for the poor.

Your support for the Christian heritage, moreover, can contribute significantly to the defeat of a culture that is now fairly widespread in Europe, which relegates to the private and subjective sphere the manifestation of one's own religious convictions. Policies built on this foundation not only entail the repudiation of Christianity's public role; more generally, they exclude engagement with Europe's religious tradition, which is so clear, despite its denominational variations, thereby threatening democracy itself, whose strength depends on the values that it promotes (cf. *Evangelium Vitae*, 70). Given that this tradition, precisely in what might be called its polyphonic unity, conveys values that are fundamental for the good of society, the European Union can only be enriched by engaging with it. It would be a sign of immaturity, if not indeed weakness, to choose to oppose or ignore it, rather than to dialogue with it. In this context one has to recognize that a certain secular intransigence shows itself to be the enemy of tolerance and of a sound secular vision of State and society. I am pleased, therefore, that the European Union's constitutional treaty envisages a structured and ongoing relationship with religious communities, recognizing their identity and their specific contribution. Above all, I trust that the effective and correct implementation of this relationship will start now, with the cooperation of all political movements irrespective of party alignments. It must not be forgotten that, when Churches or ecclesial communities intervene in public debate, expressing reservations or recalling various principles, this does not constitute a form of intolerance or an interference, since such interventions are aimed solely at enlightening consciences, enabling them to act freely and responsibly, according to the true demands of justice, even when this should conflict with situations of power and personal interest.

As far as the Catholic Church is concerned, the principal focus of her interventions in the public arena is the protection and promotion of the dignity of the person, and she is thereby consciously drawing particular attention to principles that are not negotiable. Among these the following emerge clearly today:

—protection of life in all its stages, from the first moment of conception until natural death;

—recognition and promotion of the natural structure of the family—as a union between a man and a woman based on marriage—and its defense from attempts to make it juridically equivalent to radically different forms of union that in reality harm it and contribute to its destabilization, obscuring its particular character and its irreplaceable social role;

—the protection of the right of parents to educate their children.

These principles are not truths of faith, even though they receive further light and confirmation from faith; they are inscribed in human nature itself, and therefore they are common to all humanity. The Church's action in promoting them is therefore not confessional in character, but is addressed to all people, prescinding from any religious affiliation they may have. On the contrary, such action is all the more necessary the more these principles are denied or misunderstood, because this constitutes an offense against the truth of the human person, a grave wound inflicted onto justice itself.

Dear friends, in exhorting you to be credible and consistent witnesses of these basic truths through your political activity, and more fundamentally through your commitment to live authentic and consistent lives, I invoke upon you and your work the continued assistance of God, in pledge of which I cordially impart my blessing to you and to those accompanying you.

20

Bells of Europe: The Reasons for My Hope: Interview with Fr. Germano Marani, S.J.

Published on October 16, 2012

On October 15, 2012, at the end of the session of the Synod of Bishops, a film entitled *Bells of Europe—Campane d'Europa* was shown in a special screening for the Synod Fathers. The film, produced by the Vatican Television Centre, deals with the relationship between Christianity, European culture, and the future of the continent. It includes excerpts from a series of interviews with important religious leaders and with leading figures from the world of politics and culture. The full text of the interview with Benedict XVI is given below.

Question: Your Holiness, your Encyclicals present a compelling view of man: a man inhabited by God's charity, a man whose reason is broadened by the experience of faith, a man who possesses social responsibility thanks to the dynamism of charity received and given in truth. Holiness, it is from this anthropological standpoint—in which the evangelical message exalts all the laudable aspects of mankind, purifying the grime that covers the authentic countenance of man created in the image and likeness of God—that you have repeatedly stated that this rediscovery of the human countenance, of evangelical values, of the deepest roots of Europe, is a cause of great hope for the European continent and not only for the European continent. Can you explain to us the reasons for your hope?

Answer: The first reason for my hope consists in the fact that the desire for God, the search for God, is profoundly inscribed into each human soul and cannot disappear. Certainly we can forget God for a time, lay him aside, and concern ourselves with other things, but God never disappears. Saint Augustine's words are true: we men are restless until we have found God. This restlessness also exists today and is an expression of the hope that man may, ever and anew, even today, start to journey toward this God.

The second reason for my hope lies in the fact that the Gospel of Jesus Christ, faith in Jesus Christ, is quite simply true; and the truth never ages. It too may be forgotten for a time, it may be laid aside and attention may turn to other things, but the truth as such does not disappear. Ideologies have their days numbered. They appear powerful and irresistible, but, after a certain period, they wear out and lose their energy because they lack profound truth. They are particles of truth, but in the end they are consumed. The Gospel, on the other hand, is true and can therefore never wear out. In each period of history it reveals new dimensions, it emerges in all its novelty as it responds to the needs of the heart and mind of human beings, who can walk in this truth and so discover themselves. It is for this reason, therefore, that I am convinced there will also be a new springtime for Christianity.

A third reason, an empirical reason, is evident in the fact that this sense of restlessness today exists among the young. Young people have seen much—the proposals of the various ideologies and of consumerism—and they have become aware of the emptiness and insufficiency of those things. Man was created for the infinite, the finite is too little. Thus, among the new generations we are seeing the reawakening of this restlessness, and they too begin their journey making new discoveries of the beauty of Christianity; not a cut-price or watered-down version, but Christianity in all its radicalism and profundity. Thus I believe that anthropology, as such, is showing us that there will always be a new reawakening of Christianity. The facts confirm this in a single phrase: Deep foundations. That is Christianity; it is true, and the truth always has a future.

Q.: Your Holiness, you have repeatedly said that Europe has had, and continues to have, a cultural influence on the entire human race, and it cannot but feel a particular sense of responsibility, not only for its own future, but also for that of mankind as a whole. Looking ahead, is it possible to discern the contours of the visible witness Catholics, Orthodox, and Protestants in Europe from the Atlantic to the Urals must show as, living the Gospel values in which they believe, they contribute to the building of a Europe faithful to Christ, more welcoming and united, not merely safeguarding their cultural and spiritual heritage but also committed to finding new ways to face the great challenges that characterize the postmodern and multicultural age?

A.: This is an important question. It is clear that Europe has great weight in today's world, in terms of economic, cultural, and intellectual importance; as a consequence of this it also has great responsibility. But Europe, as you said, still has to find its true identity in order to be able to speak and act in keeping with her responsibility. In my opinion, the problem today does not consist in national differences, which, thank God, are differences not divisions. In their cultural, human and temperamental differences, nations are a rich asset which together give rise to a great symphony of cultures. Basically, they are a shared culture. The problem Europe has in finding its own identity consists, I believe, in the fact that in Europe today we see two souls: one is abstract anti-historical reason, which seeks to dominate all else because it considers itself above all cultures; it is like a reason that has finally discovered itself and intends to liberate itself from all traditions and cultural values in favor of an abstract rationality. Strasburg's first verdict on the crucifix was an example of such abstract reason that seeks emancipation from all traditions, even from history itself. Yet we cannot live like that, and, moreover, even "pure reason" is conditioned by a certain historical context, and only in that context can it exist. We could call Europe's other soul the Christian one. It is a soul open to all that is reasonable, a soul that itself created the audaciousness of reason and the freedom of critical reasoning, but that remains anchored to the roots from which this Europe was born, the roots that created the continent's fundamental values and great institutions, in the vision of the Christian faith. As you said, this soul has to find a shared expression in ecumenical dialogue between the Catholic, Orthodox, and Protestant Churches. It must then encounter this abstract reason; in other words, it must accept and maintain the freedom of reason to criticize everything it can do and has done, but to practice this and give it concrete form on the foundations and in the context of the great values that Christianity has given us. Only by blending these elements can Europe have weight in the intercultural dialogue of mankind today and tomorrow. Only when reason has a historical and moral identity can it speak to others, search for an "interculturality" in which everyone can enter and find a fundamental unity in the values that open the way to the future, to a new humanism. This must be our aim. For us this humanism arises directly from the view of man created in the image and likeness of God.

SOURCES

Unless otherwise indicated, texts were translated from the original language by Michael J. Miller.

Introduction by His Holiness Pope Francis (original in Italian).

Preface by Pope Emeritus Benedict XVI (original in German).

PART ONE

At the Sources of European Identity: Athens, Jerusalem, Rome

1. The "European Synthesis". Homily at the Europe Day Celebration of the Pan-European Union of Bavaria, Cathedral in Munich, May 12, 1979. German original: "Verantwortung des Christen für Europa", in: *Zeitfragen und christlicher Glaube: Acht Predigten aus den Münchener Jahren* (Würzburg: J. W. Naumann, 1982), 28–32.

2. The Heart of Europe: "the humanism of the Incarnation". Homily on the occasion of a visit of a delegation of the German Bishops' Conference to the Polish Episcopate, Kraków, September 13, 1980. German original: "Wahrer Friede und wahre Kultur: Christlicher Glaube und Europa", in: *Priester aus innerstem Herzen: Beiträge im Klerusblatt aus fünf Jahrzehnten* (Munich: Klerusblatt-Verlag, 2007), 162–167.

3. Europe and Anti-Europe: True and False Democracy, True and False Modernity. Speech given at the International Symposium on "Europe and the Christians", Strasbourg, April 29, 1979. German original: "Europe —verpflichtendes Erbe für die Christen", in: *Europa und die Christen* (Munich: Katholischen Akademie in Bayern, 1979). Previously published in English in: Joseph Ratzinger, *Fundamental Speeches from Five Decades* (Ignatius Press, 2012), 157–75.

4. "Might Makes Right" and the Right to Life: Toward a European Idea of Law. Address at the Convention on the Right to Life and Europe held in Rome, December 18–19, 1987. Italian original: "'. . . Ecce homo': Il diritto alla vita e l'Europa", in: *L'Europa di Benedetto nella crisi delle culture* (Siena, 2005), 69–96.

5. Beyond Liberalism and Communism: Toward a European Idea of the Economy. Introduction to the Symposium "Church and Economics in our responsibility for the future of the global economy" at the Pontifical Urban University, November 21, 1985. German original: "Neues Zueinander von Ethik und Wirtschaft", in *L'Osservatore Romano* (German edition) 15 (1985), no. 48, p. 8.

PART TWO

Europe: Downfalls and Rebirths

6. War, Reconstruction and the Heritage of the Postwar Period: Four Talks on the Occasion of the Sixtieth Anniversary of the Landing of the Allied Forces in France. Translated from French (a–c) and German (d) by Michael J. Miller and previously published in English

in: Joseph Ratzinger, *Europe Today and Tomorrow* (San Francisco: Ignatius Press, 2007), 83–117.

7. 1968 and years of violence and disillusionment: diagnosis and rudiments of a response. Speech given on November 26, 1987, upon receiving an honorary doctorate at the University of Eichstatt. German original: "Abbruch und Aufbruch: Die Antwort des Glaubens auf die Krise der Werte", in: *Wendezeit für Europa* (Einsiedeln: Johannes Verlag, 1991), 11–29. English translation by Brian McNeil in Joseph Ratzinger, *Turning Point for Europe* (San Francisco: Ignatius Press, 1994), 15–40.

8. The Lesson of 1989: The Political Force of Meta-Political Realities. Conference at Sapienza University, Rome, February 15, 1990. Translated from Italian by Michael J. Miller. A version of the conference in a German anthology was translated into English by Brian McNeil and published in: *Turning Point for Europe* (San Francisco: Ignatius Press, 1994), 81–111.

9. A Turning Point for Europe? Speech given at the University of Regensburg, January 28, 1991. Translated from German by Brian McNeil and previously published in *Turning Point for Europe?* (San Francisco: Ignatius Press, 1994), 145–77.

PART THREE

The Church and the Rebirth of Europe: Educational Challenge and New Evangelization

10. The Objection to the Church and the Distortion of the Image of Man. Speech at the meeting with the presidents of the Doctrinal Commissions of Europe in Laxenburg (Vienna), May 2, 1989. German original: Joseph

Cardinal Ratzinger, Prefect of the Congregation for the Doctrine of the Faith, "Schwierigkeiten mit dem Glauben in Europa heute".

11. The Church's Faith and the New World's Utopia. Intervention at the Special Assembly for Europe of the Synod of Bishops. Original English text was unavailable; translated from the German version, "Die Zeichen der Zeit deuten", in: *Joseph Ratzinger Gesammelte Schriften*, 9:851–53.

12. The Educational Challenge. German original: "Der Auftrag der Religion angesichts der gegenwärtigen Krise von Friede und Gerechtigkeit", speech given on the occasion of the "Fifth Christian-Islamic Consultation" at the Orthodox Center of the Ecumenical Patriarch in Chambesy, December 12–15, 1988; published in the German edition of *Communio* 18 (1989): 113–22. English translation by Brian McNeil previously published in: *Turning Point for Europe* (San Francisco: Ignatius Press, 1994), 41–60.

13. The Responsibility of Faith to Society and to the World. Speech given on the occasion of the award of the Leopold Kunschak Prize, March 9, 1991. German original translated by Brian McNeil and previously published in *Turning Point for Europe* (San Francisco: Ignatius Press, 1994), 61–77.

14. The Church and Europe. Conference on the occasion of the presentation of the book *Svolta per l'Europa? Chiesa e modernità nell'Europa dei rivolgimenti* [English edition: *Turning Point for Europe?*] at the Università Cattolica del Sacro Cuore in Rome, February 8, 1992. Published in Italian in *30 Giorni*, 1 (1992).

PART FOUR

The True Europe and Its Mission

15. Reflections on the Ideals of Tomorrow's Europe. Conference given on September 8, 2001, in Cernobbio (Como) for business leaders and politicians. Published in German in *Werte in Zeiten des Umbruchs*, 89–97. English translation by Brian McNeil in *Values in a Time of Upheaval* (New York: The Crossroad Publishing Company; San Francisco: Ignatius Press, 2006), 151–60.

16. Why Europe Exists: Secularity and Secularism Yesterday, Today, Tomorrow. Conference given in Berlin, November 28, 2000. A modified version of the conference was given to the Senate of the Italian Republic at the invitation of its President, Marcello Pera, on May 13, 2004. Translated from German by Michael J. Miller and previously published in *Europe Today and Tomorrow* (San Francisco: Ignatius Press, 2007), 11–34.

17. Europe in the Crisis of Cultures. Conference given in Subiaco, at the Monastery of Saint Scholastica, on the occasion of the conferral of the Saint Benedict Prize "for the promotion of life and the family in Europe" on April 1, 2005. Italian original published in: *L'Europa di Benedetto nella crisi delle culture*, 29–68.

18. A New Europe. Address of His Holiness Benedict XVI to the participants in the Congress sponsored by the Commission of the Bishops' Conferences of the European Community (COMECE), Apostolic Palace, Clementine Hall, March 24, 2007. Text in English at Vatican website.

19. Non-negotiable Principles. Address of His Holiness Benedict XVI to the Members of the European People's Party on the occasion of the study days on Europe, Apostolic Palace, Hall of Blessing, March 30, 2006.

20. *Bells of Europe: The Reasons for My Hope.* Interview with His Holiness Benedict XVI by Fr. Germano Marani, S.J., excerpts from which were included in the film *Bells of Europe—Campane di Europa* on the relations between Christianity, European culture and the future of the continent. The film was shown in a special screening for the Synod Fathers during the Thirteenth Ordinary General Assembly of the Synod of Bishops (October 7–28, 2012). The full text of the interview was published the following day, October 16, 2012.

SUBJECT INDEX

SCRIPTURE INDEX